ELIZABETH

BARRETT

BROWNING,

WOMAN AND

ARTIST

Elizabeth Barrett Browning, Woman & Artist

HELEN COOPER

The University of North Carolina Press

Chapel Hill & London

© 1988 The University of North Carolina Press

All rights reserved

Library of Congress Cataloging-in-Publication Data

Cooper, Helen.
  Elizabeth Barrett Browning, woman and artist.

  Bibliography: p.
  Includes index.
    1. Browning, Elizabeth Barrett, 1806–1861—Criticism
and interpretation. I. Title.
PR4194.C66   1988   821'.8   87-40538
ISBN 0-8078-1788-0 (alk. paper)
ISBN 0-8078-4217-6 (pbk.: alk. paper)

The paper in this book meets the guidelines for
permanence and durability of the Committee on
Production Guidelines for Book Longevity of the
Council on Library Resources.

Printed in the United States of America

92 91 90 89 88   5 4 3 2 1

For

Emily, Albert, Jerome,

Clare, and Sarah

CONTENTS

ACKNOWLEDGMENTS

I am indebted to the following for their generous help: Adrienne Rich, Sandra Gilbert, Susan Gubar, Elaine Showalter, William Keach, Richard Levine, Thomas Flanagan, Margaret Homans, James Kincaid, Adrienne Munich, Sallie Sears, Sandra Eisdorfer, and Rosalie West. To George Levine, Barry Qualls, and Susan Squier I owe special thanks for their true collegiality and friendship demonstrated by rigorous readings of this manuscript through its many stages. I have received support from the State University of New York at Stony Brook in four ways: a summer faculty fellowship during the early stages of writing; release time from the department of English for its completion; students who throughout have confirmed my sense of this poet's vitality and importance; and financial support for the production of this book.

When I wrote my first article on Barrett Browning, Sandra Donaldson and Cora Kaplan were the pioneers in feminist scholarship on this poet. Since then there has been a blossoming of such critical work. Some has informed my thinking here, but so fruitful has Barrett Browning scholarship become that new work, including the feminist study by Angela Leighton, have appeared since my manuscript was completed and at the press. I welcome this vitality of critical debate.

Finally, I am deeply grateful to Jerome Tognoli and Clare and Sarah Cooper-Tognoli for enabling me to be both woman and scholar.

ABBREVIATIONS

A   *Elizabeth Barrett Browning: Hitherto Unpublished Poems and Stories with an Inedited Autobiography.* Edited by H. Buxton Forman. Boston: Bibliophile Society, 1914.

D   *Diary by E. B. B.: The Unpublished Diary of Elizabeth Barrett Barrett, 1831–1832.* Edited with an Introduction and Notes by Philip Kelley and Ronald Hudson. Athens: Ohio University Press, 1969.

HSB   *Elizabeth Barrett to Mr. Boyd. Unpublished Letters of Elizabeth Barrett Browning to Hugh Stuart Boyd.* Edited by Barbara P. McCarthy. London: John Murray, 1955.

L   *The Letters of Elizabeth Barrett Browning.* Edited by Frederic C. Kenyon. 2 vols. New York: Macmillan Co., 1897.

MRM   *The Letters of Elizabeth Barrett Browning to Mary Russell Mitford, 1836–1854.* Edited by Meredith B. Raymond and Mary Rose Sullivan. 3 vols. Armstrong Browning Library of Baylor University, Browning Institute, Wedgestone Press, and Wellesley College, 1983.

RB&EBB *The Letters of Robert Browning and Elizabeth*
Barrett Barrett, 1845–1846. Edited by Elvan
Kintner. 2 vols. Cambridge: Harvard University
Press, Belknap Press, 1969.

W   *The Complete Works of Elizabeth Barrett*
Browning. Edited by Charlotte Porter and Helen A.
Clarke. 6 vols. New York: Thomas Y. Crowell &
Co., 1900. Reprint. New York: AMS Press, 1973.

ELIZABETH

BARRETT

BROWNING,

WOMAN AND

ARTIST

INTRODUCTION

Virginia Woolf observed that "the only place in the mansion of literature that is assigned [Barrett Browning] is downstairs in the servants' quarters, where . . . she bangs the crockery about and eats vast handfuls of peas on the point of her knife."[1] This portrait of an energetic, uncouth scullery maid is a surprising description of "Mrs. Browning," that pale invalid who recorded her devotion to the hero who rescued her from her tyrannical father in "How do I love thee? Let me count the ways." Equally surprising is the fact that initial critical disquiet over Barrett Browning's work was not on account of her legendary sentimentality but for its "falsetto muscularity," its "very habit and trick of violence," and its "assertion of strength."[2] However, as recent feminist criticism proves, neither the uncouth scullery maid nor the insipid invalid accurately represent the poet whose work records her evolving sense of woman as having a distinct and responsible poetic voice. While my study as a whole traces the evolution of that poetic voice through Barrett Browning's career, this introduction draws attention to two ideas that inform my approach to her work. First, I outline the issues confronting Barrett Browning as a woman poet working within a male tradition. Second, I show how an understanding of Barrett Browning's contribution reshapes our conception of Victorian poetics.

In placing these issues in the foreground, I follow the tradition of feminist critical theory that Elaine Showalter has identified as "gynocritics." I thereby accompany those feminist critics of Barrett Browning's writing, Gilbert, Gubar, Mermin, and Rosenblum, whose work is informed by a perspective analogous to Showalter's when she says: "Gynocritics is, roughly speaking, historical in orientation; it looks at women's writing as it has actually occurred and tries to define its specific characteristics of language, genre, and literary influence, within a cultural network that includes variables of race, class, and nationality."[3] More specifically, I am indebted to Sandra Gilbert and Susan Gubar, whose rereading of Harold Bloom's work suggests that "anxiety of authorship" rather than "anxiety of influence" is a more accurate description of women poets in relation to their precursors. In doing this I subscribe to the liberal humanist position in relation to the self as an "autonomous, unified, coherent individual";[4] it is a position to which Barrett Browning's heroine, Aurora Leigh, also subscribed as she meditated on her twentieth birthday that she was "woman and artist,—either incomplete, / Both credulous of completion" (2.4–5). This study follows the development of Barrett Browning's poetry toward that "completion" in *Aurora Leigh* and, through its focus on Victorian reviews, examines Barrett Browning's work in its cultural context. It also privileges her commitment in the Preface to *Poems of 1844* to write with "a peculiar reference to Eve's alloted grief." Such a commitment implies a collectivity of women represented (and misrepresented) by Eve, whose subjectivity had gone unheard, whose selfhood was unrecognized.

I am not unmindful of Toril Moi's indictment of such a humanist program:

> Traditional humanism . . . is in effect part of patriarchal ideology. At its centre is the seamlessly unified self—either individual or collective—which is commonly called "Man." As Luce Irigaray or Hélène Cixous would argue, this integrated self is in fact a phallic self, constructed on the model of the self-contained, powerful phallus. Gloriously autonomous, it banishes from itself all conflict, contradiction and ambiguity. In this humanist ideology the self is the *sole author* of history and of the literary text: the humanist creator is potent, phallic and male—God in relation to his world, the author in relation to his text. History or the text become nothing but the "expression" of this unique individual: all

art becomes autobiography, a mere window on to the self and the world, with no reality of its own. The text is reduced to a passive, "feminine" reflection of an unproblematically "given," "masculine" world or self.[5]

Moi's perspective is akin to much contemporary French feminist theory, which emphasizes the primacy of the text and believes that "minds are intrinsically split, fragmented and self-alienated";[6] that feminine writing represents a preoedipal language rather than a gendered author; or that what is necessary is to examine the "space granted to the feminine in the symbolic contract"[7] as Kristeva does. I welcome the ongoing dialogue between "gynocritics" and "gynesis." Feminist theory and criticism will continue to develop with all that English, American, French, Marxist, psychoanalytic, and deconstructive critics can offer. However, Moi argues with the humanistic criticism of Virginia Woolf, a writer committed thematically and stylistically to querying notions of self. This study is committed to recreating the "traditional humanism . . . of the patriarchal ideology" in which Barrett Browning wrote. The Anglo-American "gynocritics" in which it has its roots allows me to read (while trying to avoid the intentional fallacy) Barrett Browning on her own terms; namely as one who saw herself as empowering the silenced Eve to speak for "women as a sex."[8] She created Aurora Leigh as one who had successfully completed a self as both woman and poet, even if, inevitably, Barrett Browning's concept of self was limited by Victorian ideology.

Gilbert describes *Aurora Leigh* as follows:

The tale of the poet-heroine's risorgimento, which parallels the plot of the poet-author's own insurrection-resurrection, begins with a fragmentation of the self that is both symbolized and precipitated by a shattering of the nuclear family, a shattering that leads to a devastating analysis of that structure. Just as significantly, the story ends with a reconstitution of both self and family that provides a visionary new synthesis of the relationships among men, women, and children.[9]

Gilbert addresses the "fragmentation of the self" ending with "a reconstitution of both self and family" in relation to *Aurora Leigh*. But this was a fictional representation of what had been a similar literary transformation for Barrett Browning as a poet. In the early poem "The Seraphim" Mary kneels at the foot of the cross "with a spasm, not a speech"; Aurora Leigh, however, boldly announces, "I write." Barrett Browning consciously committed herself to the creation of a stable "I" that would speak for "women as a sex." For too long she was dismissed because she did not fit with the periodization and concerns of male literature. She needs to have her work read on the terms in which she wrote it, before she is discussed from a postmodernist perspective in relation to the limitations of that humanist vision.

Barrett Browning, Tennyson's only serious rival for poet laureate in 1850 and more acclaimed by her contemporaries than was her husband, has until recently been considered a marginal figure in Victorian poetry.[10] A reading of her work suggests that the ideology of canon formation determines this marginality. Elaine Showalter in *A Literature of Their Own* and Sandra M. Gilbert and Susan Gubar in *The Madwoman in the Attic* pioneered the conviction that this canon, as feminist and Marxist critics agree, is a social construct that both describes and reinforces the culture's assignment of power.[11] Informing Barrett Browning's work and responsible for her literary marginality is a poetic and critical tradition that privileges male poets by assuming that their concerns are universal and that the poetic voice is male;[12] woman is the "other," the object of his vision and narrative rather than the subject of her own experience and discourse.

Barrett Browning shared the poetic ambition of male poets. In spite of the lack of literary "grandmothers," she determined to attain the standards demanded by the "divineness of poetry" rather than have them "lowered to [her] uses" as was the convention with the popular "poetesses" like Felicia Hemans and Letitia Landon, her contemporaries (*L*, 1:232).[13] However, in describing herself in the Preface to *Poems of 1844* as "*I* also an exile" from that tradition epitomized for her by Homer, Aeschylus, and Milton, she demonstrated her sense of being an outsider.[14] Simone de Beauvoir's discussion in *The Second Sex* of woman as the "Other" illuminates the nature of Barrett Browning's "exile": "In the sense in which the psychoanalysts understand the term, 'to identify oneself' with the mother or with the father is to *alienate oneself* in a model. . . . Woman is shown to us as enticed by two modes of alienation. Evidently to play at being a man will be for her a source of frustration; but to play at being a woman is also a delusion: to be a woman would mean to be the object, the *Other*."[15] De Beauvoir focuses on woman's maturational dilemma generally; she also speaks to the more specific problem facing the woman poet whose heritage is a centuries-old male poetics. As feminist critics, including Gilbert and Gubar, Juhasz, Diehl, and Homans, have argued, the woman poet's relationship to tradition is not based on the kind of influence that Harold Bloom posits for men in his oedipal reading of poetic history: namely the young poet's desiring through strife to assume the place and stature of the father, his precursor. The daughter can never imagine herself as a father. Although she may "play at being a man" in her apprenticeship, she can never fully mature as a poet with such a cross-gender identification. This suggests that a woman's poetry remains at an adolescent stage unless she can fully embrace her female subjectivity. Yet how is she to do so in a gender-based culture? As de Beauvoir states, to "play at being a woman" is as much of a delusion as to "play at being a man," because woman has historically been paralyzed within the role of silent object of male gaze and discourse. In Barrett Browning's terms, there were no "grandmothers" nor indeed mothers to whose place she could aspire. Thus a study of her career as a poet suggests answers to some crucial questions:[16] What is the nature of the daughter poet's engagement with her father poets? Does she find literary and cultural mothers? How does she form a mature poetic voice of her own?

The central issue in Barrett Browning's work is how a woman poet empowers herself to speak. This problem was not unique to poetry; women also exhibited anxiety about writing fiction—as evidenced by the pseudonymns of the Brontë sisters, of Mary Ann Evans, and of Aurore Dupin.[17] The poet, however, was dogged by two additional concerns. First, whereas the novel was essentially a middle-class form for which its writers did not need an Oxbridge education, the English poet was traditionally upper-middle-class and Oxbridge-educated, with a solid grounding in

Greek and Latin literature.[18] This restrictive profile excluded women from the ranks of serious poets as surely as they were excluded from the ranks of university students. Second, whereas the nature of fiction allowed for a narrative voice of either sex, the nature of lyric and the authority of epic dictated that the poet conventionally spoke in a male voice.

Such male authority not only kept women from claiming the role of poet, but also meant that woman was described as a male creation or projection rather than as the center of her own consciousness.[19] Charlotte Brontë dramatized her heroine's understanding of this in *Shirley* when she focused on Milton's inability to "read" woman correctly: " 'Milton's Eve! Milton's Eve! Milton's Eve! I repeat. No, by the pure Mother of God, she is not! . . . Milton was great; but was he good? His brain was right; how was his heart? . . . Milton tried to see the first woman; but . . . he saw her not.' "[20]

Brontë located what proved a crucial issue for Barrett Browning, namely the portrayal of Eve as archetypal woman by her most powerful and troubling precursor. However complexly and at times compassionately Milton presented Eve, he nevertheless endorsed the fact that only Adam, not Eve, was to have the power of naming his world and of naming Eve. Adam was to be the poet, Eve his muse.[21] Eve was not allowed to model herself after the image of the divine creator, the image that empowered the Romantic male poet's self-concept—"He for God only, she for God in him." Romantic ideology simultaneously authorized the political and visionary poetry Barrett Browning strove to write and disenfranchised her from doing so. She first challenged this disenfranchisement in her Preface to *Poems of 1844*, when she recorded how in "A Drama of Exile" she determined to write "with a peculiar reference to Eve's alloted grief, which, considering that self-sacrifice belonged to her womanhood, and the consciousness of originating the Fall to her offence,—appeared to me imperfectly apprehended hitherto, and more expressible by a woman than a man" (*W*, 2:143–44).

If an aspect of "Eve's alloted grief" is to be the Other in male poetics, then describing and ultimately rejecting that "grief" was Barrett Browning's project as a poet. Her rejection of it effected the transformation of woman from being the object of male gaze and narrative into being the subject of her own experience and discourse. She was, arguably, the first English woman poet to do so. Bloom's model, while limited, is still useful here: not as a son does Barrett Browning rewrite her strong father, but as a daughter she rewrites poetic history, from Aeschylus through medieval courtly romances, from *Paradise Lost* to *The Prelude*. In her greatest poem, *Aurora Leigh*, she both wrote a radical redefinition of the relationship between Adam and Eve in her portrayal of Romney and Aurora, and also traced the growth of a female poet's mind. Barrett Browning's career is therefore a critically important one. It simultaneously provides a paradigm for the woman poet's relationship to poetic tradition as long as the latter privileges the male voice, and initiates a challenge to that privilege by becoming the "grandmother" poet she herself lacked.

Barrett Browning not only presents such a paradigm and challenge in her work, she also reflects Victorian concerns. Put another way, it is important to ask what enabled Barrett Browning to write her poetry at that particular time in history. Thackeray's description of what distinguished the nineteenth century from earlier times illuminates such an inquiry:

We who have lived before railways were made, belong to another world. . . . It was only yesterday; but what a gulf between now and then! *Then* was the old world. Stage-coaches, more or less swift, riding-horses, pack-horses, highwaymen, knights in armour, Norman invaders, Roman legions, Druids, Ancient Britons painted blue, and so forth—all these belong to the old period. I will concede a halt in the midst of it, and allow that gunpowder and printing tended to modernise the world. But your railroad starts the new era, . . . We are of the age of steam. . . . Towards what new continents are we wending? to what new laws, new manners, new politics, vast new expanses of liberties unknown as yet, or only surmised? . . . The old world. There it lies on the other side of yonder embankments. . . . We elderly people have lived in that prae-railroad world, which has passed into limbo and vanished from under us. I tell you it was firm under our feet once, and not long ago. They have raised those railroad embankments up, and shut off the old world that was behind them. Climb up that bank on which the irons are laid, and look to the other side—it is gone. There *is* no other side. . . .

. . . We who have lived before railways are antediluvians— we must pass away. We are growing scarcer every day; and old—old—very old relics of the times when George was still fighting the dragon.[22]

Thackeray depicts here an "old world," essentially medieval. His conviction that it is irrevocably lost—"There *is* no other side"— informed much Victorian thought. Although Macaulay, in "Southey's Colloquies," attempted to dispel romantic notions about that golden age in his stress on improved material conditions in early Victorian England, nevertheless a pervasive anxiety about their times characterized the longing glances that some intellectuals gave to a past they imagined as stable and ordered even while they tried to make sense out of their deeply disturbing present. This anxiety was symbolically represented for them by the new railways; for Thackeray "those railroad embankments . . . on which the irons are laid" precluded any return to the past: "It is gone."

It is a commonplace now to describe nineteenth-century England as an age of transition, defined by its rapid industrialization, its exciting and terrifying discoveries about evolution, its widening of the franchise to all males, and the very idea that God may indeed not be in his heaven. The church still held sway over many lives, but many intellectuals, longing for the security of a belief in God, nevertheless doubted his existence. To dispel the chaos and meaninglessness spawned by their disbelief they were forced to find an alternative structure for the life of the community, whether it was Carlyle's commitment to work, Mill's to individual liberty and a humanized utilitarianism, or Arnold's to culture.

Discussions of high Victorian poetry, therefore, tend to see the work of Tennyson, Arnold, and Browning as responses to the fears rampant in their times, although recent critics recognize an energetic optimism informing Browning's poetry.[23] However, the introduction of Barrett Browning's work to that of the three male high Victorian poets suggests an alternative reading of that poetic history. Thus, I would argue that Oxbridge-educated Tenny-

son and Arnold represent those most deeply affected by the passing of the "old world." Browning, the urban, self-educated dis-
senter's son, and Barrett Browning, the socially, politically, and
culturally disenfranchised woman poet, represent a poetic middle-class entrepreneurial spirit, and as poets had much to gain
from the upheavals in nineteenth-century England. This challenge to the standard periodization of Victorian literature parallels Gilbert's reading of the modern period, in which male modernism laments the fragmentation of the old order while wom-
en's celebrates that fragmentation,[24] and Sydney Janet Kaplan's
belief that the "traditional parameters of a period may be shifted
or its predominant preoccupations reassessed if it is studied
through the perspective of women writers."[25]

With the promise of "new manners," other voices could inter-
rupt and redirect poetic tradition. Shakespeare's sister could follow her brother to London in this "age of steam" promising "vast
new expanses of liberties unknown as yet."

The following chapters offer an analysis of Barrett Browning's
intrusion into and appropriation of poetic history as she developed it from *The Seraphim, and Other Poems* (1838) to *Aurora
Leigh* (1856). Her first widely read volume, *The Seraphim, and
Other Poems*, which she felt to be the first work to mark her
"individuality" (*L,* 1:187), reveals an indebtedness to the male
poetic tradition in her modestly revisionary readings of Aeschylus and Milton in "The Seraphim" and of Wordsworth in "The
Poet's Vow." "Isobel's Child" and "The Romaunt of Margret,"
poems that have an immediate connection with the work of
the popular "poetesses," show how Barrett[26] simultaneously presented and tentatively challenged the traditional literary image
of woman—a challenge fueled by her early reading of Mary Wollstonecraft's *A Vindication of the Rights of Woman* and her enthusiasm for Madame de Stael's *Corinne,* one of the first texts to
have a woman poet as its protagonist.

The *Poems of 1844* are dominated by the poet's six years of
invalid confinement. These years allowed her the freedom to
read and write, which the conventional social life of a middle-
class woman proscribed, but she also experienced them as an
imprisonment. She came to identify this imprisonment with
her father's adherence to the patriarchal "system,"[27] which paral-

leled her imprisonment within a literary tradition dominated for her by Milton. Barrett's determination to write "with a peculiar reference to Eve's alloted grief" was initially inhibited by "Milton's glory" (*W*, 2:143–44). Yet, whereas her Preface to *Poems of 1844* evokes the male tradition that locates woman as object in the text, Barrett's sonnets "To George Sand" subvert that text, affirming the "poet-fire" of a "woman's voice." The rebellion dramatized by the courtly ladies of the 1844 ballads exhibits the young poet's initial covert questioning of male textual definitions; the ballads demonstrate both how Barrett reflects the popularity of medieval settings for both male and female poets and also how she questions the courtly ideology such settings endorse. Barrett attempts to free woman from male literary conventions while simultaneously subverting the "poetesses's" appropriation of those conventions in their commitment to woman's self-abnegating love. The 1844 poems still represent woman as Eve submissive in her Biblical and Miltonic roles. However, they rebel against both Eve's literary and Barrett's actual confinement, a rebellion that culminated in Barrett's defiance of her father, her marriage to Browning, and her departure for Italy.

Sonnets from the Portuguese record the process of this rebellion, while "The Runaway Slave at Pilgrim's Point" (1850), a pivotal poem, enacts its triumph. In the *Sonnets* Barrett transforms woman from her role as muse/helpmeet/object into poet/creator/subject, bringing "I a woman" and "I a poet" into harmony while reflecting on that transformation.[28] "The Runaway Slave at Pilgrim's Point" represents a turning point in Barrett Browning's career. Her earlier ballad narratives mature into the dramatic monologue of a black slave woman, raped and impregnated by her white master. The speaker dramatizes Barrett Browning's conviction that woman can locate her own consciousness as the central vision of poetry and speak as "I."

By the time Barrett Browning wrote *Casa Guidi Windows* (1851) and *Aurora Leigh* (1856) she possessed an authoritative poetic "I." She used it, however, quite differently in each of these major poems. Although Italian politics is the manifest subject of *Casa Guidi Windows*, Barrett Browning exploits it to assess her relationship to poetic tradition and to examine and criticize men's performance in the public and political role they have traditionally assigned themselves.

In *Aurora Leigh* the poet narrator tells the painful story of how she arrived at the union of woman and poet, thereby providing a fictional gloss for what Barrett Browning's previous work had shown. Initially, the woman poet, like any young poet, identifies with her powerful precursors. This necessitates imagining herself as male, with woman as object of her vision. Eventually this frustration yields to a crisis, in which the poet acknowledges she is a woman, as she must truly do to mature. (In Barrett Browning's case this is when she marries Browning and leaves England and her father to live in Italy; for Aurora Leigh it is her meeting with Marian Erle in Paris.) Finally she realizes her poetic maturity by embracing and recording her own subjectivity in which man is object of her gaze.

Barrett Browning was neither a sentimental invalid, nor the scullery maid in the "mansion of literature," but a committed writer fashioning a poetic career paradigmatic for many women poets. In so doing she challenged the universality of male poetry, suggesting rather that it reflects the way men construct themselves and their masculine identity in and through their art. The way woman constructs herself in Western art has been, and probably will be, different as long as Western culture perpetuates the balance of power between men and women represented in the cultural ideology of nineteenth-century England.

CHAPTER 1

The Angel

THE SERAPHIM, AND
OTHER POEMS (1838)

Heaven is dull,
Mine Ador, to Man's earth.
—"The Seraphim"

The reviewer in *Blackwood's Edinburgh Maga-*
zine who asked, "What other pretty book is this?" discovered it
to be *The Seraphim, and Other Poems* (1838) by Elizabeth Barrett
Barrett.[1] Barrett was thirty-two; she had already written an autobiography, *Glimpses Into My Own Life and Literary Character*
(1820),[2] and published three volumes of poetry, *The Battle of*
Marathon (1820), *An Essay on Mind, With Other Poems* (1826),
and *Poems, 1833. The Seraphim,* however, was her first work
both to receive a wide readership and extensive critical response,
and also to represent "with all its feebleness and shortcomings
and obscurities . . . the first utterance" of her "own individuality" (*L*, 1:188). But the expression of that "individuality" was
achieved through years of reading and imitating the male masters and of recognizing the relationship of gender to her determination to be a poet.

Her autobiography is a precocious, ebulliently self-confident
document, in which the adolescent Barrett recorded her self-conscious training to be a poet. At age seven she "began to think of
'forming [her] taste' . . . *to see what was best to write about and*
read about" (*A*, 8–9). As a consequence:

I read the History of England and Rome; at eight I perused
the History of Greece and . . . first found real delight in po-

etry. "The Minstrel," Pope's "Illiad" [*sic*], some parts of the "Odyssey," passages from "Paradise Lost" selected by my dearest Mama and some of Shakespeare's plays among which were, "The Tempest," "Othello" and a few historical dramatic pieces. . . .

At nine . . . Pope's "Illiad" [*sic*] some passages from Shakespeare and Novels which I enjoyed to their full extent. . . . At ten my poetry was entirely formed by the style of written authors and I read that I might write. Novels were still my most delightful study, combined with the sweet notes of poetic inspiration! At eleven I wished to be considered an authoress. Novels were thrown aside. Poetry and Essays were my studies and I felt the most ardent desire to understand the learned languages. To comprehend even the Greek alphabet was delight inexpressible. Under the tuition of Mr. McSwiney I attained that which I so fervently desired. . . .

[At twelve] I read Milton for the first time thro' together with Shakespeare and Pope's Homer. . . .

I perused all modern authors who have any claim to superior merit and poetic excellence. I was familiar with Shakespeare, Milton, Homer and Virgil, Locke, Hooker, Pope. I read Homer in the original with delight inexpressible, together with Virgil. [*A*, 9–15]

This astonishing record indicates that, even as a young girl, Barrett appreciated both the tradition she hoped to appropriate and also the crucial importance of the classics in the education of an English poet. That formal education she was denied by virtue of gender she sought to gain for herself. As an adolescent, she received permission to study with her brother's tutor, Mr. McSwiney. Then, as a young woman, she acted as an amanuensis to Hugh Boyd, a blind, rather pedantic, and second-rate Greek scholar, who lived near the Barrett house at Hope End, Malvern, and had written to the young poet in 1826 after the publication of *An Essay on Mind*. This educational history was not the equivalent of Eton and Oxbridge, but it demonstrates Barrett's understanding of the apprenticeship necessary for a poet.

Years later she reevaluated the time spent pondering the minutiae of Greek grammar and working on a study of the Greek

Christian poets with Boyd, recognizing it as wasted labor. In 1845 she wrote to a Miss Thompson, who had requested some translations from the Greek for an anthology: "Perhaps I do not . . . partake quite your 'divine fury' for converting our sex into Greek scholarship. . . . You . . . know that the Greek language . . . swallows up year after year of studious life. Now I have a 'doxy', . . . that there is no exercise of the mind so little profitable to the mind as the study of languages. It is the nearest thing to a passive recipiency—is it not?—as a mental action, though it leaves one weary as ennui itself. Women want to be made to *think actively*" (*L*, 1:260–61). Barrett never analyzed why Greek scholarship induces a "passive recipiency" in woman, precluding her need to "think actively." It is tempting to infer her conviction that study of the classics forces woman to read herself always as the object of male narrative, while to "think actively" necessitates claiming herself as subject of experience and discourse. However valid this mature evaluation of classical study for women may be, Barrett was wise to immerse herself in such study as a young poet. It gave her the credentials to be taken seriously by the critics and enabled her as a poet to engage in the epic terms she would finally realize in *Aurora Leigh*, not merely in the lyrical verse of the affections associated with the popular "poetesses."

The young Barrett, to use de Beauvoir's terms, "play[ed] at being a man" by linguistically "dress[ing] up in men's clothes" (*MRM*, 2:7). At fourteen, in her Preface to *The Battle of Marathon*, she declared Homer as the model for her epic poem based on the Greek defense against Persian invaders on the plains of Marathon in 490 B.C.: "It would have been both absurd and presumptuous, young and inexperienced as I am, to have attempted to strike out a path for myself" (*W*, 1:9). Yet even in this work, Barrett demonstrated strategies for appropriating the "path" that this literary father had walked. She assumed a male identity: "He who writes an epic poem must transport himself to the scene of action; he must imagine himself possessed of the same opinions, manners, prejudices, and belief; he must suppose himself to be the hero he delineates" (*W*, 1:7–8). Yet earlier she had revealed the poem's true hero: "Who can be indifferent, who can preserve his tranquillity, when he hears of one little city rising undaunted, and daring her innumerable enemies, in defense of her freedom?" (W, 1:6). The epic poet she designated, according to convention, as "he," and yet the "little city rising" she designated, again according to convention, as female. Naming her poetic self as male while creating the epic hero with whom "he" must identify not as a brave male but as a courageous female both located Barrett within a tradition and also subverted it by elevating a rebellious woman who is acting "in defense of her freedom" as subject of the story to be told.

Barrett studied Homer not only in the original but also in Pope's translation. This informed her imitation of Pope in *An Essay on Mind* (1826), a poem remarkable only for demonstrating Barrett's erudition in philosophy. Barrett then returned to classical sources, and in 1833 she published her first translation of Aeschylus's *Prometheus Bound*, a Romantic endeavor that assumes an added dimension for a woman whose disobedient act of writing resonated to Prometheus's theft of fire from the gods. In her Preface to the translation, reworked and published with her *Poems of 1850*, she described a kinship with Aeschylus as one of the "ancient Greeks [who] . . . felt passionately, and thought daringly" (W, 6:83). Barrett did not attempt a Shelleyan revision of the Prometheus myth, but her translation exhibited her classical credentials and also linked her with a writer who represented her own ambitions as woman and poet to feel passionately and be daring in thought. She recognized that "sometimes [Aeschylus's] fancy rushes in, where his judgment fears to tread" (W, 6:84), as she would later determine that the poem which eventually became *Aurora Leigh* would "rush into drawing-rooms & the like 'where angels fear to tread'" (RB&EBB, 1:31). Certainly Barrett's intentions from an early age were infused with entrepreneurial energy. Whereas Tennyson's early poems had languid heroines, Barrett boldly walked where women had for too long feared to tread; her early publications demonstrate how centrally she wished to locate herself in English poetic tradition.

She conformed to the apprenticeship of imitating the fathers, yet she was also aware very early that her gender necessitated comment:

> My mind is naturally independant [*sic*] and spurns that sub-
> serviency of opinion which is generally considered necessary
> to feminine softness. But this is a subject on which I must
> always feel strongly, for I feel within me an almost proud
> consciousness of independance [*sic*] which prompts me to
> defend my opinions and to yield them only to conviction!!!!!!!
>
> My friends may differ from me: the world may accuse me
> but this I am determined never to retract!!
>
> Better, oh how much better, to be the ridicule of mankind,
> the scoff of society, than lose that self respect which tho'
> this heart were bursting would elevate me above misery—
> above wretchedness and above abasement!!! These princi-
> ples are irrevocable! It is not—I feel it is not vanity that
> dictates them! it is not—I know it is not an encroachment
> on Masculine prerogative but it is a proud sentiment which
> will never, never allow me to be humbled in my own eyes!!!
> [*A*, 24]

Aware that "subserviency of opinion" is conventionally demanded
of women, she determined to nurture her right to an independent
mind. The style, with all its exclamation points and exaggerated
language, is adolescent in expression, yet it reveals Barrett's understanding that the independent thinking demanded of a poet
would render women the "ridicule of mankind, the scoff of society." Although many poets have suffered such scorn, the young
Barrett was aware that she would be ridiculed, not as men are for
the content of their thought, but as women are, for the act of
thinking at all.

She evidences how hard it was to sustain her commitment to
the intellectual life in her surviving diary (June 1831 to May
1832).[3] When Boyd wrote to her after reading *An Essay on Mind*,
inviting her to visit him and his family in nearby Malvern, Barrett's father forbade the visit: "as a *female*, and a *young* female"
such a visit would be overstepping the established observances of
society (*HSB*, 11). Even when the friendship was finally established and Barrett visited Boyd as often as possible to work at
Greek, her aunt "Bummy" (who cared for the family of ten after
their mother's death in 1828) and her sister Henrietta frowned on
this transgression of woman's social norm:

This evening, Henrietta proposed inviting Mrs. Griffith to drink tea here tomorrow,—upon which, Bummy insisted on my returning from Malvern sooner than I shd otherwise do!! I was annoyed & said so—& even refused going at all, in the case of my being obliged to come back, by anything else than darkness. Henrietta need not have asked Mrs. G tomorrow, —nor, if she had asked her, need *I* have been forced to receive her company. But the point was yielded at last—of course by *me*! [D, 131]

Her family was distressed at the "impropriety" of her feeling *"more friendship for Mr. Boyd than for the Martins!* . . . They have, as most people have, clearer ideas of the aristocracy of rank & wealth, than of the aristocracy of mind" (D, 104). How different must intellectual life have been for Tennyson in the company of the Apostles at Cambridge, or for Robert Browning in the home that his parents provided when he determined to be a poet, where his friendship with Carlyle developed. Her relationship with Boyd was analogous to the one Eliot imagined between Dorothea Brooke and Mr. Casaubon: "My dear friend Mr. Boyd!— If he knew how much it gratifies me to assist him in any way (I wish I cd do so in *every*way) all his '*drudgeries*' wd devolve upon me" (D, 44). Although Boyd encouraged Barrett's studies, he also trivialized her:

[Mr. Boyd] asked me to talk to Mr. Spowers at dinner: "on *his* account, he thought I ought to do it." I promised to do my best; and as I went out of the room, he said that I must remember what I had promised, & that he wd ask Mrs. Boyd if I had been "naughty or good." I in a panic of course. . . . Down to dinner. I impelled myself to talk, whether I had anything to say or not—to talk about the country, & the newspaper, & the raven, & Joanna Baillie & Lord Byron. So that when I had to answer Mr. Boyd's "naughty or good," I could say "good." [D, 58]

It is hard to imagine Tennyson, Browning, or Arnold accused of valuing intellect more than afternoon tea, of being called "naughty" at twenty-five. Yet these comparisons reveal the very different issues at the heart of creative composition for men and women bound by such cultural conventions. As surely as Dickens's childhood experiences—the blacking factory and his parents' imprisonment for debt—defined the nature of his fiction, so Barrett's experience of growing up female while determining to be a poet defined the form of her poetry. Only when the basic issue for a woman is understood to be "dare she write" (what Gilbert and Gubar refer to as the "anxiety of authorship") as much as "what to write" (the "anxiety of influence") can she be appreciated on her own terms. Whereas in her intellectual life Barrett was studying and imitating the classics, emotionally she recognized the discrepancy between the world expressed in male poetry and that inhabited by middle-class woman.

Many women and men exhorted middle-class woman to her role of wife and mother: the sentiments of Sarah Stickney Ellis (whose *Women of England* was published in the same year as *The Seraphim, and Other Poems*) were typical:

> Women, considered in their distinct and abstract nature, as isolated beings, must lose more than half their worth. They are, in fact, from their own constitution, and from the station they occupy in the world, strictly speaking, relative creatures. If, therefore, they are endowed with only such faculties as render them striking and distinguished in themselves, without the faculty of instrumentality, they are only as dead letters in the volume of human life, filling what would otherwise be a blank space, but doing nothing more.[4]

Barrett, in a letter to Kenyon about *The Seraphim, and Other Poems*, insisted that the expression of her own "individuality" represented "maturity" and belonging to the "living" (*L*, 1:187). Conversely, Ellis exhorted women to remember that because by nature they are "relative creatures" to their parents, husbands, and children, "individuality" renders them "dead letters." Ellis's rather than Barrett's convictions informed the work of the two most popular nineteenth-century "poetesses," Letitia Landon and Felicia Hemans.

Landon in her Preface to "The Venetian Bracelet" identifies love as her "source of song": "For a woman, whose influence and whose sphere must be in the affections, what subject can be more fitting than one which it is her peculiar province to refine, spiritualize, and exalt? I have always sought to paint it self-deny-ing, devoted, and making an almost religion of its truth." In the "Immolation of a Hindoo Widow" Landon takes such self-denial to its extreme in her depiction of suttee:

> The red pile blazes—let the bride ascend,
>   And lay her head upon her husband's heart,
> Now in a perfect unison to blend—
>   No more to part.

Hemans equally defines woman as a relative creature. Unlike Barrett who admired de Stael's poet heroine, Corinne, Hemans (recalling a scene in the novel in which Corinne receives the poet's laurel) concludes "Corinne at the Capitol" as follows:

> Happier, happier far than thou,
> With the laurel on thy brow,
> She that makes the humblest hearth
> Lovely but to one on earth!

For the poetesses, woman's role was usually accompanied by suf-fering in the wake of betrayal, loss, and rejection. In "Madeline," from *Records of Woman*, Hemans describes woman's destiny as being to "suffer and be still." Sarah Stickney Ellis endorsed He-mans's attitude, taking those words as the epigraph for *Women of England*.

In the "Indian Woman's Death-Song" (*Records of Woman*), however, Hemans has a mother drown herself and her daughter after her husband deserted them:

> "And thou, my babe! though born, like me, for woman's
>   weary lot,
> Smile!—to that wasting of the heart, my own! I leave
>   thee not;
> Too bright a thing art *thou* to pine in aching love away—
> Thy mother bears thee far, young fawn! from sorrow and
>   decay."

Hemans's recognition that "woman's weary lot" is intolerable represents a rage against the very condition she attempts to sup-port. This rage, rumbling under the sentimental, domestic sur-face of both her work and Landon's, is portrayed as violence that is inflicted on women by themselves or others, and ultimately expressed as death. The anger, which cannot be turned on the men who make them suffer, destroys the devoted "angels" themselves. If the frequent deaths of women in the poetesses' work are viewed not only as a morbid or sentimental strain but also as an expression of this anger inflicted by robust women writers on their long-suffering heroine victims, then such deaths can be seen as a strategy to exalt suffering woman while desiring to kill her off as an image of womanhood. It was a strategy Barrett inherited.

Although Barrett's record of her early reading focused on male writing, certainly by her late teens she was familiar with the work of the poetesses. The two poems she most liked in *The Literary Souvenir; or, Cabinet of Poetry and Romance* for 1826 were Landon's "The Forsaken" and Hemans's "The Wreck."[5] She eulogized both poets after their deaths in "Felicia Hemans" (*W*, 2:83) and "L.E.L.'s Last Question" (*W*, 3:117), revealing thorough knowledge of their work. Yet, although their verse engaged her and often found echoes in the choice, if not the treatment, of her own subject matter, Barrett recognized the limitations of both Hemans and Landon as poets as she assessed them to her friend, Mary Russell Mitford:

> If I had those two powers to choose from . . Mrs. Hemans's & Miss Landon's . . I mean the *raw* bare powers . . I wd choose Miss Landon's. I surmise that it was more elastic, more various, of a stronger web. I fancy it wd have worked out better—had it *been* worked out—with the right moral & intellectual influences in application. As it is, Mrs. Hemans has left the finer poems. Of that there can be no question. But perhaps . . & indeed I do say it very diffidently . . there is a sense of sameness which goes with the sense of excellence,—while we read her poems—a satiety with the satisfaction together with a feeling "this writer has written her best,"—or "It is very well—but it can never be better." [*MRM*, 1:235]

Barrett never placed Hemans and Landon in the same class as Homer, Aeschylus, Milton, Pope, or Wordsworth—the class to which she aspired. Nevertheless, they offered her a valuable model of women whose lives had been devoted to writing poetry. Even though they wrote of women analogous to Milton's Eve, they modeled woman actively describing herself rather than being passively described. It is qualitatively different to "suffer and be still" and to suffer and write about it. Yet at best, Hemans, Landon, and their like offered Barrett problematic models: patronized by the critics; committed to the notion that it was better for a woman to "make the humblest hearth" than to "wear the laurel on [her] brow"; and diligent in their portrayal of woman's acceptance of her "weary lot." Lacking the stature of the revered and envied precursors by which male poets were nurtured, they did not challenge the privileged male voice of English poetry.

Women prose writers pioneered an alternative image of womanhood for the young Barrett: "I read Mary Wolstonecraft when I was thirteen: no twelve! . . and, through the whole course of my childhood, I had a steady indignation against Nature who made me a woman, & a determinate resolution to dress up in men's clothes as soon as ever I was free of the nursery, & go into the world 'to seek my fortune.' '*How*,' was not decided; but I rather leant towards being poor Lord Byron's PAGE" (*MRM*, 2:7). Her "steady indignation against Nature" was Barrett's protest against woman as long-suffering relative creature. Wollstonecraft emphasized learning and education for women, even while stressing the importance of her role as educated wife and mother. However, by the time she wrote *The Seraphim, and Other Poems* Barrett had read Madame de Stael's *Corinne* three times. Here for the first time was woman, in her own "clothes," represented as a poet. De Stael juxtaposed the freedom possible in Italy for woman's artistic endeavors and sexual passion with a passive servitude and repression she depicted as required of English women. The Italian landscape and sensibility provided Barrett with a metaphor for artistic freedom (even before she lived there), which she later exploited fully in *Aurora Leigh*. These literary mothers, while not being precursors held in general esteem, provided models for Barrett's task of creating an image of woman from her felt reality. She was aware that it was in *The Seraphim, and Other Poems* that such a "reality" began to take shape.

Barrett's awareness that this volume revealed an original poetic voice was shared by reviewers whose responses appeared in many journals, including the *Examiner*, the *Athenaeum*, *Blackwood's Edinburgh Magazine*, the *Quarterly Review*, the *North American Review*, and the *English Review*.[6] They paid unusually serious attention to this unknown woman poet, placing her in a male tradition, yet treating her as a woman poet.

Echoing Barrett's sense of her "own individuality," the *Athenaeum* found *The Seraphim* "an extraordinary volume" (466), while the *Quarterly Review*, in a discussion of nine women poets, was representative in recognizing that Barrett both stood out "as well for her extraordinary acquaintance with ancient classic literature, as for the boldness of her poetic attempts," and failed to achieve a "success ... in proportion to her daring" (382–83). However, the *North American Review*, like her mentors, Boyd and Kenyon (but unlike Robert Browning), lamented that as Barrett progressed from her early male imitations into a more original voice, she violated poetic decorum. In *The Seraphim*, which "contains more of original poetry" than both her former volumes, the reviewer found that "her mind has gone through essential changes, which are not in all respects for the better. . . . Her great defect is a certain lawless extravagance" (207).

In their discussion of the title poem, "The Seraphim," reviewers saw Barrett as heir to a poetic tradition epitomized in their minds by Milton. Barrett talked of Aeschylus as her inspiration for this poem, but its focus on the Crucifixion evoked Milton's earlier treatment of the Fall. The *Examiner* felt that "sacred subjects" were "not fit for poetry," that even "Milton degraded the Deity" and "the presumption of Dante is at least equal to his genius" (387). The *Quarterly Review* judged that "The Seraphim" was "a subject from which Milton would have shrunk." However, the *English Review* allowed the poem almost unqualified approval and, without "quot[ing] Milton in defense of our author," judged Barrett fully "justified in approaching such a theme" (264).

Dante, Milton. The reviewers sensed in Barrett a poet who deserved mention with pillars of the male tradition. Yet in *Aurora Leigh* Romney argues against Aurora's being a poet:

You never can be satisfied with praise
Which men give women when they judge a book
Not as mere work but as mere woman's work,
Expressing the comparative respect
Which means the absolute scorn.

[2.232–36]

This double standard was widespread, as confirmed by the reviewers' treatment of Barrett as a woman poet.[7]

In *Blackwood's,* "Christopher North" admired Barrett's work. Yet he typifies those reviewers who in a patronizing tone created a halo round the smiling face of "our fair author," the "fair Elizabeth." He questioned, "What other pretty book is this? 'The Seraphim, and other Poems,' by Elizabeth Barnett [*sic*], author of a Translation of 'Prometheus Bound.' High adventure for a Lady —implying a knowledge of Hebrew—or if not—of Greek. No common mind displays itself in this Preface pregnant with lofty thoughts. Yet is her heart humble withal." Placing Barrett in a tradition of women poets—of Mary Tighe, Felicia Hemans ("that other Sweetest Singer")—and Letitia Landon—North queried, "Surely Poetesses (is there such a word?) are very happy, in spite of all the 'natural sorrows, griefs, and pains,' to which their exquisitely sensitive being must be perpetually alive" (281). He dismissed the tensions manifest in Barrett's work: "And our Elizabeth—she too is happy—though in her happiness she loveth to veil with a melancholy haze the brightness of her childhood— and of her maidenhood."

This sentimentality also informed the *Quarterly Review's* discussion of Barrett among nine women poets:

We feel that we never did a bolder thing than now we do, in summoning these nine Muses to our Quarter Sessions. The very ink turns blue with which we write their names.

It is easy to be critical on men; but when we venture to lift a pen against women, straightway *apparent facies;* the weapon drops pointless on the marked passage; and whilst the mind is bent on praise or censure of the poem, the eye swims too deep in tears and mist over the poetess herself in the frontispiece, to let it see its way to either. [375]

The review is, in fact, quite rigorous and insightful, but the reviewer adopted rhetoric associated with the female poet, making her a quite different species from the male. Detracting from a focus on her poetry, the *North American Review*, placing Barrett as one of the "tuneful tribe" (206), lamented, "In regard to this lady . . . [we] are ignorant of her lineage, her education, her tastes, and (last not least, where a lady is concerned,) her personal attractions" (202). Only the *English Review* addressed the issue of male prejudice against women writers: "her scholarship, solid and genuine, can defy the charge of female pedantry: that jealous cant of ignorant men is now, indeed, almost exploded; and women may not only cultivate high knowledge, but confess, and dare to show it, without disparagement to womanhood" (264).

Overall the reviewers preferred to imagine Barrett as a poetess; if, by invoking Milton's name, they saw "The Seraphim" as the quintessentially male poem of the volume, they found "Isobel's Child" the quintessentially female one—such that it was mentioned and quoted in almost every journal. Clearly they felt comfortable with that most feminine icon—mother and child. The poem is a dialogue between a mother who is willing her sick infant to live and the infant who is desiring to die, to escape earth's suffering. The *Athenaeum* devoted two sentimental columns to quoting from and summarizing the poem. "Christopher North" found that "the workings of a mother's love through all the phases of fear, and hope, and despair, and heavenly consolation, are given with extraordinary power" (279–80). The *Quarterly Review* considered this "somewhat fantastic poem . . . a fair specimen of Miss Barrett's general manner and power" (388). The *North American Review* acknowledged that it was a "poem of singular originality of conception and impassioned depth of feeling . . . suggested by an infant sleeping upon its mother's arm" (209). The *English Review* chose "Isobel's Child" as its "favorite . . . tender, thoughtful, and imaginative, the poem flows naturally on, developing with fine pathos the meaning of its text." The reviewers did not wholeheartedly endorse the poem. But neither coincidence nor aesthetics determined so many to discuss "Isobel's Child": it was surely the fact that only this poem depicted woman in her "natural role," as a mother with her baby.

To the reviewers Barrett's gender was a crucial issue, provoking both patronizing condescension and startled admiration. Either way they recognized in this volume representing her "own individuality" an original poetic voice: it was neither familiarly male nor, alarmingly and refreshingly, did it speak as a woman should.

The reviewers' recognition of Barrett both as heir to a male tradition and also as poetess dramatically presents the dialectic that operated throughout her career until she achieved her synthesis of these two roles in *Aurora Leigh*. In particular, two pairs of poems in *The Seraphim, and Other Poems* reveal this dialectic as Barrett simultaneously presents and challenges traditional literary images of woman: Barrett's revisionary reading of Aeschylus in "The Seraphim" and her "tender" "Isobel's Child"; her revisionary reading of Wordsworth in "The Poet's Vow" and her heroine of the affections in "The Romaunt of Margret."

In the Preface to the title poem, "The Seraphim," Barrett evoked a male precursor; she revealed her "thought, that had Aeschylus lived after the incarnation and crucifixion of our Lord Jesus Christ, he might have turned ... from the solitude of Caucasus to the deeper desertness of that crowded Jerusalem where none had any pity" (*W*, 1:164). "The Seraphim," not one of Barrett's enduring achievements, is ostensibly an orthodox Christian celebration of divine love made manifest through the Crucifixion. However, her "vision of the supreme spectacle" from "a less usual aspect" (*W*, 1:167), namely that of two angels, covertly, if not self-consciously, allowed Barrett to create a narrative strategy both for presenting woman's relationship to public events and also for analyzing her subjective experience of that relationship.

In Aeschylus, Prometheus and those who visit him speak; Milton's narrative allowed for extensive dialogue between the principals of the action. Barrett, although following epic tradition in designating her angels male, chose an "aspect" for them suggestive of women's relation to public events; her protagonists are spectators of, not actors in, the public drama. How consciously Barrett at this stage linked woman and angel it is impossible to know, but it was certainly an established connection after Coventry Patmore published "The Angel in the House" (1854–62).

Using the "less usual aspect" of the angels, Barrett decentered the male narrative; however, she did not allow woman's subjective experience to replace it:

> A woman kneels
> The mid cross under,
> With white lips asunder.
> And motion on each.
> They throb, as she feels,
> With a spasm, not a speech.
> [2.476–81]

The Crucifixion could not be viewed from Mary's point of view —an equally "less usual aspect"—because as woman she had to "suffer and be still," to feel with "a spasm, not a speech."

In "The Seraphim," however, Jesus, recognized by Zerah and Ador, the two angels, as both "man's victim" and "his deity" (1.248), suggests the paradox of Victorian middle-class woman's being viewed both as powerless "relative creature" in a society venerating masculine industrial power and also as "angel" worshipped for her moral integrity. Jesus thereby dramatizes woman's position, creating an analogy between the divine Jesus's assuming the human condition and woman's entering male public life. The poem's fascination with dangerous public events of earth rather than with the safe security of the angels' Heaven serves as a metaphor for female desire to be included in such events, whatever the cost.

The angels assess this public life on earth, comparing it with their protected home, Heaven. Zerah, convinced that "Heaven is dull,/ Mine Ador, to man's earth" (2.596–97), describes the former:

> The light that burns
> In fluent, refluent motion
> Along the crystal ocean;
> The springing of the golden harps between
> The bowery wings, in fountains of sweet sound,
> The winding, wandering music that returns
> Upon itself, exultingly self-bound

> In the great spheric round
> Of everlasting praises.
>
> [2.597–605]

In spite of these sensuous qualities, Zerah yearns for involvement in earthly "dust and death" (2.612): the "fluent, refluent" Heaven with its "winding, wandering music" cloys beside earth's harsher realities. Far from having "bowery wings," nature is destructive: "The yew-tree bows its melancholy head / And all the undergrasses kills and seres" (1.146–47); and, as Ador recognizes, humans are greedy: "having won the profit which they seek, / Men lie beside the sceptre and the gold / With fleshless hands that cannot wield or hold" (1.151–53). Zerah contrasts Heaven, where "seraphic faces" continually grow more "beautiful with worship and delight" (2.608–10) with earth, where the three who are crucified hang "'Ghast and silent to the sun. / Round them blacken and welter and press / Staring multitudes" (2.460–62). Barrett conveys the horror of the Crucifixion by the crowd's reaction to it as they push and shove to watch rather than by Jesus's suffering. Whereas in Heaven "light . . . burns . . . Along the crystal ocean" and the air is filled with "the springing of the golden harps," on earth light and sound reveal suffering and cruelty:

> Can these love? With the living's pride
> They stare at those who die, who hang
> In their sight and die. They bear the streak
> Of the crosses' shadow, black not wide,
> To fall on their heads, as it swerves aside
> When the victims' pang
> Makes the dry wood creak.
>
> [2.469–75]

Like the Lady of Shalott, the angels desire to be on earth, with all its suffering. Barrett fuses these male angels with female spectators desirous of some involvement in public events.

In the male world of patriarchal struggle enacted at the Crucifixion women have no part. With "a spasm, not a speech" the woman is a powerless and silent observer to the public world of male decision making (God, Herod, Pilate, Judas, Jesus, Peter, the soldiers). Barrett as a woman and a poet partially circumvents this: she assumes the persona of the powerless observer, but gives the angels (closer to androgyny than to traditional masculinity) the right to speech rather than spasm. Zerah identifies himself as "tearless" (2.514) because he is nonhuman, in contrast to Mary who weeps. This links the Miltonic angel as poet interpreter between God and man, and the notion of woman as angel so prevalent in nineteenth-century rhetoric. Fusing here her two traditions—male and female—Barrett, however consciously, dramatizes her desire to engage in activities hitherto reserved for men. It is not an easy task: the angels are fearful of leaving their sheltered domain. They experience "the fear of earth" and understand postlapsarian corruption. Nevertheless, whatever their hesitations while still in Heaven, they find earth preferable to their earlier protected existence. Their reasoning is not persuasive. There is nothing in the language that convinces us earth is a better place. The preference results merely from a belief that Christ/God, taking on human form, makes heaven dull in comparison with "man's earth" for all its corruption, suffering, and death. Such fear, yet determination, suggests the nineteenth-century "angels'" fear of leaving the male-sheltered house for creative combat in a world that denied them place.

Barrett fuses here a woman's desire to engage in the public concerns of humanity with her conviction that such an engagement is the poet's task. She embraces a poetic creed that provides an aesthetic cover for legitimizing her woman's desire for involvement in public concerns, not just domestic issues.

In the epilogue, when the speaker touches on the blasphemy of her enterprise in writing of a sacred subject, Barrett implies the parallel blasphemy of "counterfeiting" male texts by transforming the angels into female speakers whose "language [has] never [been] used or hearkened":

> And I—ah! what am I
> To counterfeit, with faculty earth-darkened,
>   Seraphic brows of light
> And seraph language never used nor hearkened?
> Ah me! what word that seraphs say, could come

From mouth so used to sighs, so soon to lie
Sighless, because then breathless, in the tomb?

[3]

Forgive me, that mine earthly heart should dare
Shape images of unincarnate spirits
And lay upon their burning lips a thought
Cold with the weeping which mine earth inherits.

[4]

The female mouth is "so used to sighs," rather than to the tran-
scendental male privilege of speech, that, having accomplished
her task of "shap[ing] images" and "lay[ing] . . . a thought," the
speaker asks forgiveness for her daring.

In contrast to the external, male-dominated setting of "The
Seraphim," "Isobel's Child" is set indoors and the protagonists
are a mother, her infant son, and his nurse. There is one brief
mention of the child's father. A three-month-old dying child is
brought by the nighttime ministrations of his nurse and his
mother, the Lady Isobel, back to health. Smiling over his recov-
ery, his mother is oblivious to the ominously raging storm outside. The tempestuous "external nature" that "broke / Into such
abandonment" mysteriously (and repressively) transforms its energies into "A sense of silence and of steady / Natural calm"
when it enters the "human creature's room" (5). Here the mother, praying for her child's life, compares herself to "Mary mild"
who was not denied "mother-joy" but was "blessèd in the blessèd child" (10). The boy lives, but after the storm mysteriously
dies down, the infant loses his "baby-looks" for the "earnest gazing deep" (26) of an old man and precociously tells his mother of
his desire for death. This "dark . . . dull / Low earth, by only
weepers trod" (27) cannot compare to his knowledge of the "happy heavenly air" (27) seen in a Wordsworthian "vision and a
gleam":

"I saw celestial places even.
Oh, the vistas of high palms
Making finites of delight
Through the heavenly infinite,

> Lifting up their green still tops
> To the heaven of heaven!"
>
> [29]

He challenges the efficacy of poetry to provide him with a comparable vision:

> "Can your poet make an Eden
> No winter will undo,
> And light a starry fire while heeding
> His hearth's is burning too?
> Drown in music the earth's din,
> And keep his own wild soul within
> The law of his own harmony?"
>
> [31]

He longs for the "little harp . . . whose strings are golden" (31) that waits for him in heaven. The mother, in her happy acceptance of her child's wish, seems unnatural. As Sandra Donaldson points out, the "theme of Christian consolation . . . seems almost formulaic" as the childless Barrett demonstrates how mothers "should be grateful their child is now in heaven. . . . By asking the mother why she would want him to live, the child pushes the theme of Christian consolation to its logical but deadly conclusion."[8]

Obviously, "The Seraphim" and "Isobel's Child" can be seen as exercises in orthodox religious thought—God's great love manifest in the Incarnation and Crucifixion, and the consolation of heaven. But what concerns me is the opposing visions these two poems represent in the context of their settings. The public male drama, played out at the Crucifixion at which Mary is speechless and powerless, makes heaven seem dull and earth, if not exciting or attractive, at least appealing in its dynamic energy. On the other hand the private female drama, enacted in the domestic interior of the Lady Isobel's castle, around which a turbulent external world whirls, exhibits only "dreary earthly love" in a world of "weepers." In comparison, the open spaces of heaven, offering "vistas of high palms" and the "sweet life-tree that drops / Shade like light across the river" (29), promise a more enticing vision to the infant, one of a future not spent with women in the castle but outside in highways of heaven bustling with a "thousand, thousand faces," where he can play his harp "tuned to music spherical, / Hanging on the green life-tree / Where no willows ever be" (31). Whereas the woman in "The Seraphim" is silent and powerless, the male infant of "Isobel's Child" convinces his mother his words should be privileged.

"The Seraphim" stresses the desire for involvement in the turmoil and joy of humanity, thereby privileging the public world, which is associated with men. "Isobel's Child" sees in the domestic world of the female only suffering on earth and finds death and heaven to be preferable states. While Christian consolation may be the overt message of both poems, covertly they repudiate the claustrophobia perceived in female-dominated internal space and endorse the attraction of "man's earth," male-dominated external space.

"The Romaunt of Margret" and "The Poet's Vow" should also be viewed as companion poems. Barrett's acknowledged intention was to show in "The Romaunt of Margret" that the "creature cannot be *sustained* by the creature," and in "The Poet's Vow" to "enforce a truth—that the creature cannot be *isolated* from the creature" (W, 1:168). However, at the same time she also challenges cultural assumptions about woman and the male poet. In "The Romaunt of Margret" woman, identified purely as a relative creature, dies. The male poet in "The Poet's Vow" is deluded when he imagines he can retreat from human interaction and substitute maternal nature for woman.

"The Romaunt of Margret" is a ballad. The poetesses had already appropriated the revived form by introducing issues of domesticity. Landon's "Song of the Hunter's Bride" (from *The Troubadour*) is a conventional tale of a woman anxiously awaiting her husband's return from hunting. As it grows late she fears he has been hurt, then complains,

> Why stays he thus?—he would be here
> If his love equall'd mine;—
> Methinks had I one fond cage dove,
> I would not let it pine.

This complaint is undercut by her joy at her husband's eventual return, "My Ulric, welcome home." But the image of woman as

analogous to a "fond cage dove" lingers. In Hemans's "Troubadour Song" a warrior fights valiantly in a grisly battle. His life of
external masculine activity is juxtaposed with the feminine passivity of the woman left behind in her "smiling home." The warrior survives the "thousand arrows" to return, but the woman
meanwhile had "died as roses die, / That perish with a breeze."
Although the poem stereotypes the knight and lady, its final
question, "There was death within the smiling home— / How
had death found her there?" suggests a murderous idle domesticity.

Barrett takes this fatal domesticity to its extreme in "The
Romaunt of Margret." A fairly conventional ballad narrative, in
which Margret dies because she has lost her love, reveals a domestic subtext dramatizing the killing of the Angel in the House.
In *Professions for Women* Virginia Woolf records how, as a writer,
she had to do battle with a phantom, suggestive of Ellis's "woman of England":

> She was intensely sympathetic. She was immensely charm-
> ing. She was utterly unselfish. She excelled in the difficult
> arts of family life. She sacrificed herself daily. If there was
> chicken, she took the leg; if there was a draught she sat in
> it—in short she was so constituted that she never had a
> mind or a wish of her own, but preferred to sympathize al-
> ways with the minds and wishes of others. Above all—I need
> not say it—she was pure. . . . Had I not killed her she would
> have killed me. She would have plucked the heart out of my
> writing.

Woolf knew that to write demands "having a mind of your own,
. . . expressing what you think to be the truth about human relations, morality, sex. And all these questions, according to the
Angel in the House, cannot be dealt with freely and openly by
women; they must charm, they must conciliate, they must—to
put it bluntly—tell lies if they are to succeed." Woolf battled
this image of woman, consuming time better spent on "roaming
the world in search of adventures." She recognized that "killing
the Angel in the House was part of the occupation of a woman
writer."[9]

Barrett's 1838 and 1844 ballads evoke a figure like Woolf's Angel. Alethea Hayter describes "Mrs. Browning's Ideal Woman, noble, constant, self-sacrificing, and all blushes, tears and hair down to the ground" as a "tiresome creature." While Hayter's sense that she is "a perfectly nineteenth-century figure" may be accurate, I would argue that it is the age's rather than Barrett's "Ideal Woman."[10] However unconsciously, "The Romaunt of Margret" reveals a narrative desire to "kill off" this "tiresome creature," not endorse her; Margret dies because she fulfilled her female duty to tend to others and it proved insufficiently life-sustaining.

Certainly Margret is a "relative creature": she embroiders her brother's "knightly scarf," attends his animals, waits at home for his return, sings "hunter's songs" to him, and pours him his "red wine"; she combs her sister's hair, gives her her own special bird, shares flowers with her, and rears her in Godliness. She is also her father's special handmaiden (more favored than the "hundred friends" in his court); denying herself the delight of watching the knights at tournament, she reads him a "weary book" and cherishes "his blessing when [she's] done." When not caring for her family, she sits by the river thinking of her "more than a friend / Across the mountains dim." She wears his "last look in [her] soul, / Which said, *I love but thee!*" Margret is indeed an ideal daughter of England, a veritable Angel in the House. Why does she die? Ellis would say that such unrequited love as Margret gives to her family and the suffering engendered by the separation from her lover merely require her to "suffer and be still." Margret dies because her daemon, the shadow that rises from the water and sits beside her, engages Margret in dialogue, confronting her with a subversive message. The narrator's response is to lament that earthly love will not last: "O failing human love! . . . O false, the while thou treadest earth!" But the daemon suggests that an existence predicated entirely on Ellis's notion of the "faculty of instrumentality," of being identified as always in a serving relationship to others, kills women. The daemon challenges the idea that the self-identified woman, with "faculties [that] render her striking and distinguished" in herself, is merely a "dead letter in the volume of human life"; she implies that the "relative creature" cannot sustain her own life. Margret's main fantasies focus on her absent lover, but it is not, as Gardner Taplin asserts, merely his death that kills her:[11] it is the gradual recognition of the murderous instrumentality of her existence. As the daemon asserts that her brother, her sister, and her father love their material possessions more than they love Margret, the physical environment around her withers, representing the withering of her own life:

> The sounding river which rolled, for ever
> Stood dumb and stagnant after.
>
> [14]
>
> You could see each bird as it woke and stared
> Through the shrivelled foliage after.
>
> [17]
>
> And moon and stars though bright and far
> Did shrink and darken after.
>
> [20]

Margret exists solely in her serving relation to others and on the fantasy of a lover: when that role proves to be futile, she dies. The daemon asphyxiates the angel.

The narrator, a troubadour, begins her singing of the "wild romaunt" in the present tense as though describing a scene unfolding before her. This continues until the daemon ("the lady's shadow") leaves the water: "It standeth upright in the cleft moonlight, / It sitteth at her side." The narrator now addresses Margret, forcing her to look at the daemon, her own death: "Look in its face, ladye." At this the narrator seems frightened by her own tale for she removes herself from the action, changes to the past tense, and the rest of the tale is a record of, rather than an involvement with, Margret's story.

Whereas in the first stanza the narrator knows her tale is of death—"The yew-tree leaf will suit"—by the last stanza she feels inadequate to telling her tale: "I have no voice for song. / Not song but wail, and mourners pale, / Not bards, to love belong." Her exclamatory ending shifts from narration to rhetorical chant and her lament certainly lends credence to the notion of the poem as one of transitory love:

> O failing human love!
> O light, by darkness known!

O false, the while thou treadest earth!
O deaf beneath the stone!

But she feels that "mourners" not "bards" belong to love (echoing Mary's feeling with "a spasm, not a speech" in "The Seraphim"). Does this imply that the poet's function is not to tell the
story of "failing human love," but to indict a society that suggests that its middle-class women can and must survive only on
love?

The confused relationship of the narrator to her tale suggests
an anxiety about the implications of her subject matter, determined to an extent by the autobiographical impulse informing
this poem. Dwelling on Barrett's invalidism, Porter and Clarke
focus on such an impulse: "Elizabeth must have been the paint-
er's manikin, serving as first model for Margret. . . . The hold on
life through the love of others in life,—for the sake of a peculiarly loved brother's love, a cherished little sister's, a fondly
proud father's,—these are all longing snatches at the life about
to elude Margret which must have quivered through the out-
stretched fingers of her own actual experience" (W, 2:vii-viii).
What Porter and Clarke fail to recognize is that life is only about
to elude Margret because she realizes that her love is not returned and that she is a drudge.

Much of the autobiographical significance lies not in Barrett's
precarious health (as Porter and Clarke imagine), but in the relationship between Barrett and her mother. The narrator offers no
explanation for the missing mother, but the implication is that
she died in the same way as Margret dies, through unrequited
self-sacrificing love. It is also ominously suggested that Margret's younger sister, who "wears / The look our mother wore"
(15) will die this inevitable female death. Margret, successfully
educated to be womanly, has taken on her mother's role: she is
sister/lover to her brother, sister/mother to her sister, and daugh-
ter/wife to her father. The poem, therefore, repeats Barrett's
own family situation with her brothers, younger sisters, and her
father.

Through study and invalidism, Barrett had sought to avoid the
female occupations, thereby incurring the wrath of her sister,
Henrietta. She was subject to the departures and returns of her

favorite brother, Edward, whose masculine freedom she envied in her youth. And, although he encouraged her writing, her father was peremptory, authoritarian, and emotionally contained. In 1828, when Barrett was twenty-two, her mother died, having given birth to twelve children (one died). Barrett wrote about her to Browning: "Scarcely was I woman when I lost *my* mother—dearest as she was & very tender, . . . but of a nature harrowed up into some furrows by the pressure of circumstances. . . . A sweet, gentle nature, which the thunder a little turned from its sweetness—as when it turns milk—One of those women who never can resist,—but, in submitting & bowing on themselves, make a mark, a plait, within, . . a sign of suffering. Too womanly was she—it was her only fault" (*RB&EBB*, 2:1012). Barrett describes her mother in language analogous to Woolf's angel, "A sweet, gentle nature. . . . One of those women who can never resist . . . submitting and bowing." To Barrett being such a woman was a "fault." The angel cannot sustain her sweet submissive nature because the "thunder" (Mr. Barrett?) "a little turned [her] from its sweetness—as when it turns milk." Barrett is ambivalent in both admiring and condemning her mother for being such a woman; yet she attributes her mother's death to embracing that role. It was not a role her eldest daughter intended to assume. And, as though dramatizing these responses to her mother's life, in "The Romaunt of Margret" she examines the fate of a woman who was "too womanly . . . it was her only fault."[12] However, the narrator never spells out the implications of her tale, that a woman who refuses to see herself as the relative creature Margret is, and who realizes herself through "such faculties, as render [her] striking and distinguished" in herself, will survive. Such a woman could be a poet.

Barrett's early resistance to marriage and her suspicion of romantic love are dramatized by Margret's death when the lover across the "mountains dim" (was he ever real?) dies. Romantic love is unreliable. Margret's death then is not merely a melancholy repetition of ballad conventions, but a questioning of their assumptions. The poem annihilates woman's self-annihilative role. The heroine's death, which we expect to mourn, becomes in fact a liberating act, freeing Barrett from the "Ideal Woman's" fate.

The protagonist's death is an equally sorrowful yet liberating act in "The Poet's Vow," Barrett's revisionary reading of Wordsworth and of Romantic ideology about Nature. Barrett's overt admiration of and covert entrapment by Wordsworth as a precursor are revealed in "The Book of the Poets," her critical essay on the history of English poetry published in the *Athenaeum* (1842). She laments how the followers of Dryden and Pope reduced poetry to "the trick of accoustical mechanics," how in their writings "thought had perished . . . and we had the beaten rhythm without the living footstep." In their work Nature had been "expelled" (W, 6:299). But Cowper, Burns, and Coleridge heralded a change consummated by Wordsworth, "the chief of the movement." These poets allowed "Nature, the long banished, [to re-dawn] like the morning." To accomplish this they abandoned, after a hard struggle, the "conventional dialects" of poets, conventional words, attitudes, and manners, consecrated by "wits." Wordsworth "in a bravery bravest of all . . . to the actual scandal of the world which stared at the filial familiarity, . . . threw himself not at the feet of Nature, but straightway and right tenderly upon her bosom . . . trustfully as child before mother" (W, 6:300). Barrett cites Wordsworth as the primary poet of Nature, suggesting that he and his rhetoric of Nature had a much stronger influence on her than other Romantic poets. Indeed, she outgrew her adolescent fervor for Byron, admired Keats, but found Shelley too cold and distant as a poet.

Wordsworth was spokesman for a literary tradition that posited Nature as a maternal figure. A psychoanalytic scenario of this would, thereby, have the male precursor poet as the father, and the female presence in Romantic poetry as Mother Nature, the silent other, the woman. The son, the young poet, engages in a struggle of desire for and separation from her, and is both subject to and yet controls her power.[13] In "The Poet's Vow" Barrett dramatizes the dilemma Wordsworth's representation of nature posed for her as a daughter poet.

The poem tells of an unnamed male poet who rejects his fellow human beings in order to live with the "touching, patient Earth" (1.12) to "feel [her] unseen looks / Innumerous, constant, deep" (1.19):

"And ever, when I lift my brow
At evening to the sun,
No voice of woman or of child
Recording 'Day is done.'
Your silences shall a love express,
More deep than such an one."
[1.20]

Barrett portrays a clichéd Romantic poet for whom nature, assuming female qualities, is preferable to a wife welcoming him home. But a new aspect of man's relationship to and exploitation of "Earth" is presented by this poet. He believes that, while God created a "very good" earth, man made it "very mournful," a violently crazed place instead of a calm and silent haven:

"Poor crystal sky with stars astray!
Mad winds that howling go
From east to west! perplexèd seas
That stagger from their blow!
O motion wild! O wave defiled!
Our curse hath made you so."
[1.13]

To restore the paradisal bond between man and nature (son and mother's breast), the poet breaks his bonds with other people. Forsaking adult concerns, he hopes again (as a child fantasizes) to control this mother turned madwoman, this woman who is neglecting his needs.

The narrator, however, establishes the error of his vision:

This poet daringly,
—The nature at his heart,
And that quick tune along his veins
He could not change by art,—
Had vowed his blood of brotherhood
To a stagnant place apart.

He did not vow in fear, or wrath,
Or grief's fantastic whim,
But, weights and shows of sensual things

> Too closely crossing him,
> On his soul's eyelid the pressure slid
> And made its vision dim.
>
> [1.9–10]

What he sees as a "touching, patient Earth," the narrator views as a "stagnant place apart." What he feels to be the "dessicating sin" of human involvement, she describes as the "weights and shows of sensual things / Too closely crossing him." Nature is not a maternal figure to the narrator, but a mere stagnant place unless populated by human intercourse.

In Part 2 ("Showing to Whom the Vow was Declared"), the poet assigns all his silver and gold to his "crowding friends." The narrator tellingly describes how the friends are "solaced" by "clasping bland his gift,—his hand / In a somewhat slacker hold" (2.1–2). Only his friend, Sir Roland, and his fiancée, Rosalind (his childhood companion), remain, and he dismisses them to marry each other, with his lands as Rosalind's dowry. Rosalind refuses to be so assigned, and, although she describes herself as "half a child" and the poet as "very sage" (2.8), it is she who will eventually demonstrate how fallacious is his romance with nature. She learns from his face the "cruel homily" of "the teachings of the heaven and earth" (2.8–9). Preferring to remain "untouched, unsoftened" by their beauty, she dissociates her female identity from "the senseless, loveless earth and heaven" (2.9). Sir Roland also tries to persuade the poet that his understanding of the relationship between people and the earth is destructive. The poet's response reveals a masochistic vision of his desired natural environment:

> "I go to live
> In Courland Hall, alone:
> The bats along the ceilings cling,
> The lizards in the floors do run,
> And storms and years have worn and reft
> The stain by human builders left
> In working at the stone."
>
> [2.22]

His "touching, patient Earth" is destructive. His retreat, a cob-webby squalor, undercuts his notion of nature's "unseen looks / Innumerous, constant, deep," and her "silences" that "love express" (1.19–20). In his male hands domestic space resembles an unfeminized gothic interior.

In Part 3 ("Showing How the Vow was Kept") Barrett wrote an uncanny counterpoint to Tennyson's "The Lady of Shalott." Although critics commented on certain similarities of style between Barrett and Tennyson, neither had read the other's work at this stage.[14] A comparison between the two is, however, illuminating. In Tennyson's poem the woman inside the tower knows only that a curse of unknown origin is on her. This confines her inside, prohibiting her from looking through her window. She longs to go outside—"I am half sick of shadows"—but remains the artist, weaving representations of the images from outside reflected in her mirror. Love finally compels her to look at the handsome Sir Lancelot, but such engagement in the world causes her death. Tennyson, the male poet who is free, whatever his psychopathology, to move in the world beyond his house and engage in its activities, projects a fantasy of escape from the public world onto a female artist whom he condemns to stay removed from the world and its destructive energies.

Barrett, a woman writer confined to a domestic sphere, transforms such domestic enclosure into the gothic habitat of a male poet who deliberately turns from love and the world, and chooses to stay within his tower. To the narrator this is a curse: "a lonely creature of sinful nature / It is an awful thing" (3.2). Unlike the Lady of Shalott, who only saw shadowy reflections in her mirror yet longed to look out, this "poet at his lattice sate, / And downward looked he" (3.4). Free to look down and walk about, he only peered through his window at the churchgoers, the bridal party, and the child who "Stood near the wall to see at play / The lizards green and rare" (3.6). The poet neither joined them nor blessed them, but purposely withdrew. This brought him not solace but fear:

> He dwelt alone, and sun and moon
> Were witness that he made

Rejection of his humanness
  Until they seemed to fade;
His face did so, for he did grow
  Of his own soul afraid.

The self-poised God may dwell alone
  With inward glorying,
But God's chief angel waiteth for
  A brother's voice, to sing;
And a lonely creature of sinful nature
  It is an awful thing.

An awful thing that feared itself;
  While many years did roll,
A lonely man, a feeble man,
  A part beneath the whole,
He bore by day, he bore by night
That pressure of God's infinite
  Upon his finite soul.

                    [3.1–3]

The psychic disturbance caused by denial of "his humanness," defined as involvement in the world outside the home, turns the poet into an "awful thing that feared itself."

Part 4 ("Showing How Rosalind Fared by the Keeping of the Vow") evokes Keats's "La Belle Dame Sans Merci." If the knight's encounter with "La Belle Dame" leaves him wasted and aimless, so Rosalind's rejection by the poet leaves her wasted: "In death-sheets lieth Rosalind / As white and still as they" (6.1). His devotion to nature makes Rosalind turn from her "rival" and, in an exaggerated reaction to the poet's own behavior, she insists that the windows in her room be closed so she hears nothing from outside and sees none of God's "blessed works" (4.3). When she is dead, she wants her corpse carried to Courland Hall via the natural landscape of her childhood—the long church grass, the river bank, the brook, the hill, the "piny forest still" and the "open moorland" (4.9–10). Nature, instead of fulfilling its promise ("the brook with its sunny look / Akin to living glee"), has been used against her; only as a corpse will she traverse it again.

In Part 5 ("Showing How the Vow was Broken") the poet (on the day Rosalind dies) revels alone in the beauty of the stars at midnight:

> They shine upon the steadfast hills,
>   Upon the swinging tide,
> Upon the narrow track of beach
>   And the murmuring pebbles pied:
> They shine on every lovely place,
> They shine upon the corpse's face.
>
> [5.2]

The poet learns that Rosalind is dead; his "touching, patient Earth" cannot preserve him from human interaction. The sterility of his aesthetic is now challenged by a woman poet: attached to Rosalind's corpse is a scroll. Written before her death, the poem is in the Hemans-Landon tradition of love-laments: " 'I have prayed for thee with bursting sob / When passion's course was free.' " She suffered silently and tearfully the years without him. Her poem, however, effects change. Rosalind insists that nature is not a substitute for woman: " 'I tell thee that my poor scorned heart / Is of thine earth.' " Dead, she can no longer pray for him:

> "The corpse's tongue is still,
>   Its folded fingers point to heaven,
> But point there stiff and chill."

Like the ancient mariner, the poet's only salvation lies with himself:

> "I charge thee, by the living's prayer,
>   And the dead's silentness,
> To wring out from thy soul a cry
>   Which God shall hear and bless!"

"Triumphant Rosalind" awakens his "long-subjected humanness," manifest as a "lion-cry" (5.6), and he weeps. Their roles reversed now, Rosalind, the "half-a-child," is a wise poet, and the male poet reveals "That weeping wild of a reckless child / From a proud man's broken heart" (5.7). The man "who so worshipped earth and sky" (5.8) is "found too weak / To bear his human pain" (5.9), and he too dies.

Sir Roland, years later, brings his little son to the grave. When the boy, like the poet before him, turns "upward his blithe eyes to see / The wood-doves nodding from the tree," his father, echoing Rosalind, tells him:

> "Nay, boy look downward, . . .
>   Upon this human dust asleep.
>   And hold it in thy constant ken
> That God's own unity compresses
> (One into one) the human many,
>
> .   .   .   .
>
>   If not in love, on sorrow then,—
>   Though smiling not like other men,
> Still, like them we must weep."
>
> [5.10]

The religious overtones of Barrett's aesthetic creed matured as her poetry became boldly feminized through her understanding that her responsibility was to speak for those women who "suffer wrong . . . everywhere" (L, 2:445). She was convinced that the real work of poets is the work women have always been rooted in—human suffering and joy—but without its attendant self-abnegation.

Barrett's conviction that the poet must engage with social and political issues had its terrors and burdens for her, a woman imagining herself as a descendent of the great male poetic tradition, as the "fear of earth" had for the angels in "The Seraphim." She suggests such anxiety in her dramatization of other prominent women in "The Virgin Mary to the Child Jesus," "Victoria's Tears," and "The Young Queen." In the first of these, Mary's meditation over her sleeping son, Mary knows that future generations will say of her, "Thou art / The blessedest of women!" (6), but Barrett examines the practical implications of this status. Mary feels that her pure son was "created from my nature all defiled" (7) and recognizes that:

> No small babe-smiles my watching heart has seen
> To float like speech the speechless lips between,

No dovelike cooing in the golden air,
No quick short joys of leaping babyhood.

[9]

Barrett imagines that Mary, knowing her son's destiny, will have
painfully ambivalent feelings about the "majestic angel whose
command / Was softly as a man's beseeching said" (1) naming her
as the chosen mother of Jesus. When she thinks of "the drear
sharp tongue of prophecy, / With the dread sense of things which
shall be done," of how her son will be called "despised" and "rejected," she feels: "I must not die, with mother's work to do, /
And could not live—and see" (10).

In "Victoria's Tears" Barrett imagines how this eighteen-year-
old girl, "Maiden! heir of kings," must feel as a woman leading a
country (in which women were disenfranchised) when she can
"no longer lean" on her "mother's breast." The contrast between
the adult woman with a public function—whether queen or poet
—deprived of such maternal nurturance, and Barrett's sense of
Wordsworth as one who "threw himself right tenderly upon [Na-
ture's] bosom" is a poignant one. Barrett stresses the great pomp
of the coronation, but

> She saw no purples shine,
> For tears had dimmed her eyes;
> She only knew her childhood's flowers
> Were happier pageantries!
> And while her heralds played the part,
> For million shouts to drown—
> "God save the Queen" from hill to mart,—
> She heard through all her beating heart,
> And turned and wept—
> She wept, to wear a crown!

Barrett suggests that token women who attain public promi-
nence feel ambivalent about their status. As she reveals her own
anxiety as a woman measuring her feet inside the shoes of her
dead literary fathers, so she imagines Victoria to be similarly
unnerved at her sudden power. In "The Young Queen," she delineates how "Her palace walls enring / The dust that was a king—/
And very cold beneath her feet, she feels her father's grave." At

fourteen Barrett had felt some comfort in walking in Homer's footsteps and not striking out a path for herself; now she imagines in chilling terms a severance from the father as woman appropriates power traditionally reserved for him. Instead of guiding her feet the precursor now numbs them with cold. It is a statement of loss; but it also determines the daughter to walk her own path.

The first tentative steps along such a path resulted from the "individuality" represented in *The Seraphim, and Other Poems*, in Barrett's conviction that in this "age of steam" the poet had to embrace the world "of dust and death" and "human pain." By taking Jesus, "man's victim" and "his deity"—with his engagement in human concerns—rather than God, the divine creator, as her model for the poet, Barrett legitimized her desire that woman engage in art and politics.

In *The Seraphim, and Other Poems* Barrett initiated her departure both from the "frustration" of the male poetic tradition, which privileged the male voice as subject of poetic discourse with woman as object and other, and from the "delusion" of following the poetesses who overtly advocated resignation to woman's "weary lot" even while covertly transgressing their own dictum. She began in these poems to place woman as the subject of her own discourse. When Kenyon expressed fond nostalgia for her early poems, Barrett dismissed *The Battle of Marathon* and *An Essay on Mind* as a "girl's exercise," convinced that "the difference between them and my present poems is not merely the difference between . . . immaturity and maturity; but that it is the difference between the dead and the living, between a copy and an individuality, between what is myself and what is not myself" (*L,* 1:187–88). Far from lamenting the past, she eagerly anticipated fashioning the "new manners" of the discourse expressing that subjectivity; her *Poems of 1844* represented a decisive challenge to the "old manners" she was outgrowing.

CHAPTER 2

An Emerging
Female Poetics

POEMS OF 1844

Eve's alloted grief.
—Preface to *Poems of 1844*

In her Preface to *Poems of 1844* and her two sonnets to George Sand, "A Desire" and "A Recognition," Barrett
explores an emerging poetics with greater consciousness of her
position in relation both to the established male poetic tradition
and also to a distinctly female literary one than she had in her
previous volume. Those six years between the publication of *The
Seraphim, and Other Poems* and *Poems of 1844* were dominated
by Barrett's invalidism and confinement. This confinement can
symbolize woman's literary imprisonment in a male poetic tradition. Conversely, to recognize Barrett's literary imprisonment
necessitates understanding the nature and function of her invalidism.

Barrett had always suffered ill health, but her doctors were so
worried in the winter of 1838 that they advised her to leave London, where her family had lived since 1835, for a more favorable
climate in Torquay on the south coast. Not until 1841 did she
persuade her doctors and father to allow her return to London.
Occasional carriage rides in the summers of 1845 and 1846 were
the only relief from her invalid's room in the Wimpole Street
house, until her secret marriage to Browning in September 1846.

Barrett's legendary invalidism is complex. Its origins may reach
back to the young teenager's recognition of the divergence of sex
roles once her favorite brother, Edward, was sent to public school:

Together have we past our infant hours,
Together sported Childhood's spring away,
Together cull'd young Hope's fast budding flowers,
To wreathe the forehead of each coming day!
Yes! for the present's sun makes e'en the future gay.

And when the laughing mood was nearly o'er,
Together, many a minute did we wile
On Horace' page, or Maro's sweeter lore;
While one young critic, on the classic style,
Would sagely try to frown, and make the other smile.

But now alone thou con'st the ancient tome—
And sometimes thy dear studies, it may be,
Are cross'd by dearer dreams of me and home!
Alone I muse on Homer—thoughts are free—
And if mine often stray, they go in search of thee!
[*"Verses to My Brother," W, 1:103*]

Betty Miller astutely explores the effect on the young Barrett of this separation between boy and girl. She suggests that the passionate, energetic child felt that her place as firstborn was usurped by the first son, Edward. He was her closest companion during their childhood, yet his increasingly privileged masculinity aroused in her, "inconsolable for not being born a man," a stormy "spirit of emulation." She was a lively "tomboy" who climbed walls, ladders, trees; roamed the countryside around Hope End; and loved the pouring rain and rolling in long grass. Scorning both the governess and the sewing assigned to the Barrett girls, she so resented that "subserviency of opinion which is generally considered necessary to feminine softness" that she insisted on studying Greek and Latin with Edward's tutor, Mr. McSwiney. But when Edward was sent to public school, Mr. McSwiney dismissed, and Barrett left behind, she recognized, "The Dream has faded—it is o'er." She could not go with Edward through the gates of Hope End to school, out into the world of men; confined within the domestic sphere of women she languished, Miller concludes, recognizing the "inescapable realities of her own femininity."[1]

After Edward's departure and the tutor's dismissal, doctors' reports reveal that Barrett experienced "pain in the head . . . very considerable debility and consequent nervous irritation, producing smallness and feebleness of the pulse—pain, and weakness in the back, which [would] not allow her sitting up, without support by pillows, and she [was] always rendered worse by exercise—The feet [were] generally cold."[2] They found her illness mysterious and resistant to diagnosis. Subsequently it has been thought possible that it was associated with early symptoms of tuberculosis. This sudden debility in such an energetic child, however, is puzzling.[3] Maybe she enacted that branch of Victorian medical thought that determined middle-class femaleness to be an inherently sickly condition, in which "many a young life is battered and forever crippled in the breakers of puberty."[4] Hampered by petticoats, confined at Hope End, witnessing her mother's yearly pregnancies and attendant weakness, Barrett's energies were transformed into exhaustion. Aurora Leigh sank into a similar lethargy under her aunt's educational practices (1.378–84), suggesting Barrett Browning's own diagnosis of her invalidism.[5] Whatever its etiology, Barrett employed her sickness as a strategy to resist activities deemed appropriate for a woman, and to gain time for study and writing.

Philip Kelley and Ronald Hudson, editors of Barrett's *Diary*, 1831–32, imagine that her "enforced idleness at this time, and her always indifferent health subsequently, turned her more and more to books and study, writing and introspection. . . . Her love of seclusion grew, and no doubt engendered the marked reluctance she later displayed whenever obliged to put aside her books and take part in the social round of visits." (*D*, xix). This is consistent with criticism that sees women's writing as compensation for a lack in their lives: viz., Dickinson wrote because she never married, Barrett Browning wrote because she was an invalid. However, Kelley and Hudson confuse cause and effect. In a culture which demanded that middle-class women be wives and mothers, women writers devised strategies for engaging and protecting their creative energies, such as refusing to marry, refusing to receive visitors, even invalidism. Barrett knew she needed time and room for her art; invalidism allowed her both.[6]

Barrett Browning's contemporary, Florence Nightingale, understood, and for many years enacted, this ideology of invalidism. In

"Cassandra" (1859),[7] she denounced the frittering away of women's energy, intellect, and time:

> Mrs. A has the imagination, the poetry of a Murillo, and has sufficient power of execution to show that she might have had a great deal more. Why is she not a Murillo? From a material difficulty, not a mental one. If she has a knife and fork in her hands during three hours of the day, she cannot have a pencil and a brush. Dinner is the great sacred ceremony of this day, the great sacrament. To be absent from dinner is equivalent to being ill. Nothing else will excuse us from it. Bodily incapacity is the only apology valid. (30)
>
> How do we explain then the many cases of women who have distinguished themselves . . . ?
>
> Widowhood, ill-health, or want of bread, these three explanations or excuses are supposed to justify a woman in taking up an occupation. (33)
>
> Women have no means given them, whereby they *can* resist the "claims of social life." They are taught from their infancy upwards that it is wrong, ill-tempered, and a misunderstanding of "a woman's mission" (with a great M.) if they do not allow themselves *willingly* to be interrupted at all hours. (35)

Sickness provided time and "room of one's own" for a middle-class woman's engagement in intellectual pursuit. When at twenty-five Barrett was forbidden by her father to stay a few days to help her friend, Mr. Boyd, with his work, she wrote, "You know I cannot do everything I like, or everything *when* I like. I only *rule* in my own room—where there are no *subjects* to be ill-governed—except the literary inanimate" (*HSB*, 74). Barrett needed a valid "excuse" to spend time in that room. She recorded in her *Diary* how, after a day in which her aunt made her join "Mrs. Cliffe's pic nic," she returned "unwell with overfatigue. These kind [*sic*] of things do not agree with me" (*D*, 134–35). On the next day her aunt wanted her to visit Mrs. Martin, but again she became ill:

> I felt so unwell, that I negatived the proposal,—& this set B's combustible particles on fire. She spoke crossly to me,—& I

who was on the very verge of hysterics, & required only a
finger touch to impel me forwards, burst into tears, & had
that horrible dead precursive feeling all thro' my hands &
feet. . . . I lay down on my bed after my breakfast, because I
cd scarcely sit up—and yet when time drew near for us to
meet Mrs. Martin, I sent Henrietta in to Bummy to carry my
palinodia. I wd go, if she wished it so. No!—it wd not do. (D,
135–36)

Once Henrietta and Bummy had departed, however, she "read
Mr. Beverly's pamphlets . . . ; the letter to the Archbishop of
York, & the Tombs of the prophets . . . a good deal of Lamar-
tines,—second volume of Meditations poetiques et religieuses"
(D, 136).

I do not mean to suggest that Barrett consciously feigned illness to write. Rather, the illness, whether formed from or inten-
sified by a complex reaction to the consciousness of her femaleness in adolescence, enabled Barrett to adopt invalidism as a
strategy for finding freedom at least in her own room. However,
after years of such invalidism Barrett recognized her dilemma:
such a self-protective life resembled imprisonment. She gave a
stark account of her situation to a friend (October 1843):

I live in London, to be sure, and except for the glory of it I
might live in a desert, so profound is my solitude and so
complete my isolation from things and persons without. I lie
all day, and day after day, on the sofa, and my windows do
not even look into the street. To abuse myself with a vain
deceit of rural life I have had ivy planted in a box, and it has
flourished and spread over one window, and strikes against
the glass with a little stroke from the thicker leaves when
the wind blows at all briskly. [L, 1:158]

Barrett revealed how hard it was to inhabit such "a desert" in a
later letter to Mrs. Martin (December 1845) about the closing of
the "prison doors":

Do you think I was born to live the life of an oyster, such as
I do live here? And so, the moaning and gnashing of teeth
are best done alone and without taking anyone into confidence. . . .

... For me, I am not yet undone by the winter. I still sit in my chair and walk about the room. But the prison doors are shut close, and I could dash myself against them sometimes with a passionate impatience of the needless captivity. I feel so intimately and from evidence, how, with air and warmth together in any fair proportion, I should be as well and happy as the rest of the world, that it is intolerable. [*L*, 1:274–75]

The "moaning and gnashing of teeth," that restless captive energy, were eased in Barrett by opium. When Browning expressed concern about its use, she explained that sleep "will not easily come near me except in a red hood of poppies" (*RB&EBB*, 1:437) and acknowledged,

It might strike you as strange that I who have had no pain . . no acute suffering to keep down from its angles . . should need opium in any shape. But I have had restlessness till it made me almost mad—at one time I lost the power of sleeping quite . . and even in the day, the continual aching sense of weakness has been intolerable . . besides palpitation . . as if one's life, instead of giving movement to the body, were imprisoned undiminished within it, & beating & fluttering impotently to get out, at all the doors & windows. So the medical people gave me opium . . . [and] the tranquillizing power has been wonderful. [*RB&EBB*, 1:437]

The image of Barrett as pale invalid yields to that of monster, housing restlessness enough to make her mad: in her third-floor room Barrett moaned and gnashed her teeth. As isolated as Bertha Mason, she was confined to one room where her father visited her daily to say prayers, and where the male doctors tranquilized her "restlessness" with opium; among them was a doctor who believed that for a woman to be a poet "was a mortal malady & incompatible with any common show of health under any circumstances" (*RB&EBB*, 1:151). She was the madwoman in the straightjacket. The invalidism she exploited when younger to gain time for her studies became an instrument of the patriarchy to subdue her. She must always have been subliminally aware that her father desired her imprisonment; it was clarified for her the year after the publication of the *Poems of 1844* when doctors warned that for Barrett to live she had to winter in Italy. Mr. Barrett refused to allow this, forcing Barrett to realize that the father she adored would "rather see me dead at his foot than yield the point" (*RB&EBB*, 1:421).

There is so much legend surrounding Elizabeth Barrett, Robert Browning, and Mr. Barrett that I do not wish to add to it. I am not interested here in the psychological complexities surrounding this daughter-father relationship. It is, however, necessary to outline how Barrett described the relationship and transmuted it into her art, in order to illuminate the latter.

Concerning Mr. Barrett, she explained to Browning, "[His] principle of passive filial obedience is held . . drawn (& quartered) from Scripture. He *sees* the law & the gospel on his side" (*RB&EBB*, 1:408). Barrett felt that her father both cared for his ten children and took seriously "all those patriarchal ideas of governing grownup children 'in the way they *must* go!' " She appreciated that there could never be a "truer affection in a father's heart" but condemned the "evil [that] is in the system" to which her father subscribed: "to make happy according to his own views of the propriety of happiness—he takes it to be his duty to rule like the Kings of Christendom, by divine right" (*RB&EBB*, 1:169). While many Victorian fathers may have behaved similarly toward their sons and daughters, the Barrett children were subject to a peculiarity in their father, namely his attitude toward their sexuality and possible marriage: "he never *does* tolerate in his family (sons or daughters) the development of one class of feelings" (*RB&EBB*, 1:196). Elizabeth Barrett was not the only child disowned by Mr. Barrett because of her marriage; her sister, Henrietta, and her brother, Alfred, were also cut from Mr. Barrett's life and will. The other surviving children remained single.

Barrett described her father as an exaggeratedly authoritarian upholder of the patriarchy; yet, she imagined the isolation that resulted for him with an empathy that reveals as much about her situation as her understanding of his: "We can alter nothing by ever so many words. After all, he is the victim. He isolates himself—& now and then he feels it . . the cold dead silence all round, which is the effect of an incredible system. If he were not stronger than most men, he could not bear it as he does"

(*RB&EBB*, 1:422). However, her compassion did not blind her to his contribution to her isolation. When he declared she would incur his grave displeasure if she wintered away from home,[8] she submitted to his will, "taking up [her] chain again" (*RB&EBB*, 1:233) and remaining in her "cage" (*RB&EBB*, 1:238). As her desire to live, encouraged by Browning, grew, she understood how her isolation had been "imprisonment" and her father the "gaoler."[9]

Barrett recognized how different her life as a young female poet had been from Browning's as a young male one:

What you say of society draws me on to many comparative thoughts of your life & mine. You seem to have drunken of the cup of life full, with the sun shining on it. I have lived only inwardly,—or with *sorrow*, for a strong emotion. Before this seclusion of my illness, I was secluded still—& there are few of the youngest women in the world who have not seen more, heard more, known more, of society, than I, who am scarcely to be called young now. I grew up in the country .. had no social opportunities, .. had my heart in books & poetry, .. & my experience, in reveries. My sympathies drooped towards the ground like an untrained honeysuckle. ... It was a lonely life—growing green like the grass around it. Books and dreams were what I lived in—& domestic life only seemed to buzz gently around, like the bees about the grass. And so time passed, and passed—and afterwards, when my illness came & I seemed to stand at the edge of the world with all done, & no prospect (as appeared at one time) of ever passing the threshold of one room again,—why then, I turned to thinking with some bitterness ... that I had stood blind in this temple I was about to leave .. that I had seen no Human nature, that my brothers & sisters of the earth were *names* to me, .. that I had beheld no great mountain or river—nothing in fact. I was as a man dying who had not read Shakespeare .. & it was too late!—do you understand? And do you also know what a disadvantage this ignorance is to my art—Why, if I live on & yet do not escape from this seclusion, do you not perceive that I labour under signal disadvantages .. that I am, in a manner, as a *blind poet*? Certainly, there is a compensation to a degree. I have had much of the inner life—& from the habit of selfconsciousness of selfanalysis, I make great guesses at Human Nature in the main. But how willingly I would as a poet exchange some of this lumbering, ponderous, helpless knowledge of books, for some experience of life & man. [*RB&EBB* 1:41]

Barrett offered no feminist analysis of her adolescence, of her "seclusion," of her invalidism, beyond her complaint that she "had no social opportunities." There was social intercourse at Hope End for "ladies," but none for a poet. Barrett imagined her art as limited by her social restrictions; Woolf offered a similar analysis: "It cannot be doubted that the long years of seclusion had done her irreparable damage as an artist. She had lived shut off, guessing at what was outside, and inevitably magnifying what was within."[10] A restricted environment does not automatically limit a writer, secure in the subjectivity of that experience;[11] when, however, the experience belongs to the realm of the female "other," it has traditionally been trivialized.[12] Barrett and Woolf both internalized this masculine notion when they found "disadvantage' or "irreparable damage" to Barrett's art as resulting from her seclusion.

In that early letter to Browning, Barrett reflected on how her years of confinement affected her art and how "as a *blind poet*" she would "exchange some of this lumbering, ponderous, helpless knowledge of books, for some experience of life & man" (*RB&EBB*, 1:41); her feelings echoed or resulted from the reviewers' response to *Poems of 1844*. They continued to admire her work, but lamented that Barrett's poems originated in books, not life. Sarah Flower Adams in the *Westminster Review* summed up this critical reservation: Barrett's being "an exile ... secluded from society" resulted in a "style, not unfrequently, wanting the ease of colloquial expression. Books her only companions, she [was] led to adopt their language," which "weakened instead of assisting the development of real power."[13] Barrett herself grew "to despise book-knowledge & its effect on the mind ... when people *live by it*" because they cloister "their souls under these roofs made with hands, when they might be under the sky.

Such people grow dark & narrow & low, with all their pains"
(*RB&EBB*, 1:167).

Barrett imagined she "stood blind in this temple [she] was
about to leave . . that [she] had seen no Human nature," but her
art is not diminished because she represented those experiences
of being woman and artist that shaped her aesthetic. Her solitude
can be seen not as detrimental to her art but rather as a fortu-
itous and essential stage in her progress toward a mature poetic
voice. Certainly Browning did not share Barrett's feelings about
her work: he recognized there an integrity of voice that he felt
eluded his own work: "Your poetry must be, cannot but be, infi-
nitely more to me than mine to you—for you *do* what I always
wanted, hoped to do, and only seem now likely to do for the first
time. You speak out, *you,*—I only make men & women speak—
give you truth broken into prismatic hues, and fear the pure
white light, even if it is in me: but I am going to try (*RB&EBB*,
1:7). We value Browning precisely because he made "men &
women speak," prefiguring modernism in his recognition that
truth is not absolute but "broken into prismatic hues." However,
this appreciation of Barrett's work, even allowing for the enthusiasm of a new lover, was genuine and enduring.

Alice Meynell cast light on the apparent contradiction between
Barrett's fear that poetic limitation would result from her seclusion and Browning's recognition that her work was sincere. Meynell preferred the "Mrs. Browning" who "rose from her sofa,
stood at a husband's side, received his friends," to the Barrett
"lurking in that delusive bower which secluded writers—those
who are women—are apt to build for themselves out of their
fancies as to what they probably seem to be in the mind and
thought of the world of their readers." Nevertheless, she understood that "nothing but the secrecy of a dark sick-room and a
sofa could give a sensitive woman the strange courage of Elizabeth Barrett's poems. Out of sight she had no fear of the vocifer-
ous though sweet part she took in the world."[14]

Barrett may have felt limited by solitude and encumbered by
book knowledge, but she also appreciated how her "strange courage" was fostered by her isolation: she refused an invitation to
visit Mrs. Martin in 1846, saying, "I can lose nothing here, shut

up in my prison, and the nightingales come to my windows and sing through the sooty panes. If I were at Hastings I should risk the chance of recovering liberty, and the consolations of slavery would not reach me as they do here" (*L,* 1:276). Although the rhetoric of "shut up," "prison," and "sooty panes" belies the notion of contentment in that room, Barrett recognized that her poems ("the nightingales singing at her window") were the "consolations of slavery":

> Have I not felt twenty times the desolate advantage of being insulated here & of not minding anybody when I made my poems?—of living a little like a disembodied spirit, & caring less for supposititious [*sic*] criticism than for the black fly buzzing in the pane?—*That* made me what dear Mr. Kenyon calls "insolent,"—untimid, & unconventional in my degree; and not so much by strength, you see, as by separation—*You* touch your greater ends by mere strength; breaking with your own hands the hampering threads which, in your position wd have hampered *me.* [*RB&EBB,* 1:263]

Barrett knew that to reach the "greater ends" of poetry each poet must break "the hampering threads" that bind her or him. To Bloom this would mean the threads of the precursor's poems that bind the imagination of the son. In Barrett's case it meant that, and also the "hampering threads" of woman's role. It is an ironic image, reflecting as it does the sewing that occupied middle-class women's fingers instead of the pen. Browning had the advantage of strength, a male power; Barrett the advantage of seclusion, a female condition. If she had moved as freely as Browning in literary society, she would have been "hampered" from touching her "greater ends." She explained: "I never learnt to talk as you do in London. . . . If my poetry is worth anything to any eye,—it is the flower of me" (*RB&EBB,* 1:65). The "desolate advantage" of her isolation freed her from woman's role; protected her from exposure to criticism of her writing and herself; and cut her off from the way "to talk . . . in London," from the "threads which . . . wd have hampered *me,*" so she could hear her own voice, see her own vision, be " 'insolent,'—untimid, & unconventional," be unladylike.

Barrett paid for freedom of imagination with imprisonment

of body: her confinement produced a rhetoric of imprisonment, which in turn impelled her—who knows how consciously—both to expose woman's textual imprisonment and to revise the assumptions of poetic tradition. Her Preface to *Poems of 1844* reveals her awareness of the former, whereas her sonnets to George Sand, "A Desire" and "A Recognition," illustrate that her identification with Sand encouraged her to attempt the latter.

The Preface to *Poems of 1844* demonstrates Barrett's "anxiety" about Miltonic "influence" and about her own "authorship." Her self-consciousness about his influence suggests a possible strategy for solving the dilemma of the daughter's struggle with the strong precursor father poet. A clue to this strategy lies in Barrett's dedication to the 1844 volume, "To My Father." Protest against the authority of the father—that "alien tyranny / With its dynastic reasons of larger bones / And stronger sinews" ("A Drama of Exile," 1865–67)—rumbles under and sometimes explodes through the surface obedience of many poems in the volume. Yet the energy and even violence manifested are absent in the sweetness of the dedication in which she recalls "the time far off when I was a child and wrote verses, and when I dedicated them to you who were my public and my critic." She expresses gratitude for an "existence which has been sustained and comforted by you as well as given," culminating in her feeling—as a thirty-eight-year-old woman—that though "somewhat more faint-hearted than I used to be, it is my fancy thus to seem to return to a visible personal dependence on you, as if indeed I were a child again; to conjure your beloved image between myself and the public, so as to be sure of one smile,—and to satisfy my heart while I sanctify my ambition, by associating with the great pursuit of my life its tenderest and holiest affection" (*W*, 2:142–43). Barrett set her "ambition" at the age of ten: "No woman was ever before such a poet as she would be. As Homer was among men, so would she be among women,—many persons would be obliged to say that she was a little taller than Homer if anything."[15] She also understood the cultural imperative that to be a good (middle-class) woman was not to be a poet "taller than Homer" but to have the qualities of a child.[16] Her emphasis in the dedication on imagining herself "a child again" and in the Preface on her "lowness" and "weakness" suggests acceptance of, while in fact rebelling against, the "alien tyranny" that defined her as woman-child in both literature and life. Barrett's comments in the Preface on the composition of "A Drama of Exile," a lyric drama about Adam and Eve just after their expulsion from the Garden of Eden, enact this strategy. The long passage merits careful study.

The subject of the Drama rather fastened on me than was chosen; and the form, approaching the model of the Greek tragedy, shaped itself under my hand, rather by force of pleasure than of design. But when the excitement of composition had subsided, I felt afraid of my position. My subject was the new and strange experience of the fallen humanity, as it went forth from Paradise into the wilderness; with a peculiar reference to Eve's alloted grief, which, considering that self-sacrifice belonged to her womanhood, and the consciousness of originating the Fall to her offence,—appeared to me imperfectly apprehended hitherto, and more expressible by a woman than a man. There was room, at least, for lyrical emotion in those first steps into the wilderness,—in that first sense of desolation after wrath,—in that first audible gathering of the recriminating "groan of the whole creation,"—in that first darkening of the hills from the recoiling feet of angels,—and in that first silence of the voice of God. And I took pleasure in driving in, like a pile, stroke upon stroke, the Idea of EXILE,—admitting Lucifer as an extreme Adam, to represent the ultimate tendencies of sin and loss,—that it might be strong to bear up the contrary idea of Heavenly love and purity. But when all was done, I felt afraid, as I said before, of my position. I had promised my own prudence to shut close the gates of Eden between Milton and myself, so that none might say I dared to walk in his footsteps. He should be within, I thought, with his Adam and Eve unfallen or falling,—and I, without, with my EXILES,—*I* also an exile! It would not do. The subject, and his glory covering it, swept through the gates, and I stood full in it, against my will, and contrary to my vow,—till I shrank back fearing, almost desponding; hesitating to venture even a passing association with our great poet before the face of

the public. Whether at last I took courage for the venture, by
a sudden revival of that love of manuscript which should be
classed by moral philosophers among the natural affections,
or by the encouraging voice of a dear friend, it is not interesting to the reader to inquire. Neither could the fact affect the
question; since I bear, of course, my own responsibilities. For
the rest, Milton is too high, and I am too low, to render it
necessary for me to disavow any rash emulation of his divine
faculty on his own ground; while enough individuality will
be granted, I hope, to my poem, to rescue me from that im-
putation of plagiarism which should be too servile a thing
for every sincere thinker. After all, and at the worst, I have
only attempted, in respect to Milton, what the Greek dramatists achieved lawfully in respect to Homer. They con-
structed dramas on Trojan ground; they raised on the buskin
and even clasped with the sock, the feet of Homeric heroes;
yet they neither imitated their Homer nor emasculated him.
. . . To this analogy—the more favourable to me from the
obvious exception in it, that Homer's subject was his own
possibly by creation,—whereas Milton's was his own by illustration only,—I appeal. To this analogy—*not* to this comparison, be it understood—I appeal. For the analogy of the
stronger may apply to the weaker; and the reader may have
patience with the weakest while she suggests the application. [W, 2:143–45]

Barrett initially denies responsibility for the subject matter of
"A Drama of Exile": "it rather fastened on me than was chosen."
She places herself in a male tradition when she claims that her
poem was "approaching the model of Greek tragedy," but immediately undercuts such assertiveness, "I felt afraid of my position." Yet the ensuing description of the poem reveals not fear,
but a confident exposition of her subject matter as "the new
and strange experience of the fallen humanity." She elaborates
on the aspect of the Fall that most interests her, "Eve's alloted
grief," then quietly challenges Milton: this aspect has been "imperfectly apprehended hitherto, and [is] more expressible by a
woman than a man." Her assertion is tempered, however, by an
apologetic justification, as though she already felt her own posi-

tion challenged: "There was room, at least, for lyrical emotion in those first steps into the wilderness." She imagines "that first silence of the voice of God," as both a "desolation after wrath" and also a silence that allows her "pleasure . . . in the Idea of EXILE." Her concern for "Eve's alloted grief" shifts to the male actors in this drama: "I took pleasure in driving in like a pile, stroke upon stroke, the Idea of EXILE,—admitting Lucifer as an extreme Adam, to represent the ultimate tendencies of sin and loss." Yet Barrett ends the burst of verbal "masculine" energy on the anticlimactic "feminine" notes of "Heavenly love and purity."

Like Milton's, Barrett's rhetoric indicates a greater delight in the energies of the exiled than the obedience of the pure. Having embraced her commitment to "Eve's alloted grief" and the vigor of the "Idea of EXILE," she follows her tame commitment to "love and purity" by reiterating "I felt afraid." Her fear is that of a daughter who has "dared to walk in [the father's] footsteps." As though confessing an "anxiety of influence," Barrett states that she had tried to "shut close the gates of Eden between Milton and myself." This is the first mention of Milton's name, though his presence haunts the Preface. In a reversal of conventional gender roles, Barrett tries to confine Milton inside a place of domestic innocence: "He should be within . . . with his Adam and Eve unfallen or falling." Barrett places herself outside in the male world of experience: "and I, without, with my EXILES,—*I* also an exile!" This crucial claim has a felt urgency inexplicable from the context. Its meaning can only be surmised as speaking to her sense of exile as a writer from the Miltonic tradition. This is not, however, a totally negative position: her rhetoric reveals delight in her usurpation of the masculine sexual rhythms implicit in her "pleasure in driving in like a pile, stroke upon stroke, the Idea of EXILE." Yet "exile" also dramatizes her felt duty to abandon such energy for the submissively asexual female world of "love and purity."

The Preface states what "A Drama of Exile" demonstrates, Barrett's failure to achieve a truly visionary rereading of Milton's poem. She could not keep Milton confined in his text, in his garden of innocence; she could not rewrite his poem from her exiled female perspective. The Preface speaks more clearly to this issue than does the poem itself: "The subject, and his glory covering it, swept through the gates, and I stood full in it, *against my will*, and contrary to my vow,—till I shrank back fearing, almost desponding" (emphasis mine). The "alien tyranny" of Milton's text overpowered her, not because she believed in man's supremacy, but because she was subject to it "against [her] will." Although she rallied, "took courage for the venture" and wrote her poem, the result is dominated by Milton's male ideology.

Barrett's closing remarks on the "Drama" rationalize her attempt to speak to "Eve's alloted grief" and the "Idea of EXILE." Sensitive to criticisms of and expectations about women's work, she clears herself from charges of imitation and emasculation by claiming that her work in relation to Milton's is analogous to what "the Greek dramatists achieved lawfully in respect to Homer." Homer's "subject was his own possibly by creation" whereas Milton's was his "by illustration only." Milton interpreted the gender economy according to his ideology; Barrett claims implicitly the right to redefine that economy her way. She rationalizes her right through legal language, reflecting on what the Greek dramatists "achieved lawfully" and reiterating that hers is a case she can rightfully "appeal." But the woman who dedicated herself as a child to her biological father ends the dialectic between assertion and submission with the latter, referring to herself, Milton's literary daughter, as the "weakest" writer.

The Preface is the key to Barrett's poetics: "Eve's alloted grief . . . imperfectly apprehended hitherto, and more expressible by a woman than a man." Yet its very rhetoric dramatizes the difficulties she had in realizing her aesthetic. The traditionally male rhetoric in which Barrett expresses her determination to explore the hitherto male territory of "the wilderness . . . in that first silence of the voice of God," gives way to the rhetoric of the "poetesses," rife with "fear," "love," "purity," and weakness. She juxtaposes the assertive woman's usurpation of patriarchal power with the woman-as-child-as-poetess's appeasement of the "alien tyranny" of the Father—be it God, Milton, or Mr. Barrett.

If Milton's voice was the paternal influence inhibiting Barrett's portrayal of Eve in "A Drama of Exile," George Sand's was the maternal voice confirming Barrett's attempts to liberate herself from the "alien tyranny" of Milton's vision. Barrett first mentioned Aurore Dupin, Baronne Dudevant, George Sand, in a letter to Mary Russell Mitford, dated November 21, 1842, in which she confessed her "secret" of "reading . . . the new French literature." She questions, rather coyly, whether Mitford thinks "it is very naughty of [her] to read naughty books." "Curious beyond the patience of [her] Eve-ship," she justifies such reading because she lives "out of the world altogether" and is "lonely enough & old enough & sad enough & experienced enough in every sort of good & bad reading, not to be hurt personally by a French superfluity of bad." Among those writers she mentions is the "*shameless*" George Sand (*MRM*, 2:85). It is unclear whether Barrett's reference to her "Eve-ship" refers to her writing of "A Drama of Exile" or to her impatience with the role of innocence, silence, and submission culturally assigned to the suffering Eve/woman. However, George Sand's novels of female passion and assertion, of questioning the inequality in marital relationships, modeled an alternative that soothed some of her earlier "steady indignation against Nature who made [her] a woman" (*MRM*, 2:7).

Her reading of French novels, and especially of the "shameless" George Sand, invited charges of shamelessness against herself. Barrett reveals in her letters on the subject curious contradictions. She writes Mitford that Sand is "a true woman of genius" (*MRM*, 2:85) and allows to Browning that she is one woman who does not demonstrate an intellectual inferiority to men, who has "all that breadth & scope of faculty which women want" (*RB&EBB*, 1:114); her *Consuelo* is "a sort of rambling Odyssey, a female Odyssey" (*RB&EBB*, 1:160). Yet she also refers to Sand as "this brilliant monstrous woman" (*MRM*, 2:127–28), as one who is "eloquent as a fallen angel" (*MRM*, 2:85), as a woman who "has something monstrous in combination with her genius" (*RB&EBB*, 1:113). Barrett's sense of Sand as "monstrous" is, she explains to Mitford, "a bare expression of the sort of feeling with which one regards a woman whenever she leans to the aggrandizement of the physical aspect of passion" (*MRM*, 2:85). Sand's frank portrayal of female sensuality may have caused Barrett less embarrassment than a feeling of duty to express such sentiments to the proper Miss Mitford, who felt "righteous indignation on the subject of Madame Dudevant" (*MRM*, 2:127). Barrett allows that *Lelia* is a "serpent book" of "soul-slime"

(*MRM*, 2:127), the reading of which made her blush "in my solitude to the ends of my fingers" (*MRM*, 2:93). Such "vileness"
notwithstanding, French literature, and Sand's work in particular, made Barrett's "whole being" ache so that her quotidian existence at home seemed "all so neutral tinted and dull and cold by
comparison." She respected this literature's refusal to be bound
by convention: "It is as if the soul of the thinker were given to
the four winds & the multitudinous waters, without hold or
compass,—& as if in this great tornado of being she lost sight of
the localities & relations both of Heaven & Earth" (*MRM*, 2:86).

Sand offered Barrett womanhood beyond the "love and purity" of her "Eve-ship": "she who is man & woman together"
(*RB&EBB*, 1:159), "this brilliant monstrous woman." Barrett
claimed Sand's passionate intellect while apparently repudiating
it by calling her "monstrous." Sand united Jane Eyre with Bertha
Mason, harmonizing the "angel" and "monster" of female experience documented by Gilbert and Gubar in *The Madwoman in
the Attic*.[17] In her admiration of Sand as a writer who is "eloquent as a fallen angel," Barrett embraced the satanic implications of Sand's work for women.

Whatever ambivalences Barrett felt or was obliged to feel about
Sand, she acknowledged her "naughty secret" publicly by pub-
lishing her two sonnets addressed to Sand in the *Poems of 1844*.
She told Mitford: "Mr. Kenyon told me I was 'a daring person' for
the introduction of those sonnets. He had heard an able man say
at his table a day or two before, that no modest woman would or
ought to confess to an acquaintance with the works of George
Sand" (*MRM*, 2:460). Maybe part of the daring was embodied in
the form of the poems. Although Milton, Wordsworth, and Keats
had adapted the sonnet, its origins lay in love. Certainly Barrett
was aware of the original "very strictest Italian form" (*MRM*,
2:52), and Patricia Thomson underscores this resonance: "The
love affair of Elizabeth Barrett with George Sand is much less
celebrated than her romance with Browning, but, in its own way,
it was as intense, as liberating and as clearly, if not as fully, documented."[18] Barrett's two sonnets, "To George Sand, A Desire"
and "To George Sand, A Recognition," overtly documented this
literary affair.

In the opening of "To George Sand, A Desire," Barrett addresses George Sand by her "self-called" male name, evoking the God-like creativity and male power over words that Sand has usurped. Sand violates the accepted gender economy by valorizing her woman's intellect with man's emotions. The "lions" of her "tumultuous senses," with which her soul answers "roar for roar," represent her "monstrous" aspect. Barrett recognizes, however, that Sand's readers misperceive her passionate soul and senses when they respond to her as to an "applauded circus"; her sexuality has become a popular act. In the second quatrain she wishes Sand to transcend, therefore, her lionlike physicality and represents her soul as a demiangel with powerful swan wings beating from her "strong shoulders." The masculine force of the lion is still implied in the power necessary for this ascent. Rescuing Sand's "nobler nature" from the "tumultuous senses" that her readers vulgarize, Barrett imagines how Sand's true genius, her "strength and science," could be freed from the contamination of her sexuality to flood the world with "holier light." The sestet desexes Sand totally: the swan's wings become angel's wings, the setting is neither earth nor sky, but Heaven. Barrett separates Sand's soul from physicality, purifying the woman whose life is imaged as an "applauded circus." She represents her as one whom an innocent "child and maiden" can "embrace" and "kiss upon [her] lips a stainless fame." Sexual passion is transformed into a kiss of innocence, the woman artist into the domestic angel.

The poem works with exaggeration, both of the gross way in which readers turn Sand into an "applauded circus" and of the purity which is the alternative. It demonstrates the monster-angel dichotomy of woman and is unable to offer any integration of the two. The sonnet's language and rhythm emphasize its anticlimactic nature: the assertive stresses of the opening line, "Thou large-brained woman and large-hearted man," are dramatically contrasted with the almost tripping rhythm of the last, "To kiss upon thy lips a stainless fame." It is hard to tell whether this transformation of Sand represents Barrett's true feelings, or whether, as Thomson hypothesizes, it is "revealing, both of Elizabeth Barrett's own deep involvement and her consciousness of a censorious public, whom she attempts to propitiate with such terms as 'angel,' 'pure,' 'holier,' 'stainless,' 'maiden,' 'nobler.' "[19] It does allow Barrett both to acknowledge her admiration for Sand publicly and also to defend herself from the criticism that "no modest woman would or *ought* to confess an acquaintance with the works of George Sand."

"To George Sand, A Recognition" is quite another kind of sonnet. Again it uses the Petrarchan form, but carries none of the Petrarchan idealizing of the beloved that "A Desire" exploits. Having appeased her public with the first sonnet, in the second Barrett states the nature of Sand's importance for her. This sonnet speaks to the dialectic between Milton's influence and Sand's own. If the recitative is Barrett's statement in the Preface that she intends to speak with "peculiar reference to Eve's alloted grief," then the aria in "A Recognition" elaborates on that "grief," and on Sand's articulation of it.

The opening quatrain is a question. Drawing from her notion that George Sand is "she who is man & woman together" (*RB&EBB*, 1:159), Barrett emphasizes that masculine qualities can never disguise Sand, who is a "true woman" possessed of a "woman's nature" that connects her to "the gauds and armlets worn / By weaker women in captivity." Recognizing women as a class, Barrett questions whether Sand for all her apparent "manly scorn" can ever deny belonging to that class. "Ah, vain denial" dismisses such severance as impossible. This connects her with Sand: the 1844 poems demonstrate both Barrett's own separation from the traditional role of woman and also her very real sense of "captivity."

This sonnet seeks to define woman ("true woman," "woman's nature," "weaker women," "woman's voice," "woman's hair," and "woman-heart"); it is a bleak definition. The Biblical notion of "Eve's alloted grief" triumphs: woman is in "captivity," she sobs and speaks with "voice forlorn," and knows "dishevelled strength in agony." She is, however, beyond "Eve-ship" in her capability of speaking about her lot with a "revolted cry." Barrett recognizes Sand's accomplishment as resonating to her own purposes: to be a spokeswoman for those who are not privileged and who feel with "spasm, not a speech," a Promethean usurper of the God-granted male power of language.

The second quatrain (which extends into the ninth line) answers the question the speaker poses in the first. No costume can mask woman's essential nature, and woman, traditionally assigned to a life of suffering, must express her condition. She will, thereby, find her strength, symbolized by the wild hair that is freed or tamed in so much of Victorian literature as either expression or suppression of woman's passion and imagination.[20]

If the second quatrain answers the first, the sestet explains the answer, with a curious dichotomy between the "world" and "we." "The world" sees Sand as a poet burning in a "poet-fire," but "we" see "thy woman-heart beat evermore / Through the large flame." The "world" implies men (or all readers who—wittingly or not—read within patriarchal blinkers) who know her as a writer; whereas "we," the women, recognize how Sand's "woman-heart" informs her work. Women's literature was conventionally patronized and trivialized. However, women writers who, defying their cultural roles, wrote "through the large flame" of the hitherto male "poet-fire"—as did Sand, and as Barrett aspired to do—challenged the identification of male with universal. Sand wrote of the "revolted cry" of woman, Barrett of "Eve's alloted grief": women, if not the "world," recognize the shift in gender and poetic assumptions when the "poet-fire" is informed by a "woman-heart."

"A Recognition" is essentially an aesthetic manifesto, rooted (if a little spasmodically) in the actual world. But the last two and a half lines are curious: with a quick switch, echoing "A Desire," Barrett imagines Sand again unsexed on the "heavenly shore," a spirit. Although there is a linguistic/imagistic transition from "the woman-heart" beating to "beat purer, heart," the rhetorical and emotional transition feels forced. The final image is of death, the "heavenly shore." Only there will God "unsex" Sand, liberate her from the demands her "poet-fire" puts on her "woman-heart." The switch from earth to heaven is analogous to the switch in Barrett's Preface from the assertive energy of imagining the "pleasure in driving in, like a pile, stroke upon stroke, the Idea of EXILE" to the passive stasis of "heavenly love and purity." It may repudiate the "dishevelled strength in agony" of woman's lot, but it also detracts from the passion of the "body" of the sonnet, by "purifying" it into spirit. The religious language of the last lines, "purer," "unsex," "heavenly," "unincarnate," "purely," deflect from Sand's and Barrett's earthly purpose as women writers.[21]

The influence of Milton and Sand, demonstrated so dramatically in the Preface and the George Sand sonnets, dominates the *Poems of 1844*. Milton evokes the male tradition that locates woman as his object: Sand confirms Barrett's subversion of that text. When woman speaks back, hers will be a different and equally important story. The *Poems of 1844* reveal some progress toward this latter ideal over *The Seraphim, and Other Poems*, but they demonstrate most noticeably a dialectic between, not a synthesis of, the two influences.

Barrett's seclusion led her, in *Poems of 1844*, both to recognize and rebel against her literary confinement: whereas the Preface and the George Sand sonnets speak to those issues, her ballads are the most interesting dramatization of them. Poe, for all his reservations about Barrett's idiosyncratic work, recognized and admired its "happy audacity of thought and expression never before known in one of her sex."[22] If the conscious awareness of Milton inhibited Barrett when she attempted to imagine the Fall from woman's perspective, the revisionary program she identified in her Preface is obliquely manifest in the rebellion against the patriarchy dramatized by the courtly ladies of her ballads. They foreshadowed Barrett's own rejection of what she painfully came to understand as imprisonment in her father's room.

CHAPTER 3

Rebellion

EVE'S SONGS OF

INNOCENCE

The "system" of man.
—The Letters of Robert Browning
and Elizabeth Barrett Barrett,
1845–1846

The 1844 ballads were enormously popular. According to reviewers of the *Poems of 1844*, they contained "some of the best ballad-writing we have met with for many a day": in the ballads Barrett "has struck out many new tones in the rhythmical scale; rich and recondite harmonies, full of originality"; "Lady Geraldine's Courtship" was the "best performance of the whole, because the most real, the most closely allied to the work-day world around us all"; "Rhyme of the Duchess May" as "a ballad and for merit of various kinds, may rank with the highest of the class."[1] The *Athenaeum* favored the ballads, recognizing the contrast between Barrett's poetic voice and the poetesses' work: "Between her poems and the slighter lyrics of most of the sisterhood, there is all the difference which exists between the putting on of 'singing-robes' for altar-service, and the taking up lute or harp to enchant an indulgent circle of friends and kindred."[2]

Like her Romantic precursors and her immediate contemporary, Tennyson, Barrett represented the present in the costumes of the past. Her ballads, reminiscent of "The Eve of St. Agnes," "La Belle Dame Sans Merci," "Christabel," and "The Lady of Shalott," portray gender relations in a medieval setting.[3] The male poets locate a mystery in the nature of sexual experience itself, whereas Barrett dramatizes woman's challenge to "the 'system' of man" (*RB&EBB*, 1:341).[4]

Barrett's most intimate observation of marriage was of her father's "thunder" and her mother's submission, which caused the latter a "mark, a plait, within, . . a sign of suffering" (*RB&EBB*, 2:1012). She saw too often marriages of convenience without happiness, and consequently had never sought the state herself. She believed that "women generally *lose* by marriage" (*L*, 1:330) and therefore had a "loathing dread of marriage as a loveless state." She "always did certainly believe in love" (*L*, 1:312), defined as mutual passion and intellectual equality, but found that "a fulness of sympathy, a sharing of life, one with another, . . . is scarcely ever looked for except in a narrow conventional sense. Men like to come home and find a blazing fire and a smiling face and an hour of relaxation. Their serious thoughts, and earnest aims in life, they like to keep on one side. And this is the carrying out of love and marriage almost everywhere in the world— and this, the degrading of women by both."[5] Barrett, cognizant of the double standard applied to marital infidelities—"the crushing into dust for the woman—and the 'oh you naughty man' ism for the betrayer"—protested this "injustice which cries upwards from the earth" (*MRM*, 1:295). When Browning criticized women's calculating behavior, she upbraided him, describing contemporary marriages as "worse than solitudes and more desolate":

> The falseness and the calculations!—why how can you, who are *just, blame women* . . when you must know what the "system" of man is towards them,—& of men not ungenerous otherwise? Why are women to be blamed if they act as if they had to do with swindlers?—is it not the mere instinct of preservation which makes them do it? These make women what they are. . . . Why there are, to be sure, cold & heartless, light & changeable, ungenerous & calculating women in the world!—that is sure. But for the most part, they are only what they are made . . & far better than the nature of the making. [*RB&EBB*, 1:340–41]

Her early observation of "the 'system' of man" and of marriage convinced her that it too seldom provided happiness for women.

Barrett's examination of the sexual economy of courtship and marriage in poems with medieval settings locates her within a tradition that favored the ballad form and "the lyrical narrative of dramatic confrontation."[6] My discussion here will focus on six poems. "Bertha in the Lane," akin to the work of the poetesses, represents woman enacting "love's divine self-abnegation" (34). "The Romaunt of the Page," "The Lay of the Brown Rosary," and "Rhyme of the Duchess May" reject the conventions both of courtly love and of female self-abnegation. In each poem Barrett narrates an Eve who transgresses—by refusing her role of subservient, silent woman—and is punished by death. "Lady Geraldine's Courtship" both presents and questions courtly rhetoric and ideology, but its heroine lives. Finally, "The Romance of the Swan's Nest" prefigures Barrett's rejection of the ballad form as too confining.

Barrett's early ballads, "The Romaunt of the Ganges" (1838), "The Romaunt of the Page" (1839), and "The Lay of the Brown Rosary" (1840), were published in *Findens' Tableaux*. This annual of verse, edited by Mary Russell Mitford, published a few sentimental poems by minor male poets, but the majority of its contributors were women. The *Findens' Tableaux* in which "The Romaunt of the Page" appeared carried the full title *Findens' Tableaux of the Affections: A Series of Picturesque Illustrations of the Womanly Virtues* (1839). The "affections" and "womanly virtues" establish the ideology to which the annual subscribed. Inclusion apparently located Barrett's work in a female genre whose allegiances were to such womanly virtues; however, the 1844 ballads suggest a redefinition of what constitutes the virtuous woman.[7]

That such a redefinition involved a rejection of the poetess's as much as of the male poet's voice is manifest in "Bertha in the Lane," a poem that admirably demonstrates woman's self-abnegation. It resonates to the work of the poetesses, acting, therefore, as a touchstone from which to judge Barrett's subversion of that female genre in the other ballads. The speaker, Bertha's older sister, is the only female protagonist in the 1844 poems who narrates her own tale. Her rebellious sisters in the other ballads are under the control of a narrator. This narrative represents woman at her most self-sacrificially virtuous. The speaker overhears that her fiancé, Robert, loves Bertha (who is seven years younger) but will dutifully marry his betrothed whom he "esteems." Apparently making her own wedding dress, the speaker surprises Bertha by offering her the dress and Robert. Asking Bertha to help her to bed, she complains, "Though the clock stands at the noon / I am weary" (1). The speaker's virtue is not, however, self-willed but learned from her mother, now dead:

> Mother, mother, up in heaven,
>   Stand up on the jasper sea,
> And be witness I have given
>   All the gifts required of me,—
> Hope that blessed me, bliss that crowned,
> Love that left me with a wound,
> Life itself that turneth round!
>
> [6]

The price she is "required" by her mother to pay—hope, bliss, love, and life—is steep; and she cannot always sustain the façade of easy compliance. Initially she welcomes her mother's spiritual presence in the room:

> Mother, mother, thou art kind,
>   Thou art standing in the room,
> In a molten glory shrined
>   That rays off into the gloom!
>
> [7]

But the word "gloom" ushers in a more realistic vision—a fear of the death the mother demands from her daughter:

> But thy smile is bright and bleak
> Like cold waves—I cannot speak,
> I sob in it, and grow weak.
>
> Ghostly mother, keep aloof
>   One hour longer from my soul,
> For I still am thinking of
>   Earth's warm-beating joy and dole!
>
> [7–8]

The striking image of her mother's "smile bright and bleak /
Like cold waves" transforms the dutiful daughter into one who
fears death and resents self-sacrifice.

In a flashback the speaker tells Bertha how she learned of
the love between her and Robert, then gives instructions for
her burial—evoking the ghastly image of the living death she
imagines:

> On that grave drop not a tear!
>   Else, though fathom-deep the place,
> Through the woollen shroud I wear
>   I shall feel it on my face.
>
> [31]

She will not die easily, requesting Bertha to kiss her eyes, so that
as she dies the light will go

> Sweetly, as it used to rise
> When I watched the morning-grey
> Strike, betwixt the hills, the way
> He was sure to come that day.
>
> [32]

She remembers the love she longs for but succumbs to her fate,
"no more vain words be said!" She asks her mother to "smile
now on thy Dead, / I am death-strong in my soul" (38). Under her
mother's bright, bleak smile she connects her own female suffering with that of Jesus:

> Jesus, Victim, comprehending
>   Love's divine self-abnegation,
> Cleanse my love in its self-spending,
>   And absorb the poor libation!
>
> [34]

The emotional impact of the poem enforces the notion that
women's self-sacrifice is learned from mothers, the subtle, successful agents of patriarchy. Yet the poem's last line, "I aspire
while I expire," in which the speaker imagines her ascension into
Heaven, is so bad, its verbal play so inappropriate, that the poem's seriousness is undercut and we question how virtuous is the
speaker's self-sacrifice.

None of Barrett's other heroines die so meekly, but the rebellion against such a destiny is voiced far from the "Sidmouth town" of "Bertha in the Lane." Barrett's defiant heroines wear medieval costume, props so popularized by the early nineteenth-century revival of interest in the Middle Ages that they disguised the subversive nature of the poems' propositions. Barrett's early steps onto her own poetic ground enticed but did not incite her readers. Three poems that challenge the patriarchal assumptions of courtly literature and the "womanly virtues" extolled by the poetesses are "The Romaunt of the Page," "The Lay of the Brown Rosary," and the "Rhyme of the Duchess May." Each dramatizes an Eve who refuses Milton's dictum "He for God only, she for God in him," and each, because of her defiance, dies.

"The Romaunt of the Page" was written in 1838 (just before Barrett's eight years of chronic invalidism) in response to an engraving sent to her by Mitford, the editor of *Findens' Tableaux*. Mitford often sent engravings to poets as subject matter for poems. The underlying assumption that women can produce verses to order determined that the poetry was unrepresentative of the writers' concerns—except when such pictures were in the hands of a poet like Barrett who refused the role of poetess even as she relinquished the assumed role of male poet. The engraving about which Barrett wrote "The Romaunt of the Page" "represents a girl dressed as a squire or page but . . . obviously feminine in appearance. . . . She is kneeling at the foot of a tree and looking with a wistful expression toward the back of a fully armed knight on a horse that is pawing the air and is about to charge away. On the ground in front of the page are a casque and a murderous-looking instrument, which seems to be a combination of crossbow and battle-axe."[8] It is the stuff of which the young adolescent Barrett dreamed when she acknowledged, "Through the whole course of my childhood, I had a steady indignation against Nature who made me a woman, and a determinate resolution to dress up in men's clothes . . . & go into the world 'to seek my fortune.' '*How*,' was not decided; but I rather leant towards being poor Lord Byron's PAGE" (*MRM*, 2:7). Reminiscent of Shakespeare's romantic comedies, the poem employs disguise to enable the woman to test her lover before committing herself to him.[9] Although the protagonist, dressed as a page, is married to the knight she serves, the rushed midnight wedding before the knight's departure to the crusades results in an unconsummated marriage in which husband and wife are ignorant even of each other's appearance. The woman-as-page is strong and brave, one who " 'fearest not to steep in blood / The curls upon [his] brow,' " and who " 'once in the tent, and twice in the fight,' " saved her master, Sir Hubert, from a " 'mortal blow' " (2). The page talks of the " 'bloody battle-game' " (3), and when the knight imagines introducing his page to his wife, he tells her " 'her bower may suit thee ill' " for " 'fitter thy hand for my knightly spear / Than thy tongue for my lady's will' " (10). The page is thus established as capable in the violence of battle and more suited to the male "battle-game" than the female "bower."

Only in retrospect do we understand the mention of "his" curls and why "no lady in her bower . . . / Could blush more sudden red" (11) than "he." The page "slowly and thankfully" accepts the knight's praise not because "he" imagines his valiant future as a knight, but because *she* assumes that the knight's pleasure in her suitability for the battlefield rather than lady's rooms confirms his acceptance of her unorthodox actions. The page's blushing assertion, " 'thy lady's bower to me / Is suited well' " (11), indicates not the titillation of a page in training as a warrior and courtly lover, but reveals the woman's relief that her mystery husband has passed her test and will welcome his valiant, assertive wife. In this ironic moment, the knight—and initially the reader—understands one meaning, and the page—and eventually the reader—quite another.

At this ambiguous moment a dirge is heard from the "convent on the sea, / One mile off" where nuns mourn the death of their Lady Abbess, *"Beati, beati, mortui!"* ("Blessed be the dead.") The nuns' long laments (12, 44) function as a Greek chorus. Although the relevance of their grief is inexplicable here, its ominous note that "wheeleth on the wind around" eerily undermines the page's confidence in "his" suitability to the "lady's bower." The protagonist's unconventional actions seem jeopardized when her blushing self-absorption in her own future well-being tunes out the nuns' chanting. They mourn a woman's death: "And the knight heard all, and the page heard none," but instead talks on confidently.

The woman provokes the knight into revealing his feelings

about his wife and her beauty. Her ruse works, but the story she hears about herself is a bitter one; it is rife with slander, duels, murders, and vengeance, which necessitated the knight's upholding his honor by marrying the daughter of a man who avenged his father's murder while he was away riding "the lists at court" (16). The speedy marriage before he left for the crusades—" 'the steed thrice neighed, and the priest fast prayed' " (23)—occurred in the dead of a moonless night. He has, therefore, no idea of his wife's appearance. The knight is a victim of the gender economy he perpetuates; without parents the daughter had no honorable place. The knight to be honorable had to marry her.

When the page discusses how "her sister" disguised herself as a page to fight by her knight/husband, the pleasant intimacy between knight and page abruptly ceases. Deaths must be avenged, marriages arranged, and knights leave their wives for the battlefield; a lady must not leave her castle to join her husband in battle. In this "system of man," the wife whom the knight resents must act according to the "womanly virtues": " 'My love, so please you, shall requite / No woman, whether dark or bright, / Unwomaned if she be' " (25). From the safety of her male disguise, the page/wife challenges such hypocrisy:

> The page stopped weeping and smiled cold—
>   "Your wisdom may declare
> That womanhood is proved the best
> By golden brooch and glossy vest
>   The mincing ladies wear;
> Yet it is proved, and was of old,
> Anear as well, I dare to hold,
>   By truth, or by despair."
>
> He smiled no more, he wept no more,
>   But passionate he spake—
> "Oh, womanly she prayed in tent,
>   When none beside did wake!
> Oh, womanly she paled in fight,
>   For one belovèd's sake!—
> And her little hand, defiled with blood,
> Her tender tears of womanhood
>   Most woman-pure did make!"

—"Well done it were for thy sistèr,
  Thou tellest well her tale!
But for my lady, she shall pray
  I' the kirk of Nydesdale.
Not dread for me but love for me
  Shall make my lady pale;
No casque shall hide her woman's tear—
It shall have room to trickle clear
  Behind her woman's veil."

—"But what if she mistook thy mind
  And followed thee to strife,
Then kneeling did entreat thy love
  As Paynims ask for life?"
—"I would forgive, and evermore
Would love her as my servitor,
  But little as my wife.

"Look up—there is a small bright cloud
  Alone amid the skies!
So high, so pure, and so apart,
  A woman's honour lies."
The page looked up—the cloud was sheen—
A sadder cloud did rush, I ween,
  Betwixt it and his eyes.

Then dimly dropped his eyes away
  From welkin unto hill—
Ha! who rides there?—the page is 'ware,
  Though the cry at his heart is still:
And the page seeth all and the knight seeth none,
Though banner and spear do fleck the sun,
  And the Saracens ride at will.

[26–31]

Challenging a "wisdom" that reveres the superficial "golden
brooch," "glossy vest," and "mincing ladies," the page extols a
womanhood not limited to costumes and postures, but manifest
in enduring qualities, "By truth, or by despair." In her system the
"sister's" active loyalty to her husband in the field, rather than
her passive waiting in the domestic interiors of the castle, is

what makes her truly "woman-pure." Whatever we may feel about the morality of advocating war as superior to domestic life, there is an integrity in the page's assertion that a virtuous woman is one who takes creative initiative, involves herself in the public sphere, is physically strong and courageous, and expresses her love by cooperation not by dependency. The knight refuses such a woman: his response to a wife who mistook his mind by following him into battle would be to forgive her and "love her as [his] servitor, / But little as [his] wife." Though he bridles at marriage, he proves a textbook knight and courtly lover with exalted notions of woman: "Look up—there is a small bright cloud / Alone amid the skies! / So high, so pure, and so apart, / A woman's honour lies." A woman whose hair is "steep[ed] in blood" (2) and whose "hand, defiled with blood" can "ward [him] a mortal blow" (2) is abhorrent to a man who idealizes and trivializes woman as "so high, so pure, and so apart."

The page failed to hear the nuns' ominous funeral lament because she was so confident in her bright future as the knight's trusted wife. Likewise the knight, idealizing his wife's (distant) place in the future, proves inadequate as a soldier. He is so absorbed in his sentimental rhetoric, so bound in by his fictional world, that he fails to hear the approach of the very Saracens he has come to fight; "the page seeth all and the knight seeth none" (31). She, seeing the Saracens, sends the knight to safety, excusing her own lingering,

> "For I must loose on saddle-bow
>   My battle casque that galls, I trow,
> The shoulder of my steed."
>
>   [33]

The knight smiles "free at the fantasy," destined to be enacted, that the page will join him later " 'as parted spirits cleave / To mortals too beloved to leave' " (34), and fails to notice her distress. "Had the knight looked up to the page's face," he might have averted the tragic outcome. He exhibits no such sensitivity leaving the page "alone, alone," where she bitterly reveals her true identity: " 'Have I renounced my womanhood, / For wifehood unto *thee*?' " (36). Although she asks " 'God save thee' " (37), she wishes the knight a wife " 'more woman-proud and half as true' " as herself who is " 'false page, but truthful woman' " (39). Her authority succumbs to the knight's system, "How bright the little cloud appears" (38).

Yet her final act is defiant: she bloodies herself saving the knight's life instead of staying "so apart" from earthly turmoil. The ending is violent indeed with its "tramp of hoof," and "flash of steel," with the Paynims who "smote her low" and "cleft her golden ringlets through." The gruesome final vision reveals how she "felt the scimitar gleam down, / And met it from beneath" (43). Yet accompanying all this violence is her smile, "bright in victory."

We may ask, what is her "victory"? She has succeeded, through self-sacrifice, in saving her husband; the poem, therefore, appears to dramatize the extreme of womanly self-abnegation. And yet, she has also usurped the male role by dying in battle to protect her family. The knight seems incapable of protecting himself without his page to notice the enemy's approach and ward off "mortal blows." Her victory is her indictment of the knight's system: far from being "so high, so pure, and so apart," the woman proves her competence outside the home. And yet, within patriarchy, the woman, whatever her strength, is sacrificed by the knight: to irrelevancy at home, to death outside of it. The poem dramatizes a macabre counterpoint to "The Lady of Shalott." The page is slaughtered and the poem ends with the nuns' lament:

> Dirge for abbess laid in shroud
> Sweepeth o'er the shroudless dead,
> Page or lady, as we said,
> With the dews upon her head,
> All as sad if not as loud.
>   *Ingemisco, ingemisco!*
> Is ever a lament begun
> By any mourner under sun,
> Which, ere it endeth, suits but *one*?

The dirge of the "weary nuns" binds their cloistered existence to their sister's cultural imprisonment.

Although the ending of "The Romaunt of the Page" is punitive, the poem indicts courtly worship of woman and its misogynistic heart. It thereby subverts the acquiescent female tradition to which its publication in *Findens' Tableaux* suggests that it belongs.

"The Lay of the Brown Rosary" also first appeared (as "The Legend of the Brown Rosarie") in *Findens' Tableaux* (entitled that year *The Iris of Prose, Poetry, and Art for 1840*). The poem was republished in 1844 in the New York *Ladies' Companion and Literary Expositor*, emphasizing the poem's identification with a female literary tradition. The picture for this poem had "in the margins around the central picture of two women and a little boy in a chapel . . . faint representations of a 'brown rosarie,' an 'old convent ruin,' a nun, angels, an 'evil spirit,' the 'bridegroom' and 'Leonora' both on horseback, and 'the priest at the altar' with his 'grave young sacristans.' "[10] Barrett described writing this poem to her sister, Arabel: "When you once begin a story you can't bring it to an end all in a moment—and what with nuns and devils and angels and marriages and death and little boys, I couldn't get out of the mud without a great deal of splashing."[11] The "splashing" reveals a superficially Christian framework for the poem, the struggle between God and the Devil for Onora's soul, concealing an alignment of men with God and women with the Devil. The Eve who repudiates Lucifer in "A Drama of Exile" understands her allegiance with the feminized Devil who rebels against male authority. The male figures, however,—God, father, brother, angels, priest, and bridegroom—outnumber and outweigh the female ones, Onora, nun, and mother.

The poem centers on the appearance of Onora's dead father to his daughter in her dreams. God has ordained that Onora should also die, although God and her father become indistinguishable as the originator of the summons: "God decreed my death and I shrank back afraid. / Have patience, O dead father mine!" (2.161–62). Onora wishes to live because "Love feareth death," and she longs for her "lover [who] to battle is gone" (1.28); she has "barter[ed] love; / God's love for man's" (2.116–17). She is aided in refusing God's order by an Evil Spirit represented as a nun, cruelly interred alive in the convent wall for her refusal to confess to the Priest. The choice between submission to male authority and rebellion that brings the punishment of death-in-life is, it is implied, a choice that unites women.

The poem is structurally fascinating. Parts 1 and 3 have stanzas of five lines of amphibrachs. Part 2 contains Onora's dream, first of the angels, and then of her dialogue with the Evil Spirit dressed as the nun. The angels, God's messengers, speak in brisk octosyllabics, whereas the extended dream dialogue between Onora and the nun/Evil Spirit, to whom Onora repeats her vows to the Devil, is in rhyming fourteener couplets. This latter form is repeated in Part 4 in which Onora dies. This repetition is crucial: although Onora submits to the rule of God and her father, her death is represented rhythmically by a structure that ties her not to God's angels but still to the nun, to her female tradition of rebellion. Structurally Barrett implies that men may appropriate women but cannot finally change their form/body/being. Women, for her, remain different from men and resistant even in apparent submission. This poem would have been very different had she written Part 4 in the octosyllabics the angels use to represent God's will.

Parts 1 and 3 represent conventional ballad lore, such that without Parts 2 and 4 they would make a complete poem. A knight is away at battle. He survives the world of male heroics only to return to the destructive powers of woman. These two sections, although told by a narrator, reveal Onora's young brother's perspective. He, in Part 1, warns their mother that Onora sits with the nun of the brown rosary in a ruined convent:

"The old convent ruin the ivy rots off,
Where the owl hoots by day and the toad is sun-proof,
Where no singing-birds build and the trees gaunt and grey
As in stormy sea-coasts appear breasted one way—
    But is *this* the wind's doing?

"A nun in the east wall was buried alive
Who mocked at the priest when he called her to shrive,
And shrieked such a curse, as the stone took her breath,
The old abbess fell backwards and swooned unto death
    With an Ave half-spoken."

[1.41–50]

Our sympathies are divided between the boy's horror at female disobedience enacted initally by the nun and now by his sister, and the nun, victim of this gruesome punishment. Onora, making no mention of the nun, quells her mother's alarm at the boy's tale and anticipates her lover's return from battle. Part 1 ends with mother and daughter planning the marriage, and with the boy "half-ashamed and half-softened" (1.101).

Part 3 opens with a "morn for a bridal":

> While down through the wood rides that fair company,
> The youths with the courtship, the maids with the glee,
> Till the chapel-cross opens to sight, and at once
> All the maids sigh demurely and think for the nonce,
>   "And so endeth a wooing!"
>
> And the bride and the bridegroom are leading the way,
> With his hand on her rein, and a word yet to say;
> Her dropt eyelids suggest the soft answers beneath,
> And the little quick smiles come and go with her breath
>   When she sigheth or speaketh.
>
> [3.225–34]

This conventional portrait presents the bridegroom reining in Onora's horse while she prepares for her role as demure wife. At the chapel her young brother tries to prevent the marriage because Onora wears the nun's brown rosary. But the wedding guests just laugh and the priest retorts, "Thou art wild, pretty boy! Blessed she / Who prefers at her bridal a brown rosary / To a worldly arraying" (3.297–99). The happy wedding scene is interrupted by a laugh heard at the altar (3.304); the bride looks "as if no bride she were, / Gazing cold at the priest without gesture of prayer" (3.307–8); the priest "whenever the Great Name [is] there to be read, / His voice [sinks] to silence" (3.312–13); and the bridegroom gives his bride the kiss fatal to himself. The boy's accusations are finally justified. Onora rips the brown rosary from her neck:

> She dashed it in scorn to the marble-paved ground
> Where it fell mute as snow, and a weird music-sound
> Crept up, like a chill, up the aisles long and dim.
>
> [3.355–57]

With no reason to live, she throws herself on her dead husband: "I am ready for dying" (3.354).

As such the poem would be emotionally and structurally conventional, even if a little mysterious. The boy would be exonerated and woman proven still to be destructive. The drama in Part 3 represents an exaggerated version of "La Belle Dame Sans Merci": instead of being Keats's "wretched wight, / Alone and palely loitering" after he had "shut her wild sad eyes— / So kiss'd to sleep," the knight in "The Lay of the Brown Rosary" "kisseth the bride" and "fell stark at her foot" (3.326, 328). It is arguable that sudden death is preferable to the "death-pale" life of which Keats's knight dreams in which "starv'd lips in the gloom / With horrid warning gaped wide": either way sexual involvement with a woman is dramatized as destructive.

However, quite a different tale emerges when Part 2 intrudes into this ballad narrative. Onora's dream explains both her commitment to the nun and also the strange events of her wedding day; the destructive woman is transformed into one who enacts strategies for survival against the destructive power of *male* authority. In her dream two angels appear. One, hearing Onora is a sinner, is eager to save her:

> She so young, that I who bring
> Good dreams for saintly children, might
> Mistake that small soft face tonight,
> And fetch her such a blessèd thing.
> [2.109–13]

The other sternly rebukes him—"It is not WILLED" (2.127)—and they depart. The angels, although often associated with women in nineteenth-century rhetoric, are here manifestations of male will and authority, whereas the Devil, whose incarnation as Lucifer was masculine, inhabits the rebellious, sexual spirit of the female in this poem. With the departure of the angels, the nun, who dressed as an Evil Spirit embodies the cultural view of unorthodox womanhood, appears in the dream where Onora walks, "among the fields, beneath the autumn-sun, / With [her] dead father, hand in hand, as [she had] often done" (2.137–38). She longs to stay with her father, whose feet are "tied . . . beneath the kirkyard stone" but who in dreams calls, " 'Come forth, my daughter, my beloved, and walk the fields with me!'" (2.142–45). Barrett's strategy for revealing Onora's story lies in the nun's insistence that Onora repeat it aloud for when her thoughts wander "too near heaven" (2.130):

> "Stand up where thou dost stand
> Among the fields of Dreamland with thy father hand in
>   hand,
> And clear and slow repeat the vow, declare its cause
>   and kind,
> Which not to break, in sleep or wake thou bearest on
>   thy mind."
>
> [2.152–55]

Step by step Onora tells her story until she finally rehearses her vow to the nun. She sold her soul to the Devil, "because that God decreed [her] death" (2.161); she could not suffer on the day she was engaged "to lie content and still beneath a stone, / And feel [her] own betrothed go by" (2.170–71). She vows to the nun, "upon thy rosary brown," she will never repeat God's name (2.200–208), thereby allying herself with the woman who also refused patriarchal authority. She chooses life and love, not death and God. She describes her final dream image: " 'my love! I felt him near again! / I saw his steed on mountain-head, I heard it on the plain!'" (2.207–209). On waking she is uneasy, but "her hands tremble fast as their pulses and, free / From the death-clasp, close over—the BROWN ROSARY" (2.218–19).

Onora's pact with the Devil infects the wedding day with tension. The boy's anxiety is revealed to have a basis in truth, and the strange altar behavior of the priest is clarified. Because Onora has resisted to some degree, she wins a limited victory. The bridegroom dies, not Onora herself. The victory is limited because although she lives, she does not have love on earth, and hence her despair, " 'I am ready for dying'" (3.354). Instead, she must linger on, dead in life, knowing her guilt, aware that everything around her has life and vitality: " 'only I am dreary, / And, mother, of my dreariness behold me very weary'" (4.364–65). She submits to slow death:

> Then breaking into tears,—"Dear God," she cried, "and
> must we see
> All blissful things depart from us or ere we go to THEE?
> We cannot guess Thee in the wood or hear Thee in the
> wind?
> Our cedars must fall round us ere we see the light
> behind?"
>
> [4.386–89]

Part 3 ends on death and Onora's recognition of her sin; Part 4 reveals her still challenging God's will. When she finally dies, it is not out of obedience to God's call, but because earth excludes a woman who defies male authority: Onora perishes "mute for lack of root, earth's nourishment to reach" (4.400). This Eve also allies herself with Lucifer, and is punished.

The dramatization of the "nun in the east wall . . . buried alive" because she defied male authority is emblematic of woman's condition. The absolute trust the mother has in Onora's allegiance to the nun is pitted against God, father, son, and essentially against priest and bridegroom. The father's apparently gratuitous summoning of his daughter to death, and the punitive killing of her husband, thereby denying her happiness, sex, and love, ultimately render the women powerless against this masculine will. Certainly the desire of patriarchal society to immure woman was becoming a peculiarly personal concern of Barrett's as she lingered in her invalid's room. The strength of the protest against it is vivid here, even if submission is the outcome.

"Rhyme of the Duchess May," however, records a heroine who refuses submission. Although she also dies, her death results from self-assertion for which she feels no remorse. The poem first appeared in *Poems of 1844*, a year after its composition.[12] Barrett wrote it after reading George Sand's work, which may account for this heroine's refusal of courtly and marital economies. Barrett dramatizes medieval marriage as an economic, not affectionate, arrangement. The Duchess May, "a Duke's fair orphan-girl," was ward of her uncle, the earl, who "betrothed her twelve years old, for the sake of dowry gold, / To his son Lord Leigh the churl" (8). But the Duchess May, who loved Sir Guy of Linteged, rejected such traffic in women inherent in the sex/

gender economy of marriage. When she refused to marry her cousin, the earl commented, " 'Good my niece, that hand withal looketh somewhat soft and small / For so large a will, in sooth' " (11). To which his niece astutely replied, in a sing-song nursery rhythm that mocked her uncle's diminution of her, " 'Little hand clasps muckle gold, or it were not worth the hold / Of thy son, good uncle mine!' " (12). Her cousin invoked might as right; he "jerked his breath, and sware thickly in his teeth" that " 'He would wed his own betrothed, an she loved him an she loathed, / Let the life come or the death' " (13). The Duchess May resisted intimidation and refused to acquiesce, declaring, " '[a] woman's will dies hard' " and " 'orphaned girl and dowered lady, / I deny you wife and ward' " (15). She married Sir Guy of Linteged at midnight in secret and rode off with him through the "night-storm," reflecting in the natural world the upheaval she had created in the social order.

After three months of marriage Earl Leigh and his son with their forces attacked Linteged:

> Down the sun dropt large and red on the towers of
>   Linteged,—
>   *Toll slowly.*
> Lance and spear upon the height, bristling strange in
>   fiery light,
>   While the castle stood in shade.
>
>   [3]

For fourteen days, reflecting the red sun, the castle "seethed in blood" (5). The violence dramatized male rage at woman's assumption of power over her own life. Lord Leigh gleefully anticipated the moment he would "wring thy fingers pale in the gauntlet of my mail" (32). Leigh, whose "thin lips . . . scarcely sheathe the cold white gnashing of his teeth" (26), imagined a cruel revenge. But the Leighs were not the only ones to assault the integrity of Duchess May. Sir Guy equally objectified her when he suggested ending the slaughter of his soldier kinsmen by voluntarily dying and returning his wife to Lord Leigh. He valued his men's lives over his wife's, although to assuage such betrayal he pictured an idealized ending to the affair, not the torture Leigh fantasized:

"Then my foes shall sleek their pride, soothing fair
my widowed bride
  Whose sole sin was love of me:

"With their words all smooth and sweet, they will
front her and entreat"—
  Toll slowly.
"And their purple pall will spread underneath her
fainting head
  While her tears drop over it.

"She will weep her woman's tears, she will pray her
woman's prayers"—
  Toll slowly.
"But her heart is young in pain, and her hopes will
spring again
  By the suntime of her years."

[49–51]

It is a patronizing attitude and a fictional vision; nothing in
the spunky young Duchess suggested such submission of "her
fainting head." When she heard that Sir Guy intended to kill
himself and return her to Lord Leigh, she cried and "Low she
dropt her head, and lower, till her hair coiled on the floor" (56).
But her coiling hair suggested strength, not "the fainting head"
of the Duke's picture of her grief. Her grief was short-lived and
transformed into action; she decided to die with her chosen husband. The Duchess's actions affirmed what neither the beloved
Sir Guy nor the loathed Lord Leigh understood: she was not an
object whose disposition men decide; she was not an object
whose fate could be decided by displays of male strength; she was
not an object who passively submitted to men's will.

She decided her own fate, jumping to death with her husband. Terrified but determined, once on horseback seconds before death, "she clung wild and she clung mute with her shud-
dering lips half-shut" (87). Her abundant hair is a symbol of passion, energy, and assertion as she insists "by all my womanhood"
(75) and "by wifehood's verity" (76) on dying with her husband,
to avoid Lord Leigh. Reminiscent of Landon's "Hindoo Widow,"

this protagonist is more closely allied to Morris's Jehane in "The Haystack in the Floods": she decides her fate rather than ceding to custom. Unlike the knight in "The Romaunt of the Page," Sir Guy accepts the Duchess's authority. Barrett dramatizes the balance of determination and fear in the Duchess's Pyrrhic victory through the horse's terrified balancing on the tower top "in stark despair, with his front hoofs poised in air" (92) before the three plunge to "the headlong death below."

In the conclusion the narrator, a bell-ringer, thinks on "the ancient Rhyme." He notices a grave: " HERE, UNDEFILED, LIETH MAUD, A THREE-YEAR CHILD, / EIGHTEEN HUNDRED FOR-TY-THREE." He does not contrast her innocence and the lovers' guilt, but rather likens them:

> Though in passion ye would dash, with a blind and
> heavy crash—
> > *Toll slowly—*
> Up against the thick-bossed shield of God's judgement
> in the field,—
> > Though your heart and brain were rash,—
>
> Now, your will is all unwilled; now, your pulses are
> all stilled:
> > *Toll slowly.*
> Now, ye lie as meek and mild (whereso laid) as Maud
> the child
> > Whose small grave was lately filled.
>
> > > [5–6]

Although the Duchess May defied patriarchal authority and both lovers defied God in their suicidal leap, the narrator gives his and, he feels sure, God's blessing on them, "I smiled to think God's greatness flowed around our incompleteness,— / Round our restlessness, His rest" (11).

This conclusion, together with the prologue, frames the Duchess May's story: the bell-ringer claims to "read this ancient rhyme" (6) while sitting in a churchyard hearing the bells peal. This story within a story functions as a distancing device, reducing Barrett's apparent responsibility for her unorthodox story.

However, the tone relates less to the heroine's triumph than to the grief for her death, suggested by the mood of mourning and the solemn ringing of the bells. The bell-ringers announce, " 'Ours is music for the dead' " (1). The solemn tone is achieved by Barrett's manipulation of the ballad form and its refrain; by reading the refrain in the middle of each stanza the reader hears the bell toll against the unfolding narrative rather than as a conclusion to each stage.

What is the lament for which the bell tolls throughout this "ancient rhyme"? Like "The Romaunt of the Page" and "The Lay of the Brown Rosary" the poem ends with the death of both man and woman: the knight in "The Romaunt of the Page" seems incompetent to save his life without his page/wife and may well meet as bloody a death as she; the bridegroom dies upon kissing his bride in "The Lay of the Brown Rosary" before she herself declines into death; and in a more triumphant death Sir Guy and Duchess May decide their own fate. These ballads expose the destructiveness to both men and women of the sex/gender economy defined as courtly behavior and often as Victorian ideology.

If these three poems were popular, "Lady Geraldine's Courtship" truly won its readers' hearts in spite of Barrett's apprehension over its modernity: "it is a 'romance of the age,' treating of railroads, routes, and all manner of 'temporalities,' and in so radical a temper that I expect to be reproved for it by the Conservative reviews round" (L, 1:177). The poem is a strange hybrid: self-consciously modern in theme, yet persistently courtly in rhetoric. Yet Barrett finally allows an assertive heroine to live, even if only within limiting conventions.

In the first part (1-92) the poet, Bertram, writes to a friend about his love for and apparent rejection by Lady Geraldine; the narrator in the conclusion reveals Bertram's mistake. The poem's modernity is established from the outset:

> She has halls among the woodlands, she has castles by
>   the breakers,
> She has farms and she has manors, she can threaten
>   and command:

And the palpitating engines snort in steam across her
    acres,
As they mark upon the blasted heaven the measure of
    the land.

        [3]

The rhythmic repetition of "she has . . . she can" is as ordered as
the structured social system that allows for Lady Geraldine's inherited lands and power; however, the movement through the
last two lines is analogous to the trains piercing those pastoral
country estates. Bertram describes how he and Lady Geraldine
discussed at length rural scenes and concerns, books, and the
problematics of progress:

"We are gods by our own reck'ning, and may well
    shut up the temples,
And wield on, amid the incense-steam, the thunder of
    our cars.

"For we throw out acclamations of self-thanking, self-
    admiring,
With, at every mile run faster,—'O the wondrous
    wondrous age!'
Little thinking if we work our souls as nobly as our
    iron,
Or if angels will commend us at the goal of pilgrimage.

"Why, what *is* this patient entrance into nature's deep
    resources
But the child's most gradual learning to walk upright
    without bane!
When we drive out, from the cloud of steam, majestical
    white horses,
Are we greater than the first men who led black ones
    by the mane?

"If we trod the deeps of ocean, if we struck the stars
    in rising,
If we wrapped the globe intensely with one hot electric
    breath,

'Twere but power within our tether, no new spirit-
    power comprising,
And in life we were not greater men, nor bolder men
    in death."

[50–53]

Through Bertram, the poet, Barrett confronts some crucial artistic, social, political, and spiritual issues of her day: To what extent should poetry represent contemporary concerns? What place
does the language of industry have in the rhetoric of poetry? Is
progress in and of itself good? What happens to the soul under
technological advance? The poem's modernity is also expressed
in Bertram's entertaining Lady Geraldine by reading not only
from Spenser and the "subtle interflowings / Found in Petrarch's
sonnets" (40) but also:

At times a modern volume, Wordsworth's solemn-
    thoughted idyl,
Howitt's ballad-verse, or Tennyson's enchanted
    reverie,—
Or from Browning some "Pomegranate," which, if
    cut deep down the middle,
Shows a heart within blood-tinctured, of a veined
    humanity.

[41]

This was a modernity that won Robert Browning's heart.

The poem seemed "so radical" to Barrett because of its preoccupation with class, dramatized in the union of the poor, low-
born poet with the wealthy and noble Lady Geraldine, which
suggests that the life of the mind makes a poet as rich as an
aristocrat. However, it also questions the premise of courtly love
that informed nineteenth-century rhetoric about women. Thus
Bertram resembles a sonneteer in his languishing after a lady
whom he believes totally unattainable, and whose very unattain-
ability fuels his passion:

I was only a poor poet, made for singing at her casement,
As the finches or the thrushes, while she thought of
    other things.

Oh, she walked so high above me, she appeared to
     my abasement,
In her lovely silken murmur, like an angel clad in wings!

[5]

His memory of "the blessèd woods of Sussex . . . / With their
leafy tide of greenery still rippling up the wind" is transformed
into "the cursèd woods of Sussex! where the hunter's arrow
found me, / When a fair face and a tender voice had made me
mad and blind!" (18) Bertram exploits the courtly image of the
slaying of the lover by Cupid's "arrow" as he imagines himself
one of Cupid's victims. Lady Geraldine is as beautiful as any
troubadour's or sonneteer's mistress:

Thus, her foot upon the new-mown grass, bareheaded,
     with the flowing
Of the virginal white vesture gathered closely to her
     throat,
And the golden ringlets in her neck just quickened by
     her going,
And appearing to breathe sun for air, and doubting if
     to float.

[24]

His love for her is platonic:

And I loved her,
     loved her certes
As I loved all heavenly objects, with uplifted eyes and
     hands;
As I loved pure inspirations, loved the graces, loved
     the virtues,
In a Love content with writing his own name on
     desert sands.

Or at least I thought so, purely.

[54–55]

He pursues her with humiliating persistence: "Why, her grey-
hound followed also! dogs—we both were dogs for scorning— /
To be sent back when she pleased it" (37). And he lives in "end-
less desolation" (80).

It is not clear how deliberately overt was Barrett's mockery of the attitudes and rhetoric of the courtly lover. What is apparent is that this traditional language of woman worship is what was available to a woman imagining herself as a male poet writing about a woman. This courtly system crumbles, however, when Bertram overhears Lady Geraldine tell a wealthy admirer, " 'Whom I marry shall be noble, / Ay, and wealthy. I shall never blush to think how he was born' " (66). Bertram, ignorant of her love for him, is also ignorant that she is describing the "wealth" of the poet, equating the poet's genius to an inherited title. A true courtly lover, Bertram upbraids Lady Geraldine for her cruelty, for her delight in her superiority and, in fact, for the very qualities he has been worshiping:

> "What right have you, madam, gazing in your palace
>   mirror daily,
> Getting so by heart your beauty which all others must
>   adore,
> While you draw the golden ringlets down your fingers,
>   to vow gaily
> You will wed no man that's only good to God, and
>   nothing more?"
>
> [76]

Her response to this tirade is to look up "as if in wonder, / With tears beaded on her lashes, and [say]—'Bertram!' " (82). Traditionally the lady is silent: the lover adores, berates, and desires the lady, and humbles himself with no verbal response. Bertram experiences an extravagant reaction to her thus tenderly naming him, shattering the courtly code: "her gentleness destroyed me whom her scorn made desolate"; he is "struck backward and exhausted by that inward flow of passion":

> By such wrong and woe exhausted—what I suffered
>   and occasioned,—
> As a wild horse through a city runs with lightning
>   in his eyes,
> And then dashing at a church's cold and passive wall,
>   impassioned,

Strikes the death into his burning brain, and blindly
   drops and dies—

So I fell, struck down before her—do you blame me,
   friend, for weakness?
'Twas my strength of passion slew me!—fell before her
   like a stone;
Fast the dreadful world rolled from me on its roaring
   wheels of blackness:
When the light came I was lying in this chamber and
   alone.

[87–88]

Not only has the courtly lady spoken in gentleness to her lover,
but in a further role reversal, the man, overcome by emotion,
swoons at the woman's feet. Lady Geraldine's acknowledgment
of love for the poet signals Barrett's dismantling of a literary tradition that rhetorically maintained woman in an idealized, dis-
tanced, and unrealistic position; it is as though the knight in
"The Romaunt of the Page" had finally understood that it is only
a male fantasy to talk of "a small bright cloud / Alone amid the
skies" as revealing woman's honor.

But that is not how the poem ends; this ballad, which subverts
conventions and in which (finally) the lovers live and the only
violence is Bertram's faint, has some puzzling elements. First,
Barrett persists in her inability to imagine a woman poet; thus,
like "The Poet's Vow," "Lady Geraldine's Courtship" subscribes
to the convention of a male poet whose vision is modified or
clarified by a female muse. The use of this convention maintains, even in what Barrett saw as the poem's radical temper, a
basically conservative vision. Second, there is the episode surrounding the statue, Silence (29–35). This statue, built in a foun-
tain on one of Lady Geraldine's estates, represents man's fantasy
of woman at his most adoring and misogynistic: she is a work of
art cast in marble; she is called Silence; she sleeps; and she holds
a rose, referred to as her "symbol-rose." The statue's origin is in
Egyptian mythology, in which the god, Heru P-Khart, was represented as a youth with one finger pointing to his mouth. The
Greeks adopted him as their god of silence, Harpocrates, and leg-

end has it that Cupid gave Harpocrates a rose to bribe him not to betray Venus's part in a love affair he happened to witness. The rose, which to the Greeks was a symbol of the male god of silence, and in the courtly love tradition was a symbol of woman, is fused here to represent a silent woman, a woman such as Carlyle admired doing her "silently important" duties and "lead[ing] noiselessly" under man's protection.[13] Bertram and Geraldine disagree over the relation of the essential meaning to the symbolic nature of the statue. Bertram describes Lady Geraldine's beauty, thus aroused:

> Half in playfulness she spoke, I thought, and half in
>   indignation;
> Friends, who listened, laughed her words off, while
>   her lovers deemed her fair:
> A fair woman, flushed with feeling, in her noble-
>   lighted station
> Near the statue's white reposing—and both bathed in
>   sunny air!
>
> [35]

Lady Geraldine, linked with the "statue's white reposing," becomes associated with the silent woman: as two women they are "both bathed in sunny air" and beautiful to their admirers. The introduction of the statue seems an irrelevant intrusion except to reinforce the idea of woman as object of man's gaze.

The narrator of the poem's conclusion recalls the scene, however, when Bertram finished his letter in despair; having made such a foolish outburst, he had determined to leave Lady Geraldine's house early in the morning. Looking up, however, he saw Geraldine, whom he described as a silent statue: "Soh! how still the lady standeth! . . . / 'Twixt the purple lattice-curtains how she standeth still and pale!" (2). He saw her "Shining eyes, like antique jewels set in Parian statue-stone!" and recognized how "underneath that calm white forehead" she was "burning torrid" (3); Lady Geraldine's statuesque quality was emphasized by the movement around her that so contrasted with her own stillness:

> With a murmurous stir uncertain, in the air the purple
>   curtain

Swelleth in and swelleth out around her motionless
    pale brows,
While the gliding of the river sends a rippling noise
    for ever
Through the open casement whitened by the moonlight's
    slant repose.

[4]

Bertram commanded her, " 'Vision of a lady! stand there silent, stand there steady!' " and invoked again courtly rhetoric for " 'the lips of silent passion, / Curved like an archer's bow to send the bitter arrows out' " (5). To aid his illusion of her as a courtly mistress, "Ever, evermore the while in a slow silence she kept smiling, / And approached him slowly, slowly, in a gliding measured pace" (6). He could not separate reality from fantasy, and she concurred with this illusion: " 'Bertram, if I say I love thee, . . . 'tis the vision only speaks' " (10). He "quickened to adore her, on his knee he fell before her" (11). The image of woman as a statue on a pedestal with a man worshiping at her feet was finally undercut as "she whispered low in triumph" that a poet is rich and noble, and " 'I shall not blush in knowing that men call him lowly born' " (11). The final iconoclastic lines of the poem are given to a woman who refuses her silent role and, in acknowledging her love, expresses the fact that, underneath the "calm white forehead" men perceive in women, she does in fact have passions "ever burning torrid" (Conclusion, 3).

The speaking statue acts as a symbol of change, not its enactment. Although marriage between Bertram and Lady Geraldine may be radical, its rhetoric is conservative. That Barrett stresses the poem's modernity in such rhetoric, and creates a male poet as protagonist, suggests that her situation has certain parallels to a courtly lady's. The conventions of both the Middle Ages and the nineteenth century make the union of woman and poet difficult.

Although Barrett wrote a few ballads after this, such as "Amy's Cruelty" (*Last Poems*, 1862), she never repeated such concentration and such strategies again. *Aurora Leigh* indicates why: reflecting on her success as a poet, Aurora declares,

My ballads prospered; but the ballad's race
Is rapid for a poet who bears weights
Of thought and golden image.

[5.84–86]

I do distrust the poet who discerns
No character or glory in his times,
And trundles back his soul five hundred years,
Past moat and drawbridge, into a castle-court,
To sing—oh, not of lizard or of toad
Alive i' the ditch there,—'twere excusable,
But of some black chief, half knight, half sheep-lifter,
Some beauteous dame, half chattel and half queen,
As dead must be, for the greater part,
The poems made on the chivalric bones;
And that's no wonder: death inherits death.

[5.189–99]

Aurora Leigh speaks to Barrett's conviction that the poet's "sole work is to represent the age, / . . . this live, throbbing age" (5.202–3), not to "[trundle] back his [*sic*] soul five hundred years" to medieval times. Aurora's rejection of a poetics that limits woman, "some beauteous dame," as "half chattel and half queen," and one that is "dead" because forged from "chivalric bones," parallels Barrett's own rejection. Although in these medieval ballads and courtly love poems Barrett dramatized Victorian middle-class woman's position in the sex/gender economy of marriage, the medieval context proved constricting for her development as a female poet.

"The Romance of the Swan's Nest," which first appeared in *Poems of 1844*, demonstrates the inadequacy of such a poetics for a woman poet, signaling Barrett's rejection of making poems from "chivalric bones." Little Ellie is refreshingly free from sentimentality, except perhaps for the reference to her "shining hair and face." She has freedom: "Little Ellie sits alone / 'Mid the beeches of a meadow, / By a stream-side on the grass" a mile's walk from home (a freedom comparable to that of the narrator in Barrett's lyric, "The Lost Bower"). It is refreshing in its tactful and open avowal of childhood eroticism:

> She has thrown her bonnet by,
>   And her feet she has been dipping
>   In the shallow water's flow:
> Now she holds them nakedly
>   In her hands, all sleek and dripping,
>   While she rocketh to and fro.

To talk of the poem as relating Ellie's sexual fantasies may be a little crude, but certainly a young girl's stroking her wet naked feet and rocking to and fro thinking of a handsome knight who is riding his red-roan steed to visit her is certainly as suggestive in its way as the more passionate eroticism of "Goblin Market." Little Ellie's fantasies center on the stock features of romance that must have constituted her reading: a noble lover who woos ladies with his lute and kills men with his sword. Ellie imagines he will prefer her to knightly glory, but she will test him, sending him on dangerous missions before finally giving in: "I may bend / From my pride, and answer—'Pardon / If he comes to take my love.' " Merging fantasy with reality, Ellie imagines showing this heroic lover her secret, the "swan's nest among the reeds." However, while Ellie had daydreamed, "Lo, the wild swan had deserted, / And a rat had gnawed the reeds!": what she holds valuable in the actual world is destroyed. Dreaming courtly fantasies, Barrett implies, gnaws at women's energy, sexuality, and identity as the swan has left the nest and the rat eaten the reeds. This poem, placed almost at the end of the volume, repudiates a literary convention that served but ultimately confined Barrett.

The ballads in *Poems of 1844* reflect the popularity of medieval settings for both male and female poets. Thus Barrett is neither writing as a mere poetess nor appropriating a form, such as the epic, seen exclusively as male. The ballads contain, however, a set of conventions that imprison woman as silent object. Barrett moves toward freeing woman from such objectification by an assertion that simultaneously subverts the poetesses' commitment to self-abnegating love. The violence within and the deaths at the end of the ballads represent both the punishment of such assertion and a dramatization of the violence wrought upon both women and men by courtly conventions. The ballads are as assertive as Barrett's reading of Sand on her invalid couch, yet as confining as Barrett's imprisonment in her father's house. They are Songs of Innocence, still imagining Eve as submissive to her Biblical and Miltonic forms, yet initiating a rebellion against both Eve's literary and Barrett's actual confinement, a rebellion that culminated in Barrett Browning's departure for Italy. The *Sonnets from the Portuguese* record the process of this rebellion, and "The Runaway Slave at Pilgrim's Point" enacts its triumph.

CHAPTER 4

Eve's Songs of Experience

POEMS OF 1850

> *Your white men*
> *Are, after all, not gods indeed.*
> —"The Runaway Slave at
>   Pilgrim's Point"

In selecting which 1838 and 1844 poems to publish in *Poems of 1850*, Barrett Browning explained to Mitford, "I gave much time to the revision, and did not omit reforming some of the rhymes, although you must consider that the irregularity of these in a certain degree rather falls in with my system than falls out through my carelessness" (*L*, 1:436). To her Florentine friend, Mrs. Ogilvy, she lamented, "[the volume] contains *all* my poems worth a straw, though many which I should like to burn as stubble & cant. It is difficult to recover one's misdeeds from the press."[1] Barrett Browning's experiments with rhyme, claiming them as her "system" rather than her "carelessness," indicate her desire to question formal conventions. She designated her earlier work as including "stubble & cant" and "misdeeds." Although the *Poems of 1850* included previously published work, a new voice emerges in the *Sonnets from the Portuguese* and "The Runaway Slave at Pilgrim's Point," poems that drew little interest from nineteenth-century reviewers.

Although biographical explanations for literary texts open up a Pandora's box, the parallel between Barrett's description of her relationship as a daughter with her father and her relationship as a poet with her male precursors is illuminating. *Sonnets from the Portuguese* and "The Runaway Slave at Pilgrim's Point" demonstrate how Barrett's refusal of her father's authority enabled Barrett Browning to appropriate male literary authority to her purposes. Recording sexual desire in the *Sonnets*, Barrett defied her father's refusal to "tolerate in his family . . . the development of one class of feelings" (*RB&EBB*, 1:196). This was not merely a projection of repressed sexuality on Barrett's part, as exemplified by her description of her father's treatment of her younger sister, Henrietta, when she wanted to marry:

> Yet how she was made to suffer—Oh, the dreadful scenes!— and only because she had seemed to feel a little. I told you, I think, that there was an obliquity . . an eccentricity—or something beyond . . on one class of subjects. I hear how her knees were made to ring upon the floor, now! — she was carried out of the room in strong hysterics, & I, who rose up to follow her, though I was quite well at that time & suffered only by sympathy, fell flat down upon my face in a fainting-fit. Arabel thought I was dead." [*RB&EBB*, 1:394]

Barrett suffers "by sympathy" with her sister, but in falling down as though "dead" she seems to obey her father's edict denying passion. However, her disobedience in choosing " 'Not Death, but Love' " (Sonnets, 1) with Robert Browning defies her father and echoes Eve's transgression: eating of the tree of knowledge is identified as Eve's sexually assertive act. Barrett's ballads focused on woman's desire for authority; not, however, until she disobeyed the paternal edict against passion and self-determination was she able to realize an authoritative protagonist and a confident female poetic "I."

The *Sonnets* first bring into harmony "I" a woman and "I" the poet, separated in "The Poet's Vow," "A Vision of Poets" (*Poems of 1844*), and "Lady Geraldine's Courtship." The *Sonnets* record the transformation of woman from muse/helpmeet/object into poet/creator/subject. That act allowed Barrett Browning to transform earlier ballad narratives into dramatic monologues—"The Runaway Slave at Pilgrim's Point" and "Bianca Among the Nightingales" (*Last Poems*, 1862)—and the epics and dramas modeled on the Greek poets and Milton into the first-person female narratives of the long political poem, *Casa Guidi Windows*, and of her fictional autobiography, *Aurora Leigh*.

Barrett wrote the *Sonnets from the Portuguese* during her courtship of 1845–46. She only hinted of their existence to Browning, informing him on July 22, 1846, "You shall see some day at Pisa what I will not show you now" (*RB&EBB*, 2:892). Browning insisted on their publication in 1850, and to disguise their personal nature he, master of masks, suggested their title, an allusion to Barrett's "Catarina to Camoens" (1844), which he admired. This history of the *Sonnets* is crucial: the privacy surrounding their composition, and the fact that Barrett did not write them for publication, empowered her voice.

Contemporary critics have too often judged Barrett's achievement not by the standards of poetry, but of maleness. Hayter writes, "Mrs. Browning's sonnets express the love of one particular individual for another; they are personal, even idiosyncratic. Most love poems are written by, or in the character of, a young man. The *Sonnets from the Portuguese* are written by a mature invalid woman. . . . They are not enough removed from personal relationship to universal communication."[2] Lorraine Gray criticizes the *Sonnets* for failing to "express the universal wisdom expressed in the love sequences of Dante, Petrarch, Sidney, Spenser, Shakespeare and Meredith, poets who narrated man's failure to translate his ideals into the actual world."[3] Only Dorothy Mermin acknowledges the sequence as an attempt to create a female poetic voice in a male tradition; she sees the lack of irony in the *Sonnets* as resulting from Barrett's desire to locate her place within the literary tradition rather than to replicate her male contemporaries' concern to reveal "the disjunction between the passionate certainties of literature, and the flawed complexities of life."[4]

Barrett's *Sonnets* do not have the traditional "young man" as speaker, nor do they address "man's failure to translate his ideals into the actual world"; yet they should not be dismissed as "personal, even idiosyncratic." Instead of the young man's conventional lament, the mature woman starts from a known world and uses the sonnets as a process of discovery in transforming that world into one hitherto unimagined, a world created in art that she can then inhabit. The *Sonnets* enact the process whereby the speaker resolves the tensions inherent in being both poet and also the object of another's narrative into at last being the subject of her own story, able to speak in the first person of her passion.[5]

The basic plot of the amatory tradition, as with all courtly lyrics, was "a poet reiterating his plaint eight hundred, nine hundred, a thousand times; and a fair lady who ever says 'No.' "[6] Shakespeare had already added sonnets addressed to a young man and refused the elaborate tributes to the mistress: "My mistress when she walks treads on the ground"; and the speaker in Spenser's *Amoretti* found a fair lady who finally said, "Yes." Barrett, however, by adopting the Petrarchan form, rather than the English developments enacted in the Shakespearean form, implies a return to the conventions of the sonnet's Italian origins, although, like Spenser's, her sequence ends happily.

The *Sonnets* fall into three groups: in 1 and 2 the speaker portrays woman as the object of man's love, 3–40 record the speaker's wavering between objectifying herself and claiming her own creative and sexual subjectivity, and 41–44 demonstrate the poet's arrival at her own subjectivity, which displaces her allegiance to the conventions of the male tradition and reveals her confidence in the voice which that subjectivity elicits.

The first two sonnets, in which the speaker is initiated into love as the traditional object, are located in the past tense. The speaker remembers,

> a mystic Shape did move
> Behind me, and drew me backward by the hair;
> And a voice said in mastery, while I strove,—
> "Guess now who holds thee?'—"Death," I said.
> But, there,
> The silver answer rang,—"Not Death, but Love."

> [1]

The conversational tones of Sidney and Donne echo in these lines; by splitting the last one to create a seven-line sestet, Barrett delays the startling revelation at the end. The reference is to the *Iliad*, 1.204: as Athene prevented Achilles from fighting Agamemnon, so the "mystic Shape," imagined here as male "in mastery," pulls the speaker from Death and into Love. The subject-object arrangement is announced in the second sonnet, "Thee speaking, and me listening!" (made problematic by an unspoken "and me writing"). Yet Barrett transforms the convention such that the lovers are separated, not by the woman's capricious "No," but by divine prohibition: " 'Nay' is worse / From God than from all others" (2). The power attributed to the cruel ladies who scorned their poet lovers had little reality under a patriarchal authority that determined women's lives.

The third sonnet, rejecting the conventions that made woman the object, moves the sequence out of the past tense of the first two sonnets into the present. Here the speaking statue of "Lady Geraldine's Courtship" finds human form:

> Thou, bethink thee, art
> A guest for queens to social pageantries,
> With gages from a hundred brighter eyes
> Than tears even can make mine, to play thy part
> Of chief musician. What hast *thou* to do
> With looking from the lattice-lights at me,
> A poor, tired, wandering singer, singing through
> The dark, and leaning up a cypress tree?
> The chrism is on thine head,—on mine, the dew,—
> And Death must dig the level where these agree.

The female speaker's role is complex. She is the humble lover, "A poor, tired, wandering singer," who admires the beloved, perceived as exalted, "A guest for queens to social pageantries." She is also the woman whose eyes are bright with "tears," receiving the poet lover's attentions,—"What has *thou* to do / With looking from the lattice-lights at me?"—only to reject them: "The chrism is on thine head,—on mine, the dew,— / And Death must dig the level where these agree." Her rejection is not capricious, however, but from her own closeness to death. Her description of herself as "A poor, tired, wandering singer" is conventional as a description of a courtly poet. It is also realistic; her rejection of the lover stems from the distance she recognizes between them, not because of social status, but because his involvement in the "social pageantries" of life contrasts with her own preoccupation with death. The speaker's spatial allegiances here identify her with the poet as subject, rather than with the woman as object.

She is the object of his "looking"; nevertheless she places the man, beloved, poet lover, and "chief musician" in the domestic interior the woman usually inhabits, while she, the speaker, is outside in the dark "leaning up a cypress tree." Both the "dark" and "a cypress tree" function here primarily as reminders of death; this reversal of the spheres conventionally inhabited by men and women contributes, however, to the dilemma over gender roles that informs this sonnet.

The speaker's acceptance of the distance to be maintained between the beloved/lover and herself is emphasized by the perfect Petrarchan form of the fourth sonnet: the first quatrain focuses on the beloved, the "most gracious singer of high poems"; the second elaborates on the "golden fulness" of his "music," which he brings to the speaker's house, too poor for the beloved; and the sestet shifts the speaker's focus to the desolation of the house (reminiscent of the poet's house in "The Poet's Vow") where she lives with "the casement broken in, / The bats and owlets builders in the roof." The sestet answers the importuning of the "most gracious singer" by stressing the necessity that each one stay "alone, aloof" from the other. The speaker maintains her stance of inadequacy as a poet beside the beloved: "My cricket chirps against thy mandolin"; she "weeps" while he "sing[s]."

Such stasis cannot be maintained, however: the very images of decay that convince the speaker of the impossibility of love are also indicative of action and energy. The subsequent poems record both the woman's struggle to risk the unknown terrain of love rather than embrace the familiar territory of death, and also the poet's struggle to become confident in her own subjectivity. The brisk commands and argumentative linguistic structures of juxtaposed sonnets—"Stand farther off then! go" (5) followed by "Go from me. Yet I feel" (6)—express her struggle, as do her contradictory feelings. She acknowledges that "the face of all the world is changed" by the beloved who has "taught the whole / Of life in a new rhythm" (7), and she admits, *I love thee* (10). Yet convinced she must renounce her beloved to his face (11), she imagines herself as object, who in "the silence of [her] womanhood" is "unwon, however wooed," as a strategy for refusing to "fashion into speech" the love to which she does not feel enti-

tled because of her "grief" (13). The speaker argues her way into
being overpowered by the beloved: "noble and like a king, / Thou
canst prevail against my fears and fling / Thy purple round me"
(16). Yet her acceptance of love is on male terms and on strangely
violent ones: "And as a vanquished soldier yields his sword / To
one who lifts him from the bloody earth, / Even so, Beloved, I at
last record, / Here ends my strife" (16). She cannot authorize herself to be the subject of her own passion, but yields as object of
the beloved's will, imagining herself only as his muse. She offers
herself to him:

> How, Dearest, wilt thou have me for most use?
> A hope, to sing by gladly? or a fine
> Sad memory, with thy songs to interfuse?
> A shade, in which to sing—of palm or pine?
> A grove, on which to rest from singing? Choose.
> [17]

The speaker extends her objectification as one conquered by love
into the offering of herself as muse or object for the beloved.
Although Barrett's authorship modifies the speaker's passive vision of herself, "this extreme self-abnegation," as Mermin says,
"is also an incisive commentary on male love poems . . . since
the alternatives require not only the woman's passivity and silence but her absence and finally her death."[7] Previous sonnets
record the speaker's rescue from death; this final line in which
she offers to lie in her grave for the poet's inspiration highlights
the absurdity of the sacrifice traditional sonneteers require.

Subsequent sonnets ponder not the speaker's unworthiness but
the difference between "life's great cup of wonder" and the previous year when

> I sat alone here in the snow
> And saw no footprint, heard the silence sink
> No moment at thy voice, but, link by link,
> Went counting all my chains.
> [20]

However, not only does she declare, "I yield the grave for thy
sake, and exchange / My near sweet view of Heaven, for earth
with thee!" (23), but she anxiously questions,

If I leave all for thee, wilt thou exchange
And be all to me? Shall I never miss
Home-talk and blessing and the common kiss
That comes to each in turn, nor count it strange,
When I look up, to drop on a new range
Of walls and floors, another home than this?

[35]

The speaker realizes that choosing love means losing all she has previously held dear. When the "common kiss" given her as daughter of the family is transformed, however, into a lover's kiss, she rejects innocence for experience and confidently claims her passions:

First time he kissed me, he but only kissed
The fingers of this hand wherewith I write;
And ever since, it grew more clean and white,
Slow to world-greetings, quick with its "Oh, list,"
When the angels speak. A ring of amethyst
I could not wear here, plainer to my sight,
Than that first kiss. The second past in height
The first, and sought the forehead, and half missed,
Half falling on the hair. O beyond meed!
That was the chrism of love, which love's own crown,
With sanctifying sweetness, did precede.
The third upon my lips was folded down
In perfect, purple state; since when, indeed,
I have been proud and said, "My love, my own."

[38]

The kiss on the fingers makes the speaker "clean and white," more a companion of the angels than of "world-greetings." The kiss on the forehead, suggestive of an increasing sexuality in the carelessness of its being "half missed / Half falling on the hair," "pass[es] in height" the first and is accompanied with "sanctifying sweetness." Eschewing metaphoric definitions of the kiss—the "ring of amethyst," the chrism or crown of love—the speaker concisely records, "The third upon my lips was folded down." The attempt to spiritualize physical love collapses with this kiss "upon my lips." In contrast to "height" this kiss is "folded down," suggesting physicality rather than spirituality. The speaker's response to this kiss is no longer to deny it by purifying it, but to enjoy it—"I have been proud"—and to claim it—" 'My love, my own.' "

This portrait of a Victorian "angel" enjoying passionate encounters in her stern father's house is refreshing. First, it commits Barrett to a belief in physical pleasure as an essential manifestation of love, reaffirmed both at the end of *Aurora Leigh* and in "Bianca Among the Nightingales" (*Last Poems*, 1862). Second, it positions her in relation to an aspect of Victorian thinking in which "mere" sexual passion is "half-akin to brute."[8]

The speaker's proud claim, "My love, my own," ushers in the crucial turning point in the sequence (41). The early sonnets had dramatized Barrett's attempt to find a voice as both poet and woman, fusing in the process the traditional self-abnegation of the courtly lover with the conventional humility attributed to nineteenth-century woman. The later sonnets record a speaker who assesses a changed world in which she is "caught up in love, and taught the whole / Of life in a new rhythm" (7). The last four sonnets reflect on the transformation of the speaker's voice from her early attempt to accommodate to male convention into a later security in her own subjectivity. The speaker is grateful to all "Who paused a little near the prison-wall / To hear [her] music in its louder parts" (41), yet the true timbre of her voice only the beloved appreciates who "own'st the grace / To look through and behind this mask of [her]" (39). The speaker gains confidence in her voice, transforming the beloved from the one who perceives her to the one who listens to her:

> But thou, who, in my voice's sink and fall
> When the sob took it, thy divinest Art's
> Own instrument didst drop down at thy foot
> To hearken what I said between my tears.
>
> [41]

The female "I" is authoritative once she no longer allows the male poet's "divinest Art" to compete with, appropriate, or trivialize her voice. She silences the male voice of the opening sonnets, so the beloved is object to her realized subjectivity. She can now imagine, confidently, a future as a poet in which she will "shoot / [Her] soul's full meaning into future years, / That *they* should lend it utterance." This theme is elaborated in the next sonnet, in which, quoting from "Past and Future" (*Poems of 1844*), " '*My future will not copy fair my past,*' " the speaker reflects on how once she imagined her future to be in heaven, whereas now it is to be in the world. The beloved becomes her Muse:

> I seek no copy now of life's first half:
> Leave here the pages with long musing curled,
> And write me new my future's epigraph,
> New angel mine, unhoped for in the world!
>
> [42]

The "angel," culturally associated in the nineteenth century with woman, is here used in an ambiguous way—as the earlier Seraphim had been. Barrett draws on a Biblical and Miltonic tradition that considered the angel as male, and yet the asexual quality of the angel associates the "new angel mine" as her muse with the young boy at the end of "A Vision of Poets" and the little boy whose singing would be the inspiration for *Casa Guidi Windows*.

The famous penultimate sonnet, "How do I love thee? Let me count the ways," is, in fact, less sentimental than authoritative about its speaker's desire. The "I" is confidently female, while the object of her attention is assuredly male. There is none of the hysterics of Bertram's love for Geraldine, none of the tortuous love conventions with which the ballad heroines tried to articulate their passions, none of the unfortunate and cloying images found earlier in the sonnets, such as when the crying speaker asks the beloved to "Open thine heart wide, / And fold within the wet wings of thy dove" (35). Instead the voice is as confident in its passion as it had earlier been in its sonnet of despair, "Grief" (*Poems of 1844*).

Barrett's disobedience of her father's edict against "the development of a certain class of feelings" meant eating of the tree of knowledge and entering the world of experience. She did not perceive this as a fall, which necessitated woman's suffering, but as a liberating act that allowed her imaginative freedom. In her rejection of what she wrote in "life's first half" and in her commitment to write a "new . . . future's epigraph" she also rejected her literary fathers' edict. This is exemplified in her last sonnet:

Belovèd, thou hast brought me many flowers
Plucked in the garden, all the summer through
And winter, and it seemed as if they grew
In this close room, nor missed the sun and showers.
So, in the like name of that love of ours,
Take back these thoughts which here unfolded too,
And which on warm and cold days I withdrew
From my heart's ground. Indeed, those beds and bowers
Be overgrown with bitter weeds and rue,
And wait thy weeding; yet here's eglantine,
Here's ivy!—take them, as I used to do
Thy flowers, and keep them where they shall not pine.
Instruct thine eyes to keep their colours true,
And tell thy soul their roots are left in mine.

[44]

Both the room and the texts which so long imprisoned her and in which she "lived with visions for my company / Instead of men and women" (26), have been simultaneously transformed to a place of imaginative freedom. The very invalid isolation that had freed Barrett from conformity to literary expectations about women poets also protected her from the normal chaperoned routine of upper-middle-class courtship. The freedom to experience her passion unhampered by parental physical presence, and the fact that a male poet set his own work aside to listen to hers, translated into a female "I," confident in "these thoughts which here unfolded too." Whereas the "Beloved" brings flowers, she gives back poems, which she expects him to "keep . . . where they shall not pine." The last two lines record the assurance she feels in a poetic voice identified as female, and an admonition to the male poet reader that he read her desire, not his own: "Instruct thine eyes to keep their [her poems] colours true."

These were Barrett's last sonnets. Their formal discipline substitutes for the speaker's imprisonment, a substitution that allows the speaker freedom to engage in the process of transformation I have described. It is appropriate that the sonnet sequence, which by definition had hitherto hinged on the objectification of woman, should be the arena for the self-conscious transformation of the poetic "I" of English poetry to include the female voice. But the form ultimately proved as confining as the "close room" for Barrett; like her creator, Aurora Leigh felt the poet "can stand / Like Atlas, in the sonnet,—and support / His [sic] own heavens pregnant with dynastic stars; / But then he must stand still, nor take a step" (5.86–89). Barrett fully intended to "take a step" beyond.

The decision to leave the "close room" of the *Sonnets* was paralleled by Barrett's decision to leave her room in Wimpole Street. She justified this to her friend Mrs. Martin:

> I had made up my mind to act upon my full right of taking my own way. I had long believed such an act (the most strictly personal act of one's life) to be within the rights of every person of mature age, man or woman, and I had resolved to exercise that right in my own case by a resolution which had slowly ripened. All the other doors of life were shut to me, and shut me in as in a prison. . . . Therefore, wrong or right, . . . I did and do consider . . . I sinned against no duty. (*L*, 1:293–94)

Barrett, in marrying Browning and moving to Italy, received the approval of her sisters but was repudiated by her brothers, who had grown "used to the thought of a tomb; [where she] was buried" (*L*, 1:288).[9] She refused, however, to concur with their desire that she "drop like a dead weight into the abyss, a sacrifice without an object and expiation" (*L*, 1:287). Onora's death, for choosing love, passion, and life in defiance of her father and of God, is eerily prophetic of Barrett's own situation. But Barrett refused the fate for herself that she had earlier imposed on her heroine.

The transformation that the *Sonnets* wrought on Barrett's work is exemplified by the fact that "Lady Geraldine's Courtship," with its male protagonist, was one of the last poems written before the *Sonnets* in 1844, and that "The Runaway Slave at Pilgrim's Point," with its first-person narration by a black slave woman, was one of the first written after them in 1846, after her secret marriage and departure for Italy, after her father's (and brothers') refusal to talk, write, or see her again. The last sonnet, whose pastoral echoes demonstrate the female speaker's ability to manipulate male poetic conventions to her own uses, is the culmination of Barrett's work; "The Runaway Slave," in which the poet engaged the protagonist in a natural landscape far from the domestic interior so familiar to the speaker of the *Sonnets*, is the beginning of Barrett Browning's.

Barrett Browning's first mention of "The Runaway Slave at Pilgrim's Point" is in a letter to Mitford, dated January 12, 1842. Her uncle, Richard Barrett (first cousin to her father and an influential Jamaican land and slave owner), had years previously given her "a subject for a poem about a run away negro . . . in his handwriting" (*MRM*, 1:331). She finally took his "subject" and wrote a "rather long ballad . . . at request of anti-slavery friends in America" (*L*, 1:462). She confided to her friend, Mr. Boyd, that it was "too ferocious, perhaps, for the Americans to publish: but they asked for a poem and shall have it" (*L*, 1:315). "The Runaway Slave" was first published in 1848 in *The Liberty Bell*, which was sold at the Boston National Anti-Slavery Bazaar of 1848. It has been described as a "horrifying story" of a "slave forced into concubinage," dismissed as "too blunt and shocking to have any enduring artistic worth," and toned down to a description of a "negro slave-woman with her voodoo ideas of angels sucking souls." Only recently has its subject been acknowledged; a black slave woman is "raped by her white master."[10]

"The Runaway Slave at Pilgrim's Point" is not the first of Barrett's poems of social criticism. *Poems of 1844* had included "The Cry of the Children," written after R. H. Horne had sent her the government's blue book on child labor in the factories and mines. It is a powerful poem, technically and politically:

> "For all day the wheels are droning, turning;
>   Their wind comes in our faces,
> Till our hearts turn, our heads with pulses burning,
>   And the walls turn in their places:
> Turns the sky in the high window, blank and reeling,
>   Turns the long light that drops adown the wall,
> Turn the black flies that crawl along the ceiling:
>   All are turning, all the day, and we with all.
> And all day the iron wheels are droning,
>   And sometimes we could pray,

> 'O ye wheels' (breaking out in a mad moaning),
>   'Stop! be silent for to-day!' "

[7]

The droning tedium of these exploited children's lives is suggested by the repetition of "turn," as though to recreate the factory wheels that surrounded them. Politically, the poem exposes
the powerlessness of "mothers" in the industrial "Fatherland" (2)
and also addresses the religious hypocrisy accompanying zeal for
progress. The children imagine that God "Our Father" should
spare them their miserable conditions saying, "Come and rest
with me, my child."

> "But, no!" say the children, weeping faster,
>   "He is speechless as a stone:
> And they tell us, of His image is the master
>   Who commands us to work on.
> Go to!" say the children,—"up in Heaven,
>   Dark, wheel-like, turning clouds are all we find.
> Do not mock us; grief has made us unbelieving:
>   We look up for God, but tears have made us blind."
> Do you hear the children weeping and disproving,
>   O my brothers, what ye preach?
> For God's possible is taught by His world's loving,
>   And the children doubt of each.

[11]

The idea that God is only manifest through people's actions, and
is cold and "speechless as a stone" to society's victims, reappears
in "The Runaway Slave." But, whereas the children's protest is
controlled by the quotation marks that separate their words from
the narrator's, there is no such mediation in "The Runaway
Slave," where for the first time one of Barrett's angry female
speakers narrates her story. Not without years of struggle could
Barrett Browning begin this poem with an unmediated "I."

Hemans's *Records of Woman* (1828) and Browning's *Dramatic
Lyrics* (1842) and *Dramatic Romances* (1845) suggest possible female and male influences for this poem. Hemans's poems are
tales of women, all of whom suffer with varying degrees of resignation or resentment the pangs of love, leading usually to death.

They are mainly third-person narratives, although some women narrate their stories. None has the forceful rhetoric of Barrett Browning's style, but they do center experience in female consciousness, and such titles as the "Indian Woman's Death-Song" or "The American Forest Girl" suggest, as much as Wordsworth, a genre that encompasses the lives of hitherto insignificant people as poetic material. However, none of Hemans's titles bears the irony that Barrett Browning's does in yoking the runaway slave with the oppressive descendants of the pilgrims, themselves once oppressed. Nor do the accounts of woman's suffering in love touch on the social and political complexities that Barrett Browning brings to her slave's story. The "Indian Woman's Death-Song" does, however, offer a model for a story of infanticide: the speaker, deserted by her husband for another woman, rows a canoe down the Mississippi toward a cataract, intending that she and her child should drown. The woman's dying song echoes the conventional lament of the poetesses until she addresses her daughter:

> "And thou, my babe! though born, like me, for woman's
> weary lot,
> Smile!—to that wasting of the heart, my own! I leave thee
> not;
> Too bright a thing art *thou* to pine in aching love
> away—
> Thy mother bears thee far, young fawn! from sorrow and
> decay."

There is here no serious engagement with the issue of infanticide; and the mother's suicide, while killing her daughter to protect her from "woman's weary lot," is much less audacious than Barrett Browning's speaker's action. Without committing suicide, she suffocates her infant son to deny him "the master right."

Although Barrett Browning might have imagined her poem as belonging to literary "records of woman," Browning may well have influenced the authority expressed in this "record." By the time Barrett Browning wrote "The Runaway Slave," Browning had published both his *Dramatic Lyrics* (1842) and *Dramatic Romances* (1845) which included his early dramatic monologues, "My Last Duchess," and "The Bishop Orders His Tomb at St.

Praxed's Church." When the two poets started corresponding early in 1845, they were already admirers of each other's work. In one of her earliest letters to Browning, Barrett had written, "You are 'masculine' to the height—and I, as a woman, have studied some of your gestures of language & intonation wistfully, as a thing beyond me far!" (*RB&EBB*, 1:9). Her admiration for Browning's unconventional "gestures of language and intonation" must have assured her of his sympathy with her commitment to "new *forms* . . as well as thoughts. The old gods are dethroned. Why should we go back to the antique moulds . . classical moulds, as they are so improperly called? . . . Let us all aspire rather to *Life*—& let the dead bury their dead" (*RB&EBB*, 1:43). Most of Tennyson's early dramatic monologues, spoken through such classical figures as Ulysses or Tithonus, would not have been as liberating as Browning's conversational tone, his focus on obscure (even if titled) characters, and the essential contemporaneity of his settings (even when his subjects were in fact taken from the Renaissance). Peculiarly appropriate to Barrett Browning's concerns in "The Runaway Slave" were Browning's murderers' monologues, "My Last Duchess," and "Porphyria's Lover," and his hypocritical—if persuasive—representative of religious institutions, the dying Bishop. By 1846 Barrett Browning had empowered herself to appropriate the confidence of Browning's speakers in expressing the slave's worldview.

However, if Browning's triumph enables us to sympathize with speakers such as the Duke, Porphyria's lover, or the Bishop, even as we judge them for their actions, Barrett Browning's task was quite different: she identifies our sympathy with the despised outsider and our judgement with the privileged law-abiding citizen. She thereby makes the "unnatural" act of infanticide (made monstrous by such mythic women as Medea) seem natural in a culture that violently distorts the bond between mother and child.

The slave, appropriated as a potent symbol for nineteenth-century women's oppression (as in Harriet Beecher Stowe's *Uncle Tom's Cabin*), had peculiar importance for Barrett Browning because her family had owned slaves in Jamaica for several generations.[11] Mr. Barrett returned, as a young man, to England, leaving his plantations under the management of overseers. However, as

Barrett grew in the luxury of Hope End, her family's home, her father and brothers made trips to Jamaica; slavery informed the first thirty years of her life. The loss of Hope End was precipitated by the financial decline attendant on the Proclamation of Freedom for the Slaves in 1833. Barrett wrote to a friend, "The late Bill has ruined the [white] West Indians. That is settled. The consternation here is very great. Nevertheless I am glad, and always shall be, that the negroes are—virtually—free!" (L, 1:23). Sixteen years later the slave speaker's repudiation of the unjust power of white slave owners resonates with Barrett Browning's rejection of her once slave-owning father's irrational authority in refusing to allow his children, both sons and daughters, to marry and leave his home. The request by the abolitionists that she write such a poem empowered the rage she had suppressed by years of opium as she lay on her invalid couch.

"The Runaway Slave at Pilgrim's Point" is a dramatic monologue in ballad form. The speaker, a young black slave woman, has escaped from the plantation the day before her narrative begins and has run to Pilgrim's Point, where "exile turned to ancestor" (1). Her story is in three parts. The first two she addresses to "the pilgrim-souls" at Pilgrim's Point, those who first came to America as a land of freedom, and whose descendants now own the slaves whom she represents: initially (1–8), the slave meditates on being black in a world privileging God's "white creatures" (4); in a flashback (9–28) she tells her story to these "pilgrim-souls." Finally (29–36), she addresses the "hunter sons" of the original pilgrims who have pursued her to stone her to death.

The assertive opening, "I stand," sets the tone. The speaker never falters in presenting the complexity of her situation, as a woman, a black, and a slave—a thoroughly marginal protagonist—in the white man's violent system. She recognizes that it divides women, black from white, "As white as the ladies who scorned to pray / Beside me at church but yesterday" (17). Although she dies, she finds freedom outside of that system, by shaping her own discourse.

As she describes the "pilgrim-souls" clustering around her— "round me and round me ye go"—we feel the dizziness and exhaustion of one who has "gasped and run / All night long from the whips" (2). Her purpose is to "speak" to the pilgrim-souls:

"lift my black face, my black hand, / Here, in your names, to curse this land / Ye blessed in freedom's" (3). She claims her racial identity, "I am black, I am black," and describes how such an identity imprisons her: "About our souls . . . / Our blackness shuts like prison-bars" (6). The slave employs metaphors, which Barrett Browning used in her letters to Browning describing her invalidism in a room cut off from sun, to dramatize imprisonment behind a dark skin in a world where God's work of creating black people has been cast away "under the feet of His white creatures" (4). She celebrates that the "little dark bird sits and sings", the "dark stream ripples out of sight", the "dark frogs chant in the safe morass", and the "darkest night" is host to the "sweetest stars" (5). In the natural world, unlike the human one, there is no equation of dark with bad and light with good, and no discrimination between black and white people: the sun and frost "they make us hot, they make us cold," while the "beasts and birds, in wood and fold, / Do fear and take us for very men" (8).

The slave argues for the equality of black and white before detailing her particular oppression. Like her meditation on blackness, her story begins with her assertion, "I am black, I am black" (9). Love for her fellow slave engaged her in a human emotion that united her with rather than distinguished her from white people, making her feel "unsold, unbought" (10). Her white owner, denying such common humanity, insisted that the lovers had "no claim to love and bliss" (14), to basic human emotions, and brutally separated them. His actions mirrored those of God, who silently and "coldly . . . sat'st behind the sun" (13), offering no comfort to the slaves. The owner and his men "wrung [her] cold hands out of his / They dragged him—where?" She knows only that they left her lover's "blood's mark in the dust" (14).

The white men deny the slave not only the communal human emotion of love, but also that of grief. Denial of and control over the slave's emotions were essential to the owner's supremacy: "Mere grief's too good for such as I" (15). To dramatize his ownership of the slaves' bodies, the owner beats the man and rapes the woman: "Wrong, followed by a deeper wrong!/ . . . the white men brought the shame ere long / To strangle the sob of my agony" (15). Barrett Browning's description of rape is tactful but explicit when the "wrong" is immediately followed by "I am black, I am black! / I wore a child upon my breast" (16), a child who was "far too white, too white" for her (17). The violation and control inherent in rape is "worse" than the "lash" (21).

Susan Brownmiller in *Against Our Will: Men, Women and Rape* discusses the notorious system of rape, euphemistically termed "concubinage"—literally, "cohabiting of man and woman not legally married"—in which white male slave owners assumed sexual rights over their black slave women:[12] the mulatto children of such "breeder women" were sold for the owner's financial gain. Barrett Browning expressed no surprise at her uncle's story of the runaway slave; she was probably quite familiar with the iniquitous system. As Jeanette Marks records in *The Family of the Barrett*: "That the problem of black and white connections had since the second generation in Jamaica been embedding itself in the family ramifications of the Barrett family is based on direct evidence. . . . Concubinage as 'custom of the country' was an inescapable part of slavery."[13] Whereas such novels as *Adam Bede* and *Ruth* center on the seduction of women, Barrett Browning dramatizes both here and in Marian Erle's story in *Aurora Leigh* the violence that threatens and controls women. (Pompilia's description of her enforced sexual relations with Guido in Browning's later *The Ring and the Book* would now be described as marital rape.) She examines the way sexual and racial politics warp the emotions.

The slave's maternal feelings are in conflict: in a representation of a mother-child relationship, she carries the child on her breast; however, he appears as an "amulet that [hangs] too slack"; neither mother nor child can rest—they go "moaning, child and mother, / One to another"; and there is an ominous note in "all ended for the best" (16). The speaker's complex maternal feelings dramatize a conflict between her love for her child and her hatred of the way he was conceived and of what he represents. From birth he was different, so that she "dared not sing to the white-faced child / The only song [she] knew" (19), the song of her black lover's name, feeling that "A child and mother / Do

wrong to look at one another / When one is black and one is fair"
(20). Once she has seen her child, she can never forget his conception:

> Why in that single glance I had
>   Of my child's face, . . . I tell you all,
> I saw a look that made me mad!
>   The *master's* look, that used to fall
> On my soul like his lash . . . or worse!
>
> [21]

Her "far too white" (17) son resembles his father: the sight of
him is like a reenactment of her rape. It also reminds her of what
his moaning and struggling represent: "the white child wanted
his liberty— / Ha, ha! he wanted the master-right" (18). She fears
he will claim it, scorning his dark mother as much as the "white
ladies" in church do. The white male child, even as an infant,
proclaims his mother's dispossession. (I should point out here
that Barrett Browning was operating not in accordance with the
American system, whereby any child born of one black parent
was classified and disenfranchised as a black, but according to
the Jamaican system. In the latter, the children of white owners
and black slaves could be sent to England along with the father's
"legal" white children for schooling. Hence the lighter the skin
the more a male child could claim the "master-right.")

The speaker gradually unfolds her child's story, anticipating
the final tragedy in her references to his "little feet that never
grew" (19) and to how he lies now between the mango roots (20).
To hide his white face she covers it with a handkerchief "close
and tight" (18); he struggles against this imposed darkness. She
kills the child to protect herself from the rapist she sees in him:
"I twisted it round in my shawl" because of the "*master's* look,
that used to fall / On my soul like his lash . . . or worse" (21), till
the child lay "too suddenly still and mute" (22). Clutching his
dead body, she escapes from the plantation. As she runs, she reiterates God's abandonment of black people, imagining that the
trees, and by implication God, ignore her: "They stood too high
for astonishment, / They could see God sit on his throne" (25).
However, God's "angels far, / With a white sharp finger from
every star, / Did point and mock" (26). This separation of God

and his angels from herself results not from her being a murderer cast out of Heaven, but from being black and marginalized by the white God, angels, and people.

Though horrible, this infanticide becomes, within the terms of the poem, tragically grand and inevitable, the logical conclusion to the slave's situation. She blames, not herself, but the "fine white angels (who have seen / Nearest the secret of God's power)" who "sucked the soul" of her child (23). The cultural signifiers, black and white, are now reversed: the "white angels" are murderers claiming "the white child's spirit." So liberating is the dramatic monologue for Barrett Browning (even if, as with Browning's Pompilia in *The Ring and the Book*, the language is that of an educated middle-class poet rather than of a raped teenage girl) that we accept the slave's reasoning: she is made so marginal by the white man's system that she cannot be judged by its laws. What from their white perspective seems a crazed black woman strangling her child and clutching him "on [her] heart like a stone" (24) is a brutalized woman's totally coherent act. Her behavior, although resembling madness, is, in fact, governed by her victimization in an alien system. If God's silence convinces Porphyria's lover that he is morally right, it convinces the slave that God's system, epitomized by his "white angels," is morally wrong.

Although she kills him, the speaker's love for her child is manifest in the confusion she exhibits between her own self and her son: "My little body," refers to her son; running till "I felt it was tired" (26) indicates her own exhaustion. This merging anticipates the union that becomes possible once the white child is buried in the dark earth:

> Yet when it was all done aright,—
> 　Earth, 'twixt me and my baby, strewed,—
> All, changed to black earth,—nothing white,—
> 　A dark child in the dark!—ensued
> Some comfort, and my heart grew young;
> I sate down smiling there and sung
> 　The song I learnt in my maidenhood.
>
> And thus we two were reconciled,
> 　The white child and black mother, thus;

> For as I sang it soft and wild,
>   The same song, more melodious,
> Rose from the grave whereon I sate:
> It was the dead child singing that,
>   To join the souls of both of us.
>
> [27–28]

"Song" here is an important issue. First, it evokes the slave practice of singing in the fields to survive the grueling work. Second, it draws attention to the ballad form that ties this poem to Barrett Browning's earlier works. Although "The Runaway Slave" rejects the medievalism of the 1838 and 1844 ballads, its speaker is connected to their protagonists' questioning of the white man's courtly ideology. Third, the emphatic repetition of "I sang" asserts the slave's right to narrate her story.

Initially, the slave addresses the "pilgrim-souls"—"I speak to you." Her intention is to tell her tragic story and to "curse this land / Ye blessed in freedom's" name (3). She recalls the man she loved and how:

> I sang his name instead of a song,
>   Over and over I sang his name,
>
> .   .   .   .
>
> I sang it low, that the slave-girls near
> Might never guess, from aught they could hear,
>   It was only a name—a name.
>
> [12]

The slave's initial song exemplifies the work of the poetesses; her "song" is confined to love and to her lover's name. However, in an ironic reversal, this does not prove to be safe subject matter for a woman: like love and grief, use of language threatens the white men's power.

After the birth of her "too white" son, who struggled against the blackness imposed by the slave's kerchief because, she imagines, he wanted his white male "master-right" (18), the slave is fearful: "I might have sung and made him mild, / But I dared not sing to the white-faced child / The only song I knew" (19). Even a white male infant dispossesses her of her right to sing. Her only song is of her slavery; that cannot be told to the masters. So

angry is she at being silenced that she suffocates the child, rendering him as "still and mute" (22) as he has made her. Only
when she has transformed him into a "dark child in the dark" by
burying him in the earth, which knows no discrimination, can
she sing to him. "The song I learnt in my maidenhood" (27) may
literally refer to her lover's name, but it also functions on a more
complex level. Now the subject of her story rather than the object of his, she sings to her son "soft and wild." He no longer
signifies the white male world, but inhabits her dark earth. She
centers herself and transforms the young white boy into her
muse, making her song "more melodious" (28).

The sun rises as she tells her story. While the "free sun rideth
gloriously," the pilgrim-souls become more menacing, and yet as
insubstantial "pilgrim-ghosts" they fade away at the arrival of
this new dawn in which the slave "glares with a scorn" (29). The
speaker, once frightened to imagine herself as subject in the presence of her white child, now renders the white pilgrim-souls into
objects frightened by her power. By singing to her son, the slave
wins her freedom and confronts in strength "the hunter sons"
(30) eager to whip her to death.

Although the speaker knows her death is at hand, she directs
this last scene. As the white men armed with whips approach
her "in a ring," she shouts, "Keep off" (30). Her words do not
represent hope for escape, but rather an order to listen before
stoning her. As one picks up a stone, she commands him to drop
it, charging the men with following the double standard in that
their wives "May keep live babies on [their] knee, / And sing the
song [they] like the best," while also indicating their actions of
moving in and threatening her (31). She taunts "the Washington-
race," who, "staring, shrinking back," are now afraid of her, with
the mockery they have made of language. "This land is the free
America" is an empty phrase beside "this mark on my wrist
. . . / Ropes tied me up here to the flogging-place" (32).

Facing her death, the slave imagines being rendered into a
Christ-like martyr. She remembers the silence surrounding her
frequent floggings: "Not a sound! / I hung, as a gourd hangs in
the sun" (33), identifying both with the nondiscriminatory natural world again and with the image of Christ on the cross. But
she refuses this sop:

> Our wounds are different. Your white men
>   Are, after all, not gods indeed,
> Nor able to make Christs again
>   Do good with bleeding. *We* who bleed
> (Stand off!) we help not in our loss!
> *We* are too heavy for our cross,
>   And fall and crush you and your seed.
>
> [35]

In this bitter denunciation, white men are no longer the "gods" they claim to be, and black people, exemplified by this black woman, refuse to be cast as Christ figures whose suffering can be justified as doing "good by bleeding." Their suffering is so great it will destroy the structures designed to contain and exploit it, and will kill the white man's "seed." When the slave "look[s] at the sky," she feels the "clouds are breaking on [her] brain"; the white man's Heaven crushes the dying slave, whereas she eagerly joins her white child and lover in the nondiscriminating "death-dark" earth. In her fall she will crush the white "seed."

Unlike her foremothers in Barrett's poetry, this woman is not submissive. She dies at the height of her power, but in death, though "broken-hearted," she rejects the system that marginalizes and violates her. Her initial desire "to curse this land," strengthens into leaving the white men "all curse-free / In [her] broken heart's disdain" (36). The formulaic gibberish of a curse, which enjoins supernatural aid and which the slave imagined was her only strength, yields to the power she gains by centering herself in her own discourse. She dies holding her hypocritical persecutors in "disdain" at Pilgrim's Point.

The dramatic monologue proved a powerful medium for Barrett Browning. Yoking her need to produce a public poem about slavery to her own developing poetics, Barrett Browning incorporated rape and infanticide into the slave's denunciation of patriarchy. Barrett Browning did not shrink from the unsayable, in contrast to American women like Angeline Grimké who toiled for the abolitionist movement yet felt bound by women's silence concerning their bodies and the belief that "a man's private life was beyond the pale of political scrutiny."[14] The violence visited on slave women did not inform the speech even of those most horrified by it. Barrett Browning exploits the slave's triumphant cry, "Your white men / Are, after all, not gods indeed," to speak to her own liberation from both her own once slave-owning father and also from the literary fathers who for so long held her in thrall.

Eve's songs of experience celebrate woman's refusal both to be bound by patriarchal authority and also to accept her "alloted grief" for such a refusal. Unlike Eve in "A Drama of Exile," when the slave disavows identification with Christ in suffering, she excoriates her pain rather than accepting it. This disavowal also symbolizes Barrett Browning's outgrowing the necessity to justify her poetic ambition by identifying both the woman's and the poet's task with Christ's suffering on behalf of "mankind." *Sonnets from the Portuguese* were the testing-ground for the female "I": the black slave woman exemplifies Barrett Browning's conviction that on her own authority woman can locate her consciousness at the center of poetry. Her two long poems, *Casa Guidi Windows* and *Aurora Leigh*, demonstrate what such a vision reveals.

CHAPTER 5

The Mature Voice

CASA GUIDI WINDOWS

(1851)

We do not serve the dead—the past is past.
—Casa Guidi Windows

In her Preface to *Poems of 1844* Barrett Browning referred to her effort to write "with a particular reference to Eve's alloted grief, . . . imperfectly apprehended hitherto, and more expressible by a woman than a man." Milton's "glory," however, inhibited her realization of this project. She showed Eve's suffering, yet depicted an acquiescent woman. Her 1844 ballads initiated the refusal of this "alloted grief," finally enacted in *The Sonnets from the Portuguese* and "The Runaway Slave at Pilgrim's Point," when Barrett Browning combined a female "I," who rejects her suffering role, with a self-consciousness about her task as a woman poet.

When Barrett Browning wrote *Casa Guidi Windows* (1851) and *Aurora Leigh* (1856), she assumed poetic authority as a woman. Dolores Rosenblum is right to claim that *Casa Guidi Windows* sets the aesthetic groundwork for the dramatization in *Aurora Leigh* of the fact that woman is the originator of rather than a reflection of meaning.[1] She uses her authority, however, quite differently in these major poems. In *Casa Guidi Windows*, the speaker represents Barrett Browning as she dwells both on her place in poetic tradition and on men's management of the political economy: "This poem contains the impressions of the writer upon events in Tuscany of which she was a witness. . . . It is a simple story of personal impressions, whose only value is in the intensity with which they were received" (W, 3:249). In *Aurora Leigh*, however, she employs fictional autobiography to record the painful growth of a woman poet's mind. The details of *Aurora Leigh* are fictional, but its essential movement is autobiographical: "I have put much of myself in it—I mean to say, of my soul, my thoughts, emotions, opinions; in other respects, there is not a personal line, of course" (L, 2:228). Aurora Leigh's development resembles her creator's:

> And so like most young poets, in a flush
> Of individual life I poured myself
> Along the veins of others, and achieved
> Mere lifeless imitations of live verse.
> [1:971–74]

This aptly describes Barrett's early imitations of Homer and Pope in "The Battle of Marathon" and "An Essay on Mind." Aurora's final recognition that "the old world waits the time to be renewed" with "New churches, new oeconomies, new laws / Admitting freedom, new societies" (9.940–48) reiterates Barrett Browning's vision at the end of *Casa Guidi Windows*:

> the elemental
> New springs of life are gushing everywhere
> To cleanse the watercourses, and prevent all
> Concrete obstructions which infest the air!
> [2.761–64]

> We will trust God. The blank interstices
> Men take for ruins, He will build into
> With pillared marbles rare, or knit across
> With generous arches, till the fane's complete.
> This world has no perdition, if some loss.
> [2.776–80]

Casa Guidi Windows is in two parts, each a response to a political demonstration Barrett Browning witnessed through the windows of Casa Guidi, the house where she and Browning lived in Florence. The rebellion that characterized Barrett Browning's work, whether on behalf of the poor or against literary or paternal authority, was transformed in Italy into support for Italian unification and liberation from imperial Austrian rule.[2] On September 12, 1847, the Brownings' first wedding anniversary, she cheered a patriotic demonstration celebrating the decree of Grand Duke Leopold II of Tuscany that the Florentines could form their own civic guard, taken to symbolize a step towards unification. The new pope, Pius IX ("Pio Nono") had initiated such reforms on his election in 1846. However, this liberalism was short-lived; neither Duke Leopold nor Pius IX was prepared to fight against Austria, and in 1849 a large silent gathering demonstrated against the self-exiled duke on his return to Florence accompanied by Austrian guards.

Italian politics are the manifest subject of *Casa Guidi Windows*; yet a striking feature is its assumption of the female speaker's subjectivity throughout. From this authoritative stance, Barrett Browning's focus is twofold: first, she addresses the issue of her relationship to poetic tradition. Second, she questions Victorian gender arrangements, both as a woman writing political poetry, and by her critique of men's performance in their designated role.

Reviewers were divided about this direction in Barrett Browning's work. The *Prospective Review*, while admiring the poem, wished nostalgically for the poet's "ancient pensiveness" because it was "that union of the spirit of joy, with the shadows of grief . . . that constituted to us the greatest charm of her poetry and her character. Perhaps we should not wish such things back again to the happy wife and mother."[3] However, this reactionary association of female charm with suffering was not shared by the *Athenaeum*, whose reviewer found the poet's early work "tinged" with "sentimental melancholy," whereas in *Casa Guidi Windows* "her record of personal feelings has given way to the morals which they suggest,—and the interests of the single heart have expanded into those of mankind. This, we take it, is the progress of every nature in which the poetic element is deeply rooted. . . . Her book is at once courageous and wise."[4] The reviewer is right in his assessment of the poetic maturity exhibited in *Casa Guidi Windows*. However, his comments voice prejudices inherent in the equation of her earlier focus on woman as "personal," while her focus on men here is assumed to relate to "mankind." Other reviewers, sensing that the poem's authority of voice and perspective, two qualities long associated with being male, inhabited a female subjectivity, reveal some confusion as to how to discern the gender of the poetic voice. The *Prospective Review* straightforwardly found "something at once manly and womanly in the character of her mind—energy large, and feeling deep" (320). The *Eclectic Review*, referring to Barrett Browning's encouragement of English military aid for Italian unification, declared that "in this particular instance we hold her to be wrong, illogical, and halting in her otherwise manly and prominent progression." Yet the poem was "one of the noblest productions of female genius," containing "deep and most womanly" pathos alongside "scathing vigour" and the "perfection of satiric art."[5] The *Spectator* was the most perspicacious on this issue of gender: it found the poem's "most powerful charm" derived from "the womanly faith and trust, which, though tempered by experience and enlightened by a manly power of analyzing events and facing disagreeable truths, yet shine serene and untroubled." However, it identified the poem as female in spirit, and found its answer to contemporary events one that only "a woman and a mother, with her first-born smiling at her knee," could give. Rather than trivializing this perspective, the reviewer recognized it as enriching: "To those who think that women and politics should be wide as the poles asunder, we recommend [the poem] as a proof of the feminine warmth of heart that may coexist with a vivid sympathy with the public affairs of nations, and of the deeper human interest those affairs themselves assume when thus viewed in relation to family life and from the centre of the natural affections."[6] Locating the "natural affections" in woman at the center of family life represents a convention; however, the reviewer acknowledges that public events take on "deeper human interest" when viewed from a woman's perspective, thus granting it both difference and legitimacy.

Inherent in this female speaker is the style with which Barrett Browning narrates her "personal impressions" in *Casa Guidi Windows*. The rhyme and rhythm of the Sicilian sestet are fitting for its subject of Italian politics, and its iambic pentameter scrupulously adheres to an *ababab* rhyme scheme throughout, evoking an allegiance to male poetic conventions. Flavia Alaya also identifies this allegiance: "the style of much of her political poetry was a mainstay of Victorian hortatory verse, indebted variously to Shelley, to the cadences of the Biblical prophets, and to the odic tradition."[7] However, Barrett Browning fits the Sicilian sestet to her own voice by varying stanza lengths: the latter are decided by the needs of content, not the demands of form, "For otherwise we only imprison spirit / And not embody" (*Aurora Leigh*, 5.226–27). A clue to the "spirit" that Barrett Browning attempted to "embody" in these varying stanza lengths appears in Alaya's description of Barrett Browning's prolific letters to friends in England, commenting on political affairs in Italy, as amounting to "monthly communiqués from the front—the club journalism of women to whom real clubs were closed."[8] And indeed clubs were closed to Barrett Browning by virtue of her sex; as she lamented to English friends: "*I* can read the newspapers only through Robert's eyes, who can only read them at Vieusseux's in a room sacred from the foot of woman" (*L*, 1:442). Thus Barrett Browning received the news mediated through male eyes and voice, exaggerating the fact that sex determined she be a citizen-observer affected by political decisions in which she had no legal right to engage.[9] As a woman, her involvement in political affairs had to be amateur and primarily conversational: the idea of letters as "communiqués from the front" evokes not formal debate, nor measured prose presenting settled arguments, but a series of discrete pieces of information bearing an emotional urgency and testing out or working toward opinions. Most important, it suggests that even though Barrett Browning received her information mediated by Browning and other men with access to the reading room, her response to the events was peculiarly her own, recorded in the intimacy of letters which, like journals, have historically been the repository of female thought that is excluded from more formal publication. As Barrett Browning wrote to Mr. Kenyon in 1852: "I do see with my own eyes and feel with my own spirit, and not with other people's eyes and spirits, though they should happen to be the dearest—and that's the very best of me, be certain" (*L*, 2:53).

Thus, the energy and insight of Barrett Browning's letters, brought to the scrutiny of male political endeavor, inform, stylistically, *Casa Guidi Windows*: although the poem contains clear transitions from stanza to stanza, and bears the imprint of judiciously thought-out opinion, often the import of specific stanzas is more potent than the connections between them. Its reviewers recognized this, variously, as the poem's defect or its strength. The *Athenaeum* found it "somewhat too loose and colloquial in its manner" (597), while the *Prospective Review* was altogether condescending in finding a "leading defect in this Poem": "It is letters to friends put into verse. . . . And so Mrs. Browning, having great versifying power, and being very fond of exercising it, presents us with a pleasant little volume of extracts from a journal of her residence in Florence" (319). The *Spectator*, however, identified the individuality of the style of *Casa Guidi Windows* as residing in its "episodical passages": "The subjective mode of treatment, by which the theme has been fitted to a woman's hand, and by which it acquires the unity of a work of art and at the same time dispenses with the detail of continuous narrative, enables the writer to diverge at pleasure from her direct course, and, without causing any feeling of interruption, to introduce a variety of topic and allusion" (617).

The poem's title emphasizes the political theme "fitted to a woman's hand." Barrett Browning is free of her earlier "imprisonment" in her Wimpole Street room, whose window was covered by a blind. She still writes from the domestic interior of Casa Guidi, a reminder of the restrictions placed on her sex, but focuses on public events she observes through her window. Unlike the Lady of Shalott, whom Barrett Browning had seemed to resemble when, "half sick of shadows," she "wove" her poems of a world she felt was refracted from books rather than formed by experience, she can look out onto "Camelot" or Florence without the curse descending on her.

The calm authority of the opening, "I heard last night a little child go singing / 'Neath Casa Guidi windows, by the church, / *O bella libertà, O bella*," establishes the relationship to a poetic tradition with which, as a woman poet, Barrett Browning has finally come to terms. As in "A Vision of Poets," her muse is a young boy, not the suffering woman identified as "Italy enchained" by "older singers' lips" (1.14–21). Their muse was two-faced. First, woman was monster: "childless among mothers," "widow of empires," "a shamed sister"; responsible for her own victimization—" 'Had she been less fair, / She were less wretched' "—, she represents "men and women . . . / Harrowed and hideous in a filthy lair" (1.22–29). Second, woman was angel, "some personating Image, wherein woe / Was wrapt in beauty from offending much," some suffering Cybele, Niobe, or Juliet in her coffin (1.30–33). Barrett Browning exposes those poets who appropriated woman as the image of suffering Italy, evading her reality: "'tis easier to gaze long / On mournful masks, and sad effigies, / Than on real, live, weak creatures crushed by strong" (1.46–48). Her critique is ironic in its equal application to Italy's wrongs, which the poets lamented, and to woman's suffering, with which, in their appropriation of it as metaphor, they do not concern themselves.

Meditating on the relationship of a poet to her precursors, Barrett Browning explains the authority with which she claims a young boy as her muse to represent Italy's future rather than the traditional suffering woman identified with Italy's past. In striking contrast to Arnold's reverence for past poets as models, described in his "Preface to Poems, 1853," she declares, "I kiss their footsteps, yet their words gainsay" (1.51). She both acknowledges a debt to a tradition that formed her and rejects its tenets as inappropriate for her. Claiming her own identity as a poet—"I, a singer also, from my youth" (1.155)—as well as her own muse, she refuses to lament the past:

> Nay, hand in hand with that young child, will I
> Go singing rather, "*Bella libertà*,"
> Than, with those poets, croon the dead or cry
> "*Se tu men bella fossi, Italia!*"
>
> [1.165–68]

Whereas nostalgia for the past informs much Victorian literature, Barrett Browning has no such yearning. As a poet she joins with the young boy anticipating future freedom, rather than echoing "those old thin voices" (1.162) who testily blame their unhappy condition on Italy / woman—"If only you were less beautiful, Italy." Her reasons for preferring the present and the future are very different from those that motivated Macaulay to praise his age when he measured progress in material terms; as *Aurora Leigh* makes clear, Barrett Browning is akin to Arnold in a commitment to spiritual rather than mere material advance.

However, as her poems demonstrate, there was no previous "golden age" for women; culturally they suffered and were as enchained as the country Italian poets identified with them. Woman's, and the woman poet's, hope lay in the *"bella libertà"* of the future.

With conviction, therefore, Barrett Browning asserts, "We do not serve the dead—the past is past!" (1.217). The obvious reference to "we" is to the Italian situation. However, it also describes her role in relation to the tradition she had "served" for so long: "Could I sing this song, / If my dead masters had not taken heed / To help the heavens and earth to make me strong?" (1.432–44). While rousing enthusiasm for Italy's great future, she argues for what George Eliot identified in the poem as "the true relation of the religious mind to the past,"[10] an argument unassailable, therefore, when she overtly relates it to herself as a poet. Given Barrett Browning's acknowledged indebtedness to her precursors in her earlier work, a wonderful freedom informs "the dead . . . / . . . shall abstract / No more our strength" (1.224–26). Replacing the incapacitating anxiety Milton's influence exerted on her in "A Drama of Exile," and the rebellious cry of the black slave, "Your white men are, after all, not gods indeed," is Barrett Browning's calm refusal to be bound by the past, relating both its debilitating as well as its nurturant effects:

> O Dead, ye shall no longer cling to us
>   With rigid hands of dessicating praise,
> And drag us backward by the garment thus,
>   To stand and laud you in long-drawn virelays!
> We will not henceforth be oblivious
>   Of our own lives, because ye lived before,
> Nor of our acts, because ye acted well.
>   We thank you that ye first unlatched the door,
> But will not make it inaccessible
>   By thankings on the threshold any more.
> We hurry onward to extinguish hell
>   With our fresh souls, our younger hope, and God's
> Maturity of purpose.
>
>   [1.230–42]

As a poet her "strength" has been sapped by the "rigid hands of dessicating praise" with which she feels her precursors have clung to her; they have pulled her backwards instead of empowering her to move forwards. However, she refuses any longer to compromise her own voice: "We will not henceforth be oblivious / Of our own lives, because ye lived before." She does not repudiate the poets of the past—"We thank you that ye first unlatched the door"—but accepts her task to "hurry onward to extinguish hell / With our fresh souls." She is so confident in her maturity that she does not imagine herself as marginal, but accommodates the contribution of the "dead" to her own freedom:

> None may grudge the dead,
> Libations from full cups. Unless we choose
> To look back to the hills behind us spread,
> The plains before us, sadden and confuse;
> If orphaned, we are disinherited.
>
> [1.432–41]

Her strength lies not in rejecting tradition but in building on it. After the uneasy years of struggle to both appropriate and reject "the masters," this calm dramatization of a voice confident in both its common roots in English poetry and its flowering in a woman's voice is a triumphant moment in Barrett Browning's work.

Having established her right to speak, Barrett Browning exploits the joyful crowd's celebrations to critique men's political activity.[11] She warns the Florentines that elaborate uniforms do not of themselves separate their wearers from stupid, decorated cattle:

> Those lappets on your shoulders, citizens,
>   Your eyes strain after sideways till they ache,
>
> ·   ·   ·   ·   ·   ·   ·   ·   ·   ·
>
>   ... are not intelligence,
>   Not courage even—alas, if not the sign
> Of something very noble, they are nought;
>   For every day ye dress your sallow kine
> With fringes down their cheeks, though unbesought

> They loll their heavy heads and drag the wine,
> And bear the wooden yoke as they were taught
> The first day.
>
> [1.747–58]

The difference between "lappets" and "intelligence," between costume and commitment, between appearance and reality, is at the heart of Barrett Browning's analysis of male power and informs her assessment of the heroic leader Italy needs.[12] She shares Carlyle's concern for the "Hero as King."[13] Her call for the "teacher" (1.772, 795, 812, 818), for "some high soul, crowned capable to lead / The conscious people" (1.762–63), echoes Carlyle's sixth *Heroes* lecture:

> We come now to the last form of Heroism; that which we call Kingship. The Commander over Men; he to whose will our wills are to be subordinated, and loyally surrender themselves, and find their welfare in doing so, may be reckoned the most important of Great Men. He is practically the summary for us of *all* the various figures of Heroism; Priest, Teacher, whatsoever of earthly or of spiritual dignity we can fancy to reside in a man, embodies itself here, to *command* over us, to furnish us with constant practical teaching, to tell us for the day and hour what we are to *do*. He is called *Rex* . . . ; King . . . which means . . . Able-man.[14]

The female leader of her own country, Queen Victoria, plays no part as type or example in this poem; Barrett Browning makes the pragmatic assumption that the Italian leader for unification will be male. Her concern is not with woman as leader, but with humane male leaders, rather than ones (like her father) who rely on the trappings of power rather than the morality of their office. Like Carlyle, Barrett Browning knows, "Certainly it is a fearful business, that of having your Able-man to *seek*, and not knowing in what manner to proceed about it! That is the world's sad predicament in these times of ours."[15] She addresses herself to this search in the latter half of *Casa Guidi Windows*, Part 1.

The two possible leaders were Grand Duke Leopold II, representative of earthly power, and Pius IX, representative of spiritual authority, neither of whom Barrett Browning viewed with unalloyed enthusiasm.[16] She describes the Duke's personal appearance to the crowd during the demonstration:

> Nor was it ill, when Leopold drew
> His little children to the window-place
> He stood in at the Pitti, to suggest
> *They* too should govern as the people willed.

> .   .   .   .

> . . . I like his face; the forehead's build
> Has no capacious genius, yet perhaps
> Sufficient comprehension,—mild and sad,
> And careful nobly,—not with care that wraps
> Self-loving hearts, to stifle and make mad,
> But careful with the care that shuns a lapse
> Of faith and duty, studious not to add
> A burden in the gathering of a gain.

> [1.557–71]

It is a measured estimation. His appearance with his children promises, she hopes, the *"bella libertà"* of the young boy's song with which the poem opens. She knows, however, that a leader cannot act alone, and, with all the force of one who had so recently broken her own yoke, exhorts the people: "Will, therefore, to be strong, thou Italy! / Will to be noble! Austrian Metternich / Can fix no yoke unless the neck agree" (1.661–63). Her call for unified action under a strong leader, to rid Italy of the Austrian yoke, is not a call for war, however. No adherent of confronting the "brutal with the brutal" (1.675), Barrett Browning scorns a childlike reliance on the "fist" rather than the "brain" (1.685–86). She draws her idealistic alternative to war from a nature in which she imagines "bee and finch" settling their rivalry, so

> to our races we may justify
> Our individual claims, and, as we reach
> Our own grapes, bend the top vines to supply
> The children's uses,—how to fill a breach
> With olive branches,—how to quench a lie

> With truth, and smite a foe upon the cheek
> With Christ's most conquering kiss.
>
> [1.698–704]

Her idealistic, unrealistic hope—identified by Jean Bethke Elshtain in *Women and War* as the idealism of the "Beautiful Soul"[17] —is that Italian morality will render Austrian force powerless and expose the "'glorious arms' of military kings" as "weak." Her opposition to war focuses initially on Italian resistance to Austrian force; yet in an "episodical passage" she ponders England's imperial armies, exhorting her own country to renounce war and set the world a moral example:

> Announce law
> By freedom; exalt chivalry by peace;
> Instruct how clear calm eyes can overawe,
> And how pure hands, stretched simply to release
> A bond-slave, will not need a sword to draw
> To be held dreadful. O my England, crease
> Thy purple with no alien agonies!
> No struggles toward encroachment, no vile war!
> Disband thy captains, change thy victories,
> Be henceforth prosperous as the angels are,
> Helping, not humbling.
>
> [1.715–25]

The "alien tyranny" Eve meekly accepted in "A Drama of Exile" is now rejected as the "alien agonies" of "vile war" conducted by an aggressor. In place of such masculine activity, Barrett Browning offers qualities she associates with the female: her conviction that "clear calm eyes" can overpower evil is reiterated in a letter to Thackeray in 1861, in which she trusts the "honest innocent eyes" of woman to name what "miserable women suffer" (*L*, 2:445); and her plea that England learn from "the angels" and negotiate with other nations by "helping, not humbling" evokes woman's traditional role and repudiates man's. Yet she adds the telling new quality of thinking to the female type; her hope is for a world in which "we shall have thinkers in the place / Of fighters" (1.727–28).

Having meditated on the issues involved in imagining an earthly leader, Barrett Browning scrutinizes the spiritual authority of the church and of Pope Pius's ability to be the necessary "teacher." She doubts that "with history's bell / So heavy round the neck" (1.865–66) of the papacy, it can produce a leader. She claims, "My words are guiltless of the bigot's sense" (1.942), yet insists on "Count[ing] what goes / To making up a pope, before he wear / That triple crown" (1.897–99). Although they are disturbing, she passes over the "world-wide throes / Which went to make the popedom" (1.899–900) and acknowledges without dwelling on it

> what signifies a church
> Of perfect inspiration and pure laws,
> Who burns the first man with a brimstone-torch,
> And grinds the second, bone by bone, because
> The times, forsooth, are used to rack and scorch!
> [1.926–30]

Churches, like people, err, and she allows that too often the church exemplifies rather than repudiates cruelty. However, her concern here is not with the evils of popedom, but with the pope as leader:

> So, fold by fold,
> Explore this mummy in the priestly cope,
> Transmitted through the darks of time, to catch
> The man within the wrappage, and discern
> How he, an honest man, upon the watch
> Full fifty years, for what a man may learn,
> Contrived to get just there.
> [1.972–78]

As Barrett Browning admonished the citizens not to mistake "lappets" for intelligence, so she refuses to be awed by the trappings of papal power: she likens the traditions of the papacy to a "mummy" that preserves the pope as symbol. But her concern is to discover the "man within the wrappage"; she demands that the hero exhibit sincerity as a man. She doubts that such sincerity can be preserved in a pope, because achieving the papacy necessitates so much compromise. As pope he cannot "love

truth too dangerously" but must "prefer / 'The interests of the
Church'" (1.999–1000); otherwise

> if he
> Did more than this, higher hoped, and braver dared,
> I think he were a pope in jeopardy,
> Or no pope rather, for his truth had barred
> The vaulting of his life.
>
> [1.1022–26]

Although "his heart beats warm" (1.1035), she believes the pope
will be subsumed by his office, and that "He [will sit] in stone,
and [harden] by a charm / Into the marble of his throne high-
placed" (1.1037–38). This striking image conveys not only a Prot-
estant critique of Catholicism, but also a woman's critique of
men in power and of the inevitable corruption achieving it necessitates. If "Pio Nono" does appear as a genuine leader, she
will recognize him as the "noblest" because "the heroic heart /
Within [him] must be great enough to burst / Those trammels"
that traditionally corrupted his "saintly peers in Rome, who
crossed and cursed / With the same finger" (1.1048–52).

In a stirring appeal to "pope or peasant" (1.1053) to emerge as
leader, to "take voice and work" (1.1057), Barrett Browning tem-
pers her earlier denunciation of war. Acknowledging that, "if foes
should take the field" (1.1072), and march on Florence, the Tus-
cans might indeed need to use swords and sacrifice their lives
for the cause, she pleads with them to "first bring souls!—bring
thoughts and words" (1.1085) to address the country's wrongs,
and, asserting the importance of the poet for political action, she
asks them to "bring songs too" (1.1090). She hopes for a poet
who, "through all bursts and bruits / Of popular passion, all un-
ripe and rathe / Convictions of the popular intellect," will record
the "Ideal" toward which all labor (1.1092–97). Earlier she reproved England for imperialism; now she encourages all of Eu-
rope and "even the New World" to join against Austrian imperialism.

This apparent reversal puzzled some reviewers. The *Eclectic
Review* admired Barrett Browning's denunciation of "meeting
force by brutal force" as "glorious in its intellectual strength,"
whereas her appeal for support for the Italian cause seemed that

of "an advocate, and a most energetic and dangerous one, for war." The *Athenaeum*, however, intuited the speaker's spirit in acknowledging that while she "venerates peace," Barrett Browning finds "the apathy of a nation prostrate beneath tyranny . . . to be a worse evil than the horrors of popular insurrection."[18] Her denunciation of force that relies on the "alien tyranny" of aggressors is matched by her commitment to force that leads to the freedom of those oppressed.

Barrett Browning's call to "all the far ends of the world" (1.1101) to support Italy is based on her belief that "Italy's the whole earth's treasury" (1.1165). She identifies specifically England's poetic debt:

> England claims, by trump of poetry,
> Verona, Venice, the Ravenna-shore,
> And dearer holds John Milton's Fiesole
> Than Langlande's Malvern with the stars in flower.
> [1.1125–28]

She dwells at some length on a visit she and Browning made to Vallombrosa where Milton went "ere his heart grew sick / And his eyes blind" (1.1138–39). Claiming Fiesole, rather than Malvern, as "dearer" to England makes Milton more important than Langland, but it also speaks to her rebirth in Italy rather than to her childhood at Hope End near Malvern. By naming him "John," Barrett Browning humanizes the figure who so inhibited her while writing "A Drama of Exile." Having established her right relationship to the "dead," she can make her literary peace with "John Milton." Italy provides a common ground: she can praise Milton without being threatened, because she too loves the country that she imagines "helped to fill / The cup of Milton's soul" (1.1155–56). The end of Part 1 is buoyant and confident as Barrett Browning enjoins all those who love Italy to bless "this great cause of southern men, who strive / In God's name for man's rights, and shall not fail!" (1.1201–2).

However, in Part 2, written two years later after the pope had proven timid in and the duke disloyal to the cause they seemed to espouse, the speaker's mood has changed:

I wrote a meditation and a dream,
  Hearing a little child sing in the street.
I leant upon his music as a theme,
  Till it gave way beneath my heart's full beat,
Which tried at an exultant prophecy
  But dropped before the measure was complete.

                                    [2.1–6]

The hope engendered by the child's song gives way to disillusion-
ment. Barrett Browning, identifying her role among "We thinkers
. . . / We hopers . . . / We poets" (2.17–19), questions her earlier
privileging of the hero, repenting that she "could learn / No better counsel for a simple case, / Than to put faith in princes"
(2.73–75). She has witnessed Duke Leopold, after his voluntary
exile, return under Austrian auspices. Her appeal, "Absolve me,
patriots, of my woman's fault / That ever I believed the man was
true!" (2.64–65) has an ironic twist. Her "woman's fault" is neither inferior intelligence nor excess of sentiment; but erroneous
belief in man's honor and capabilities to rule. She proves fallacious Ruskin's boast: "The man's power is active, progressive,
defensive. He is eminently the doer, the creator, the discoverer,
the defender. His intellect is for speculation and invention; his
energy for adventure, for war, and for conquest, wherever war is
just, wherever conquest necessary."[19] Her trust in the duke was
misplaced not because her judgement was bad:

I saw the man among his little sons,
  His lips were warm with kisses while he swore,—
And I, because I am a woman, I,
  Who felt my own child's coming life before
The prescience of my soul, and held faith high,—
  I could not bear to think, whoever bore,
That lips, so warmed, could ever shape so cold a lie.

                                    [2.93–99]

Barrett Browning determines that loyalty to a child is not a sentimental limitation of woman's thinking but an honorable standard, one she finds inherent in herself as woman, and one the
duke has violated.

The duke and the pope are not the only ones to betray the

"great cause," one actively, by allying himself with Austria, the other passively, by taking no action: neither leaders nor the people, who in Carlyle's terms should "loyally surrender themselves" to the "Commander over Men," are of heroic stature. In her "Advertisement" to *Casa Guidi Windows* Barrett Browning reflects on this dual failure when she laments that she "believed, like a woman, some royal oaths, and lost sight of the probable consequences of some obvious popular defects" (*W*, 3:249). Again her emphasis on her position as "a woman" is a self-criticism only as it represents her gullibility in believing men's boasts. She emphasizes the discrepancy between the role men assign themselves and their capacity to fulfill it in a long satiric speech (2.148–83) in which she imagines the Florentine men's boasting how they "wore / Black velvet like Italian democrats" and "chalked the walls with bloody caveats / Against all tyrants," and how, even if they "did not fight / Exactly, [they] fired muskets up the air, / To show that victory was [theirs] of right." She recognizes that they have made no sacrifices, but merely enjoyed the shows of political commitment; unprepared to fight they "shook the sword within the sheath, / Like heroes—only louder." Her critique of men's inability to carry political action to fruition exposes how crying "*libertà*" represents only "inarticulate rage / And breathless sobs" (2.228–29) rather than a sincere commitment to effect change. In dramatizing Mary in "The Seraphim" (1838), Barrett Browning had shown how ineffectual such feeling was by describing it as "a spasm, not a speech."

She describes the silent crowd who lined the "long-drawn street / . . . from end to end, full in the sun, / With Austria's thousands. Sword and bayonet, / Horse, foot, artillery" (2.299–302). Contrasting it with the joyful turmoil of the earlier celebration, Barrett Browning then reproaches England, which "for ends of trade / And virtue, and God's better worshipping" exalts peace rather than "those rusty wars that eat the soul," and has not aided Italy (2.374–77). Not purely a warmonger, she admits, "I, too, have loved peace" (2.379); but she prefers a just war over a peace that leaves injustices, "the wretch who grieves / And groans," the "slave's despair / [That] dulled his helpless, miserable brain," and the "starving homes" (2.390–97). She declares:

I love no peace which is not fellowship,
    And which includes not mercy. I would have
Rather, the raking of the guns across
    The world, and shrieks against Heaven's architrave;
Rather, the struggle in the slippery fosse
    Of dying men and horses, and the wave
Blood-bubbling . . . . Enough said!—by Christ's own cross,
    And by this faint heart of my womanhood,
Such things are better than a Peace that sits
    Beside a hearth in self-commended mood,
And takes no thought how wind and rain by fits
    Are howling out of doors against the good
Of the poor wanderer.

[2.399–411]

Both realism and melodrama inform her vision of war's "blood-bubbling," and we cannot avoid recognizing in this stirring summons to fight the privilege of "this faint heart of my womanhood" that urges men on to a death she will not suffer. If men have too easily relegated women to the house, Barrett Browning is certainly complicitous in relegating men to "heroic" death as cannon fodder. A later poem, "Mother and Poet" (*Last Poems*, 1862), addresses this issue when the speaker, imagined as the poet Laura Savio, recognizes her responsibility for her two sons' deaths as patriots of the Risorgimento:

    I taught them, no doubt,
That a country's a thing men should die for at need.
    I prated of liberty, rights, and about
        The tyrant cast out.

[5]

However, in 1849, seeing tyranny dominate Italy, Barrett Browning despairs at the failure of male heroism on the part of both leaders and followers. Disillusioned, she declares, "I have grown too weary of these windows" (2.430). She wants to "Shut them straight" and "sit down by the folded door, / And veil our saddened faces" (2.426–48). She retreats into the female interior and her own imagination, which can be trusted more than political slogans: "Sights / Come thick enough and clear enough in thought / Without the sunshine" (2.430–42). Inside she ponders the failure not only of the duke and the people, but of the spiritual leader also:

> Why, almost, through this Pius, we believed
> The priesthood could be an honest thing, he smiled
> So saintly while our corn was being sheaved
> For his own granaries!
>
> [2.514–17]

But the pope was no more committed than the duke "to render man more free" (2.474), and both, like the patriots, lack "soul-conviction" (2.528) for the cause.

Although she believes that Italian unification might one day "annuntiate to the world's applause" (2.576), Barrett Browning realizes that the world is less concerned with "war-trumps" (2.575) than with "Fair-going" (2.578). Meditating on the Great Exhibition of 1851, she addresses the Captains of Industry as agents of male imperial political economy as "Imperial England draws / The flowing ends of the earth" (2.578–79), "All trailing in their splendours through the door / Of the gorgeous Crystal Palace" (2.586–87). She wrote to Mitford on November 13, 1850 anticipating the event: "Well, among the odd things we lean to in Italy is to an actual belief in the greatness and importance of the future exhibition. We have actually imagined it to be a noble idea, and you take me by surprise in speaking of the general distaste to it in England." (L, 1:466). Seeing the possibilities for peace inherent in the "Fair-going world," she lauds the fact that "Every nation, / To every other nation strange of yore, / Gives face to face the civic salutation" (2.587–89). She demonstrates genuine delight in the corals, diamonds, cloths, carpets, goblets, art, and porcelain on display. But she warns against a materialism without benefit for humanity. Addressing the Captains of Industry, those "Magi of the east and of the west" (2.628) bringing their new wares, she questions, "Is your courage spent / In handwork only?" rather than in concern for the poor, for the "wicked children," and, highlighting woman's disenfranchised state, "for women, sobbing out of sight / Because men made the laws" (2.631–39). Evoking the parable of the Good Samaritan, she appeals to the world's nations for mercy for the exiled, for the slaves, for the oppressed:

> O gracious nations, give some ear to me!
> You all go to your Fair, and I am one
> Who at the roadside of humanity
> Beseech your alms,—God's justice to be done.
>
> [2.652–55]

Her appeal for "alms" challenges all imperial countries, "great nations" with "great shames"—England, Austria, Russia, America, and France—to liberate their "scourged and bound," and returns her to concern for Italy. Remembering its "patriot dead" (2.657), she grounds her revolutionary politics not only in such men as Charles Albert, who died fighting for Italy, but also in a mother's vision, quite alien to that which she later attributed to Laura Savio. She praises Anita Garibaldi, who fought at her husband's side "Until she felt her little babe unborn / Recoil, within her, from the violent staves / And bloodhounds of the world," as she herself died (2.680–82). The speaker imagines the pregnant woman's corpse:

> the sea-weeds fit
> Her body, like a proper shroud and coif,
> And murmurously the ebbing waters grit
> The little pebbles while she lies interred
> In the sea-sand.
>
> [2.685–89]

Inspired by such examples, the speaker confidently imagines Italy's future. Recalling the image of Italy as a suffering woman with which she began, she is convinced that "Niobe! still fainting in the sun" (2.726) is a "death-song" and inappropriate for the country, and she offers instead her vision inspired by a young boy:

> And I, who first took up hope in this song,
> Because a child was singing one . . . behold,
> The hope and omen were not, haply, wrong!
> Poets are soothsayers still, like those of old

Who studied flights of doves,—and creatures young
And tender, mighty meanings, may unfold.

[2.736–41]

Depressed by political apathy and inactivity, she reaffirms her
role to write of the "springs of life." Her poem ends where it
began, with her muse, "my blue-eyed prophet":

And be God's witness that the elemental
    New springs of life are gushing everywhere
To cleanse the watercourses, and prevent all
    Concrete obstructions which infest the air!
That earth's alive, and gentle or ungentle
    Motions within her, signify but growth!—
The ground swells greenest o'er the laboring moles.

[2.761–67]

Barrett Browning now addresses her own son, born in 1849, the
same year as the Grand Duke's return to Florence with Austrian
guards. The nameless young boy singing is now embodied in her
own child as muse.

In *Casa Guidi Windows* Barrett Browning, although distress-
ingly complicitous in condemning men to "blood-bubbling," does
suggest an alternative standard of honor for political economy
and establish an authoritative speaker. Comfortable with her poetic past, she identifies a young male muse to liberate her from
the dilemma of desiring to be subject as poet while regarded as
object and muse of poetic narrative. In *Aurora Leigh* she creates
a speaker who narrates the journey to that poetic maturity.

CHAPTER 6

Woman and Artist, Both Complete

AURORA LEIGH (1856)

I choose to walk at all risks.
—*Aurora Leigh*

In *Casa Guidi Windows* Barrett Browning demonstrated confidence in her mature voice: her decision to free herself from the yoke of her father's "alien tyranny" informed her commitment to Italian liberation; and the unification she desired for Italy resonated to the unification of "woman" and "poet" that *Casa Guidi Windows* enacts. Secure in her position vis-à-vis the poetic past that had both nurtured and imprisoned her, Barrett Browning made public her "highest convictions upon Life and Art" (*W*, 4:1) and dramatized in *Aurora Leigh* the process whereby she achieved that integration of woman and poet.

Bloom has asserted that all poets are both nurtured and imprisoned by their poetic past and must free themselves from their precursors' influence. As feminist criticism on Barrett Browning and other female poets has shown, however, the process of liberation is quite different for a female than for a male poet.[1] The male poet bears the same relationship to the world as his precursor; both imagine themselves as the subject of experience. *Aurora Leigh* suggests that as long as poetry is imagined as a predominantly male endeavor, a female poet enacts her liberation by transforming herself from being the object of male narrative to being the subject of her own story.

In *The Battle of Marathon*, her translation of *Prometheus Bound*, "The Seraphim," and "A Drama of Exile," Barrett Brow-

ning attempted themes and forms associated with the male poetic tradition. Encouraged by these attempts to take herself seriously as a poet, she was nevertheless inhibited by her precursors,
and those poems are interesting revelations more of the costs of
"anxiety of influence" and of "authorship" than of accomplishment. *Aurora Leigh* is her mature appropriation of the tradition.
In the blank verse of Milton's epic, Barrett Browning writes of a
heroine who refuses to be merely a helpmate. In spite of being
taught by her aunt and lectured by her cousin Romney in the
Miltonic ways of womanhood, Aurora insists on claiming for
herself the Adamic privilege of naming the world.

Although *Aurora Leigh* was published in 1856, Barrett Browning had been planning such a poem for many years. In one of
her earliest letters to Browning she wrote:

> [M]y chief *intention* just now is the writing of a sort of
> novel-poem—a poem as completely modern as "Geraldine's
> Courtship," running into the midst of our conventions, &
> rushing into drawing-rooms & the like "where angels fear to
> tread"; & so, meeting face to face & without mask the Hu-
> manity of the age, & speaking the truth as I conceive of it,
> out plainly. That is my intention. It is not mature enough
> yet to be called a plan. I am waiting for a story, & I won't
> take one, because I want to make one, & I like to make my
> own stories, because then I can take liberties with them in
> the treatment. [*RB&EBB*, 1:31]

Barrett Browning's original intention of "making" rather than
"taking" a story seems thwarted in *Aurora Leigh's* echoes of *Corinne*, George Sand, *Ruth*, *Jane Eyre*, and "The Princess," such
that the whole poem appears "an overlapping sequence of dia-
logues with other texts."[2] Nevertheless, her epic poem uniting
woman and poet tells a story essentially her own, and this early
letter identifies the crucial qualities of what came to be *Aurora
Leigh*: its insistence on modernity, on "this live, throbbing age"
(5.203); its defiance of conventions—the female poet questions
the sex/gender economy and writes of rape, prostitution, illegitimacy, and the working class; and its location of heroic action in
"drawing-rooms" rather than on the battle-fields with medieval
"Roland [and] his knights at Roncesvalles" (5.207). Barrett's refer-

ence to "rushing into drawing-rooms & the like 'where angels fear to tread'" now has an ironic cast. Identifying herself with the "fools [who] rush in" rather than with the timid angels, Barrett asserts an earthiness over a spirituality. But her statement carries for us now the paradox that the Victorian middle-class woman, who ideologically belonged in the drawing-room with her sewing, flower arranging, morning visitors, and piano, was spiritualized into Angel in the House. Barrett, however, imagines the "angels" as being afraid of drawing-rooms, implying that "angels [will] fear to tread" in the drawing-room of her design.

Even at such an early stage of her "intention," Barrett Browning named the form *Aurora Leigh* was to take, the "novel-poem." Her adoption of a persona suggests she needed "fictional characters to carry the charge of her experience as a woman artist"[3] so that she could speak "the truth . . . out plainly," and belies her intention to meet "face to face & without Mask the Humanity of the age." But her writing of a "novel-poem" is also the synthesis of the male and female traditions between which she shifted uneasily throughout her career. Aurora's assertive "I write" (1.29) is the culmination of the progression in Barrett Browning's work from "I thought" (*Sonnets from the Portuguese*), to "I stand" ("The Runaway Slave at Pilgrim's Point"), and "I heard" (*Casa Guidi Windows*); it combines a female speaker with a hitherto male-defined activity. The male epic tradition and the female novel form her voice.

The female tradition, to which *Aurora Leigh* was heir, included the influences of both women novelists and poetesses. First, the heroine of Madame de Stael's *Corinne* provided, as Ellen Moers demonstrates,[4] a generation of women writers with the typology of England as a land of repression and Italy as a place of creative and sexual possibility for women. Corinne, however, although a renowned poet, ultimately dies from lack of love. George Sand's "revolted cry," her "woman's voice," her "dishevelled strength in agony," had long influenced Barrett Browning. Sand's life-long reevaluation of gender relations is also one of Aurora's concerns and Sand's life in Paris resonates in Aurora's life as a writer in London. The initial freedom these French influences offered was reinforced by Barrett Browning's English contemporaries. She wrote to Mrs. Martin in 1853: "Tell me if you have read Mrs. Gaskell's 'Ruth.' That's a novel which I much admire. It is strong and healthy at once, teaching a moral frightfully wanted in English society. . . . 'Villette,' too . . . is very powerful" (L, 2:141–42). *Ruth* must have suggested or confirmed Barrett Browning's conviction that a story such as Marian Erle's should be the subject not only of novels but of poetry, and *Villette* shares with *Aurora Leigh* an unreliable narrator who ultimately finds professional and sexual fulfillment outside of England.

The second female influence was that of the poetesses. When Aurora finally acknowledges her love for Romney, she claims, "Art is much, but Love is more" (9.656). Whereas Barrett eschewed the "affections" of the poetesses to model her poetry after the male tradition, Barrett Browning's mature voice incorporated their concerns into art.[5] Aurora initially imagines such affections as associated with Romney's types of "doating mothers, and perfect wives, / Sublime Madonnas, and enduring saints" (2.222–23), but she comes to understand through her engagement with Marian Erle in Paris that art is enriched by the love of a "common woman." Her statement, far from a renunciation of her art, claims a denigrated female tradition as an integral aspect of poetry, yet redefines that tradition to include the subjectivity of woman's sexual passion.

Although Ruskin wrote to Browning that *Aurora Leigh* was the greatest poem in the English language and "the first poetical expression of the Age,"[6] and Swinburne recorded, "no English contemporary poet by profession has left us work so full of living fire,"[7] the reviewers' responses were more complex, providing a remarkable counterpoint to the poem; they betrayed in their discussion the very ideologies that *Aurora Leigh* addressed.

Response was mixed over what Barrett Browning was attempting in her epic infused with female concerns. The *Athenaeum* represented those disturbed by "a mingling of what is precious with what is mean—of the voice of clarion and the lyric cadence of harp with the cracked school-room spinet—of tears and small-talk—of eloquent apostrophe and adust speculation—of the grandeur of passion and the pettiness of modes and manners."[8] Although admiring the "glorious chords and melodies" of some passages, the reviewer was distressed that "Milton's organ is put

by Mrs. Browning to play polkas in May-Fair drawing-rooms."
The *Dublin University Magazine*, however, saw the contrast between Aurora's meditation on art in Book 5 and the subsequent
episode of the party at Lord Howe's as part of a tradition epitomized by Shakespeare in his depiction of "the coarse or foolish,
or the low in thought and expression, following quickly upon the
elevated and poetic." This representation was felt to be true to
"real life": "The common-place and prosaic ever touching upon
but not blending with the sublime and poetic, like colours which
set off each other when in juxta-position, but do not lose their
distinctive characters by fusion. Such a fusion the author might
easily have effected by clothing the sentiments of the ball-room
men and women in poetic language; but she would then have
been neither true to their nature nor to her own art."[9] Even
this sensitive critic did not fully appreciate Barrett Browning's
achievement: Shakespeare separated the "low in thought and expression" from "the elevated" by the use of prose rather than
poetry. Barrett Browning, however, incorporated both the "common-place and prosaic" and the "sublime and poetic" into what
the *Westminster Review* identified as the "high fever" of Aurora's narration.[10] C. Castan described more precisely "the particular tonal quality" as one in which the "narrating suffering Aurora, mov[es] along the mountain range of her passion."[11] The
crucial point here is that, while the vocabulary may represent
high and low life, the same voice narrates both the sublime and
the commonplace in the epic form: an intelligent woman's life
perforce included in easy or uneasy juxtaposition both the life of
the intellect and of the drawing-room in a way that a man's culturally did not.

The *Athenaeum* accurately predicted readers' responses to this
portrayal of woman in saying: "To some [*Aurora Leigh*] will be so
much rank foolishness,—to others almost a spiritual revelation"
(1427). Barrett Browning had "expected to be put in the stocks
and pelted with the eggs of the last twenty years' 'singing birds'
as a disorderly woman and freethinking poet!'", so she was surprised to hear of "quite decent women taking the part of the
book in a sort of *effervescence*" which led her to "modify [her]
opinions somewhat upon [people's] conventionality, to see the
progress made in freedom of thought" (*L*, 2:252). She also heard

the response she feared, "the 'mamas of England' in a body refuse to let their daughters read it" (*L*, 2:255).

Such "mamas'" fears inform the responses of even sympathetic reviewers to the issues *Aurora Leigh* addresses. The *Dublin University Magazine* is paradigmatic: "We are disposed to think that no better test can be found of the civilization and enlightenment of any people than the position which woman attains to amongst them, both in a social and intellectual point of view" (460). It lauded Barrett Browning's protest against the "social wrongs of woman" in her "greatest poem" (461–62), and yet, belying its earlier liberalism, the review ended with a reactionary conclusion:

> Indeed in the effort to stand, not on a pedestal beside man, but actually to occupy his place, we see Mrs. Browning commit grave errors. She assumes as it were the gait and the garb of man, but the stride and the strut betray her. She is occasionally coarse in expression and unfeminine in thought; and utters what, if they be even truths, are so conveyed that we would hesitate to present them to the eye of the readers of her own sex. There is nothing that detracts so much from the pleasure which the perusal of this poem has given us, as this conviction, that the authoress has written a book which is almost a closed volume for her own sex. The days when such women as Aphra Behn can hope to be palatable to the female sex are, we believe, gone for ever. Woman must be ever true to her womanly instincts if she would be the meet helper as well as companion of man. We grieve to find such a woman as Elizabeth Barrett Browning, even in a phrase or sentiment, forgetful of that nature. [470]

Unlike George Eliot, who celebrated Barrett Browning as "the first woman who has produced a work which exhibits all the peculiar powers without the negations of her sex,"[12] the *Dublin University Magazine* saw Barrett Browning as usurping man's place. The passage is rife with irony. First: the fact that she "utters . . . truths" of women's lives—work, rape, prostitution, illegitimacy, maternity, and the sex/gender economy—designates the work "a closed volume" to the women whose experience it depicts. Second: depicting women's lives in verse "coarse in expression and unfeminine in thought" violates Barrett Browning's "womanly instincts" making her "forgetful of [her] nature." Marian Erle speaks to this:

> We wretches cannot tell out all our wrong
> Without offence to decent happy folk.
> I know that we must scrupulously hint
> With half-words, delicate reserves, the thing
> Which no one scrupled we should feel in full.
>
> [6.1220–24]

The review maintains that woman's "social and intellectual" position is of concern only insofar as it conforms to patriarchal definitions of "womanly instincts" and "nature."[13] When a woman tells her own nature she "assumes . . . the gait and the garb of man." The reviewer privileges male fantasy over female experience of women. The ultimate irony is that when Barrett Browning finally wrote as "I" she was condemned as being too much like a man, whereas earlier when her femaleness wore a male disguise she was lauded as the best poetess.

The reviews manifest two misreadings of *Aurora Leigh*. The *Dublin University Magazine* epitomizes the first by arguing that the poem intended to exemplify woman in her role as "meet helper as well as companion to man." To praise the poem as Barrett Browning's "greatest" while reinterpreting it is doublespeak. The reviewer praises the revelation of woman's "social suffering" and her "highest intellectual development," yet declares the poem a failure in its refusal of Biblical and Miltonic precepts: "In the failure both of Romney and Aurora to work out to a prosperous issue their own theories, is finally exhibited to an extent, perhaps beyond what the author intended, the utter dependence of each sex upon the other, the truth that if a primaeval decree gave man the dominion, it was as much for woman's happiness as his own—a dominion which the holy principle of love turns into a blessing to both, by making obedience an anticipating assent" (462). Although *Aurora Leigh* may conceivably demonstrate the "dependence of each sex on the other," it emphatically does not illustrate "the truth that if a primaeval decree gave man the dominion, it was as much for woman's happiness as his own." It is puzzling to see how the blinded Romney exhorting

Aurora to her work and, in effect, becoming her muse could be expressing his dominion over her. The reviewer's need for such a resolution is echoed by the *Athenaeum*'s finding the "argument unnatural" (1425), by *Blackwood*'s wishing "Mrs. Browning had selected a more natural and intelligible theme," and by Coventry Patmore's dismissal of the poem in the *North British Review* because the "development of [Aurora's] powers as a poetess is elaborately depicted; but as Mrs. Browning is herself almost the only modern example of such development, the story is uninteresting from its very singularity."[14] Patmore's reasoning is especially disturbing; if being a poet is problematic for a woman because the tradition has been male-defined, then that system is perpetuated if a poem about the growth of a woman poet's mind is ignored for its "singularity."

The second misreading is represented by those who dismiss Aurora, discovering the poem's excellence in the depiction of Marian Erle. They endorse a conservative ideology restricting woman to her maternal role. Thus *Blackwood*'s regretted that "the extreme independence of Aurora detracts from the feminine charm, and mars the interest which we otherwise might have felt for so intellectual a heroine," whereas Marian "does undoubtedly attract our sympathies more than the polished and high-minded Aurora, . . . as the mother of a hapless child. There indeed, Mrs. Browning has achieved a triumph" (36). Likewise the *Westminster Review* appreciated the "picture of innocence and maternal fondness such as perhaps has never before been realized in verse," whereas the poet-narrator's "self-consciousness repels—her speculations do not much interest us" (225).

In sum, the reviewers reveal the very patriarchal ideologies that Barrett Browning was addressing: they admire the poem, but dislike Aurora's independence and exalt Marian as mother with child; they sympathize with Barrett Browning's indictment of women's "social wrongs," yet accuse her thereby of "prov[ing] her manhood"; they admire Barrett Browning's poem, yet want to see Aurora under man's dominion as Romney's helpmate; they are touched by Marian's story but dislike the coarseness with which it is expressed. In short, they reflect the age's turmoil over the representation of woman.

Aurora Leigh's story dramatizes how she reconciled these contradictions. First, as a poet she identifies with the male tradition until she realizes, to use de Beauvoir's terms with which I began this study, that "to play at being a man [is] a source of frustration." Second, through Marian Erle she owns her "woman's passion" (6.779), then experiences how "to play at being a woman is also a delusion" when she offers herself to Romney as object of his love and need. Finally, she engages sexually and intellectually as Romney's equal, and on a symbolic level she renders him (who in his blindness evokes the blind precursors, Homer, Aeschylus, Milton, and even Mr. Boyd) into her muse. Her development parallels Barrett Browning's "frustration" in her work through the *Poems of 1844*, her "delusion" in the *Sonnets from the Portuguese* until she objectifies the poet-beloved as her Muse (41), and her assertive subjectivity in "The Runaway Slave at Pilgrim's Point," *Casa Guidi Windows*, and *Aurora Leigh*.[15]

The structure of *Aurora Leigh* is significant as a representation of Aurora's transformation. Castan established the narrative time scheme of the poem: through Book 5 Aurora is twenty-seven years old, narrating her life story on the evening she decides to leave England and return to Florence; by the end of Book 5 the "youthful confident" Aurora has caught up with the "sadder" narrator who, unlike those in *Jane Eyre* and *Great Expectations*, does not know the outcome of her story, and therefore is not fully reliable; in Books 6–9 the "story has caught up with the narrator and till the end of the poem they stay together."[16]

I want to extend these observations: the later books resemble journal entries in that Aurora records events as they occur. Her readers, thereby, experience the denouement as Aurora does, rather than mediated by her mature knowledge.[17] The tightly structured plot is as important as the narrative time sequence: the events recorded in Books 1–4 are repeated in reverse order in Books 6–9, dividing the poem into two parts:

Written in England:
1. Aurora's parents' marriage, her childhood in Italy, adolescence in England, birth as a poet.
2. Romney's proposal on Aurora's twentieth birthday.
3. Aurora as a writer in London, introduction of Lady Waldemar, Marian Erle's story.

4. Marian's story continued, the abortive wedding.
5. A pivotal book: Aurora's meditation on Art, Lord Howe's party, Aurora's decision to leave England for Italy.

Written in Paris and Italy:

6. Aurora's discovery of Marian in Paris, Marian's explanation of the abortive wedding, Marian's second story.
7. Marian's story continued, the journey to Italy, letters to Lord Howe and Lady Waldemar.
8. Romney's arrival in Florence, his and Aurora's reassessment of the discussion that took place on her twentieth birthday.
9. Marian's refusal to marry Romney, Aurora's union with Romney, her rebirth as a poet.

Aurora repeats, in the last four books, the experiences of the first four, but engages in them very differently. Whereas Book 1 records the union of Aurora's parents, Book 9 celebrates the union between Romney and Aurora. Book 2 records Romney's proposal and Aurora's rejection of it, whereas Book 8 contains the cousins' reinterpretation of that day. Books 3 and 7 tell of the attempted and actual rape of Marian, whereas Book 4 records the abortive wedding and Book 6 gives Marian's explanation for her failure to appear at it. The poem describes a narrative return that can be schematized:

ENGLAND		ABROAD
1	Union	9
2	Romney and Aurora, her twentieth birthday	8
3	Marian's story	7
4	Marian's story, the wedding	6
	5 Art	

Whereas the first books offer a mediated though unfinished autobiography, the last four demonstrate in episodic fashion the stages in Aurora's integration of woman and poet, her transformation from being the object of Romney's gaze to being the subject of her own vision. The *National Review* had an inkling of this in its assessment of the poem's controversial ending:

> She learns the error of her life,—that she had striven to be an artist instead of a woman, rather than been content to be a simple woman, and let her art spring from that true basis; and the truth, which is the deepest moral of the work, overwhelms her with its sudden conviction, that great as is art, greater is the human life of the artist; and greatest, love, which is the centre of that life and of all life— . . . As the theme deepens, and the faulty artist forgets herself in the true poet, the verse runs smooth and clear.[18]

The transformation of the "faulty artist" into the "true poet" is effected by Aurora's refusal to identify "artist" as "man." Whereas the relationship of Aurora to her father and his books informs the first half of the narrative, Marian Erle's experience controls the second half; Aurora's story resolves the conflicts between the male literary and female cultural economies to which Barrett Browning was heir.

Beginning her autobiography on the evening she decides to leave England, her father's country, for Italy, her mother's land, is Aurora's first step from "faulty artist" to "true poet"; her assumed male identity no longer tolerable, she initiates the journey to womanhood:

> Of writing many books there is no end;
> And I who have written much in prose and verse
> For others' uses, will write now for mine,—
> Will write my story for my better self.
>
> [1.1–4]

Aurora will write "for [her] better self" in order to create that self.

The twenty-seven-year-old Aurora narrates two events exemplifying the sex/gender economy that circumscribes her: her reaction as a child to her dead mother's portrait (1.120–73) and her response to Romney's sudden appearance as she crowned herself poet with an ivy wreath on her twentieth birthday (2.54–72).

Aurora narrates how her mother's death when she was four left

her with a "mother-want about the world" (1.40). The young
child lacked a mother's love, but also a role model; she grew to
define being female for herself.[19] Aurora recalls her mother's
portrait, a macabre picture painted from the corpse, which was
dressed not in the customary funeral shroud, but in her red evening gown. As a young child Aurora found this picture "very
strange"; "half in terror, half / In adoration" she would gaze at
the "swan-like supernatural white life / Just sailing upward from
the red stiff silk" (1.139–40). Her gaze transformed the picture
on the canvas into different representations of woman that later
haunt her narrative. The adult Aurora realizes that as a child
she created these images "mixed, confused unconsciously" from
"whatever [she] last read or heard or dreamed" (1.147–48):

> Ghost, fiend, and angel, fairy, witch, and sprite,
> A dauntless Muse who eyes a dreadful Fate,
> A loving Psyche who loses sight of Love,
> A still Medusa with mild milky brows
> All curdled and all clothed upon with snakes
> Whose slime falls fast as sweat will; or anon
> Our Lady of the Passion, stabbed with swords
> Where the Babe sucked; or Lamia in her first
> Moonlighted pallor, ere she shrunk and blinked
> And shuddering wriggled down to the unclean;
> Or my own mother.
>
> [1.154–64]

She recognizes that woman's identity is created by the cultural
economy: as a child she read and heard not about woman as
artist, but as Muse, Psyche, Medusa, Lamia, and the suffering
Madonna. Imprisoned by such literary representations of woman
as object of narratives formed from men's terror or adoration of
her, part of Aurora's task as a poet is to test these representations
against her own experience. Only the *Westminster Review* commented on this crucial passage, denigrating it as "a perfect shoal
of mangled and pompous similes" (221). The criticism is unwit-
tingly ironic: the very muddle that the critic identifies replicates
the muddled images of woman available to Aurora.

Aurora does not assume all the roles she identifies in her
mother's portrait, but casts Lady Waldemar and Marian into its

mythic types. If Lady Waldemar dramatizes Medusa and Lamia, then Marian is cast as Psyche, "who loses sight of love," and "Our Lady of the Passion, stabbed with [metaphoric] swords / Where the Babe sucked." At Lord Howe's party, Aurora "the printing woman" feels alienated from the seductive self-presentation of Lady Waldemar with her "alabaster shoulders and bare breasts, / On which the pearls, drowned out of sight in milk, / Were lost, excepting for the ruby clasp!" (5.619–21). The white of Lady Waldemar's shoulders and breasts and the red of her ruby clasp are reminiscent of the uncanny portrait of Aurora's mother. And, whereas her "heavy ringlets" (3.444) and "that coil / Of tresses" (5.614–16) suggest Medusa, the "twenty stinging snakes" of Lady Waldemar's hatred toward Aurora confirms her as the "Lamia-woman" (7.152). Aurora writes of these women through patriarchal eyes: Lady Waldemar is neither as monstrous nor Marian as angelic as Aurora fictionalizes them.

The second event representing the sex/gender economy, which in retrospect Aurora recognizes as revealing how she had internalized woman as object of the male gaze, is her reaction to Romney's surprising her when she crowned herself poet. She narrates how on her twentieth birthday, feeling "so young, so strong, so sure of God" (2.13), she imagined wearing the poet's laurel (as Corinne had been crowned) "In sport, not pride, to learn the feel of it" (2.34). Aurora recalls choosing ivy, not laurel: "I drew a wreath / Drenched, blinding me with dew, across my brow" (2.56–57). However, Romney's appearance transformed her from a woman actively crowning herself a poet to an art object for his gaze, a transformation to which she acquiesced:

> I stood there fixed,—
> My arms up, like the caryatid, sole
> Of some abolished temple, helplessly
> Persistent in a gesture which derides
> A former purpose.
>
> [2.60–64]

At twenty-seven, though still not fully formed as an artist, Aurora understands the anachronistic nature of such a gesture. She repressed the energy with which she had earlier "bounded forth" (2.18) into stasis: "I stood there fixed." Although acknowledging the sacredness of the tradition in which she was represented as a sculpture, a "caryatid," the older Aurora knows that the "temple" or tradition that she then upheld in that role must be "abandoned." Aurora characterizes her situation: "Woman and artist,—either incomplete, / Both credulous of completion" (2.4–5). At twenty she had been "helplessly persistent" in her conformity, and yet her gesture of standing "there fixed" under the male gaze only mocked a tradition enriched in its "former purpose" by such a gesture.

Aurora's response to these two events was to assume the identity of subject and [male] poet, rather than of object and woman, an identity suggested by her early association with poetry through her dead father's books. Reading them she felt as though her father "wrapt his little daughter in his large / Man's doublet, careless did it fit or no" (1.727–29). As overwhelmed as her creator, who was inhibited by "Milton's glory" when writing "A Drama of Exile," Aurora felt "Among the giant fossils of [her] past, / Like some small nimble mouse between the ribs / Of a mastadon" (1.836–38). Yet her turbulent response to poetry—"my soul, / At poetry's divine first finger-touch, / Let go conventions and sprang up surprised" (1.850–52)—presented an alternative to the female occupations privileged by her aunt. The latter included an education in a smattering of religion, languages, mathematics, geography, history; a "general insight into useful facts" (1.414); embroidery; and the reading of books that proved woman's "right of comprehending husband's talk," "their angelic reach / Of virtue," and their "potential faculty in everything / Of abdicating power in it" (1.431–40). Until she read poetry Aurora recalls,

> I only thought
> Of lying quiet there where I was thrown
> Like sea-weed on the rocks, and suffering her
> To prick me to a pattern with her pin,
> Fibre from fibre, delicate leaf from leaf,
> And dry out from my drowned anatomy
> The last sea-salt left in me.
>
> [1.378–84]

Under her aunt's tutelage, Aurora almost sank into female invalidism, until reading and writing of poetry averted it. Her "quickening inner life" (1.1027) so distressed her aunt that Aurora, projecting her rage onto "teas[ing] / The patient needle till it split the thread," learned deception as a strategy for survival while her "soul was singing at a work apart / Behind the wall of sense" (1.1049–54). Because her aunt had inculcated in her female duties, Aurora associated poetry with male activity.

Her early poems, like her creator's, were imitations:

> And so, like most young poets, in a flush
> Of individual life I poured myself
> Along the veins of others, and achieved
> Mere lifeless imitations of live verse.
>
> [1.971–74]

At twenty-seven Aurora reflects as a male poet on her early work, on the facile ease with which she wrote it, laughing at the young self who easily summoned the muse "As if we had seen her purple-braided head, / With the eyes in it, start between the boughs / As often as a stag's." She humorously recalls her "effete results / From virile efforts," her "cold wire-drawn odes," the "bucolics," and "didactics, driven / Against the heels of what the master said" (1.981–89). Whereas Aurora will come to admire most a poetry that is "unscrupulously epic" (5.214), she remembers the "counterfeiting epics" (1.990) of her youth, in much the same way as her creator recalled her "Battle of Marathon." As Barrett Browning wrote to Kenyon that her 1838 poems in comparison with her earlier work revealed the "difference . . . between a copy and an individuality" (L, 1:187–88), so Aurora knows:

> I wrote
> False poems, like the rest, and thought them true
> Because myself was true in writing them.
> I peradventure have writ true ones since
> With less complacence.
>
> [1.1023–27]

Romney's marriage proposal was the first assault on Aurora's youthful poetic "complacency" on her twentieth birthday. Ironically, his patronizing and dismissive attitude toward Aurora and her work functioned positively for her. Romney, spokesman of a culture, represented also by Robert Southey in his famous letter to Charlotte Brontë, insisted that Aurora accept the incompatibility between being woman and poet.[20] In fact, he confirmed Aurora in her determination to write, yet forced her to recognize she was a female poet, not a male one. She could not easily discard the "frustration" of the latter any more than her creator could, but the scene signifies her first awareness of her dilemma.

Aurora recreates the dialogue between the cousins, unmediated by her older self (2.74–497). Romney's refusal to read her poetry—as he explains, "I saw at once the thing had witchcraft in't, / Whereof the reading calls up dangerous spirits: / I rather bring it to the witch" (2.78–80)—presents woman and artist as irreconcilable opposites. His reassurance only emphasizes her deviance: "I have seen you not too much / Witch, scholar, poet, dreamer, and the rest, / To be a woman also" (2.85–87). To his urging her not to defile her "clean white morning dresses" (2.96), Aurora, however, asserts, "I choose to walk at all risks" (2.106). Barrett Browning, who once had not "dared to walk in [Milton's] footsteps" (W, 2:144), has her heroine striking out her own path and fearlessly walking in it. Romney insists that she realize she is female and therefore not a serious poet; as a poetess, she will receive the "comparative respect / Which means the absolute scorn" (2.235–36) of male critics, who will dismiss her work "not as mere work but as mere woman's work" (2.234) and praise her because "Among our female authors we make room / For this fair writer . . . / . . . competent to . . . spell" (2.240–43). The tone of Romney's comments echoes the critical timbre Barrett, "the fair Elizabeth," received, especially about *The Seraphim, and Other Poems*. Romney (the voice, as Gelpi interprets him, of Aurora's internalized critic[21]) forces Aurora into verbalizing the cultural conflict between being a woman and an artist:

> "You have read
> My soul, if not my book, and argue well

I would not condescend . . . we will not say
To such a kind of praise (a worthless end
Is praise of all kinds), but to such a use
Of holy art and golden life.

.   .   .   .

                    . . . I would rather dance
At fairs on tight-rope, till the babies dropped
Their gingerbread for joy,—than shift the types
For tolerable verse, intolerable
To men who act and suffer. Better far
Pursue a frivolous trade by serious means,
Than a sublime art frivolously."

[2.245–59]

Aurora measures herself by the standards of Art; Romney judges her a woman fit only to be one of the "doating mothers, and perfect wives, / Sublime Madonnas, and enduring saints" (2.222–23). If earlier, referring to Aurora as a "witch," he conjured up the monstrous image of woman represented in Aurora's mother's portrait, he now condemns her to the portrait's angelic aspects. These, Romney imagines, qualify her as wife, as co-worker in his utopian visions of social reform for the poor. Aurora acknowledges his work as worthy but rejects it for herself as his help-meet. In refusing Romney, she refuses the Biblical dictum, reinforced in *Paradise Lost*, that "He [was] for God only, she for God in him." Aurora's declaration is analogous to Jane Eyre's rejection of St. John Rivers:

                    "What you love
Is not a woman, Romney, but a cause:
You want a helpmate, not a mistress, sir,
A wife to help your ends,—in her no end."

[2.400–403]

Aurora recognizes Romney's desire for her as object of his life, not subject of her own. Romney, mistaking totally the thrust of her argument, taunts her with being so preoccupied with literature that she desires a literary lover, a sonneteer, who would address her elaborately:

> "Lady, thou art wondrous fair,
> And, where the Graces walk before, the Muse
> Will follow at the lightning of their eyes."
>
> [2.428–30]

He misses the irony that he is the one condemning Aurora to literary and cultural myths of woman. Aurora's answer to Romney speaks not just to him, but also to Tennyson's Prince, who at the end of "The Princess" insists on the complementarity of man and woman, and, indeed, to Mrs. Ellis, who condemns woman to be a "relative creature":

> "You misconceive the question like a man,
> Who sees a woman as the complement
> Of his sex merely. You forget too much
> That every creature, female as the male,
> Stands single in responsible act and thought
> As also in birth and death. Whoever says
> To a loyal woman, 'Love and work with me,'
> Will get fair answers if the work and love,
> Being good themselves, are good for her—the best
> She was born for."
>
> [2.434–43]

> "... But *me* your work
> Is not the best for, nor your love the best."
>
> [2.450–51]

> "I too have my vocation,—work to do."
>
> [2.455]

That women should have work of prime importance is as incomprehensible to Romney as to Aurora's aunt. Aurora echoes Carlyle's insistence on work, but applies it to women as well as men; and whereas Romney echoes Macaulay's and the utilitarians' concern with material needs, Aurora reflects the Victorian emphasis of Carlyle and Arnold, who insisted on feeding the spirit also. Once people are fed, Aurora asks, "What then, / Unless the artist keep up open roads / Betwixt the seen and unseen?" (2.467–69).

At twenty Aurora confidently rejected Romney to pursue her commitment as poet. However, when she was questioned by her aunt on Romney's sudden departure Aurora's submissiveness demonstrates how fragile that confidence was: "The lion in me felt the keeper's voice / Through all its quivering dewlaps; I was quelled / Before her,—meekened to the child she knew" (2.561–63). Culturally Aurora was seen as "child," or potential wife, as she struggled to be poet, "lion." Reflecting on that day she faces Romney's objections and is ambivalent about her decision. As poet she cannot, she feels with some longing, be a "common woman." By refusing to be "child," or wife, she has rejected being

> happier, less known and less left alone,
> Perhaps a better woman after all,
> With chubby children hanging on my neck
> To keep me low and wise.
>
> [2.513–16]

In Lady Waldemar's words, Aurora records the cultural economy that creates this separation:

> "You stand outside,
> You artist women, of the common sex;
> You share not with us, and exceed us so
> Perhaps by what you're mulcted in, your hearts
> Being starved to make your heads: so run the old
> Traditions of you."
>
> [3.406–11]

Such a statement of her own psychic dilemma, voiced by one she loathes, reinforces Aurora's conflict; it is not, however, the monstrous woman who effects the reconciliation of "artist woman" and the "common sex" but the one whom Aurora imagines as angelic. Much of her autobiography records Marian Erle's life; to tell that life, however, Aurora uses different narrative techniques before and after leaving England. In England she emphasizes that the story is in her own language, not Marian's. Practically, this solves a narrative problem for Barrett Browning, allowing her to employ a diction close to her own rather than attempting—as Eliot, Dickens, and Gaskell did—a working-class speech alien to her protected middle-class experience; it also functions structurally in the book. Aurora records:

> We talked. She told me all her story out,
> Which I'll retell with fuller utterance,
> As coloured and confirmed in after times
> By others and herself too.
>
> [3.827–30]

> I tell her story and grow passionate.
> She, Marian, did not tell it so, but used
> Meek words that made no wonder of herself
> For being so sad a creature.
>
> [3.847–50]

> She told the tale with simple, rustic turns,—
> Strong leaps of meaning in her sudden eyes
> That took the gaps of any imperfect phrase
> Of the unschooled speaker: I have rather writ
> The thing I understood so, than the thing
> I heard so. And I cannot render right
> Her quick gesticulation, wild yet soft.
>
> [4.151–17]

Aurora acknowledges her embellishments of Marian's story: she gives it "fuller utterance," with a passion missing in Marian's version. She is sympathetic to the suffering in Marian's world: to how Marian's father "cursed his wife because, the pence being out, / She could not buy more drink. At which she turned / . . . and beat her baby in revenge / For her own broken heart" (3.867–70); to how Marian's mother wanted to prostitute her daughter to the squire: " 'He means to set you up, and comfort us' " (3.1057); to how Marian's friends turn to prostitution: " 'Poor Rose, . . . / I heard her laugh last night in Oxford Street' "; and to how the sempstresses must live:

> "we've used out many nights,
> And worn the yellow daylight into shreds
> Which flapped and shivered down our aching eyes
> Till night appeared more tolerable, just

That pretty ladies might look beautiful,
Who said at last . . . 'You're lazy in that house!
'You're slow in sending home the work,—I count
'I've waited nearly an hour for't.' "

[4.243–50]

But whereas Marian speaks "simple, rustic turns" with "imper-
fect phrase," Aurora writes not what Marian said but her interpretation of it. The alienation from Marian this implies is reflected in Aurora's subsequent self-reproach "I have been wrong"
(4.439), and her acknowledgement:

I had done a duty, in the visit paid
To Marian, and was ready otherwise
To give the witness of my presence and name
Whenever she should marry . . .
                                    . . . I felt
Tired, overworked.

[4.446–49, 457–58]

The result is a fiction, apparently empathic with the plight of the
poor, yet one that appropriates Marian to Aurora's own likeness:

She told me she was fortunate and calm
On such and such a season, sat and sewed,
With no one to break up her crystal thoughts,
While rhymes from lovely poems span around
Their ringing circles of ecstatic tune,
Beneath the moistened finger of the Hour.

[3.1015–20]

This echoes Aurora's own solace during her adolescent hours of
sewing with her aunt. Aurora's middle-class fiction allows her,
like Romney, to feel charity toward a poor sufferer while scorning her class. Such scorn informs her attitude to the poor who
came to Marian's wedding:

They clogged the streets, they oozed into the church
In a dark slow stream, like blood.

[4.553–54]

> Those, faces? 'twas as if you had stirred up hell
> To heave its lowest dreg-fiends uppermost
> In fiery swirls of slime.
>
> [4.587–89]

Aurora finds a kinship with Marian as a woman, even though they are divided so crudely along class lines. When Romney preaches of his "common love" for the "loveless many," Aurora records:

> I turned
> And kissed poor Marian, out of discontent.
> The man had baffled, chafed me, till I flung
> For refuge to the woman
>
> .   .   .   .   .   .
>
> She, at least,
> Was not built up as walls are, brick by brick,
> Each fancy squared, each feeling ranged by line.
>
> [4.346–54]

Aurora's frustration with the system of man allows her to identify with a woman of a different class for a brief "refuge," which is prophetic of her later meeting with Marian in Paris.

What is radical about this fiction, however, even at this stage of Aurora's development, is the inclusion of Marian as a major character in her epic autobiography. Although Aurora objectifies Marian, as Romney does (and as Dante Gabriel Rosetti objectifies the prostitute in "Jenny"), her record of her is a powerfully ironic juxtaposition to Romney's patronizing praise,

> "You, at least,
> Have ruined no one through your dreams. Instead,
> You've helped the facile youth to live youth's day
> With innocent distraction."
>
> [4.1114–17]

Although Romney no longer labels her "witch," he condemns her as a poetess in his summary of her work as an "innocent distraction" and with his injunction, "Dear, be happy. Sing your songs, / If that's your way" (4.1202–4). Writing her "better self," Aurora's task is to make clear the difference between her "song" and that expected of the poetesses, and to refuse to be hampered by "this vile woman's way" of caring more for one man's (Romney's) approval, than for "Art's pure temple" (5.59–62). This task informs Aurora's review both of her career as poet and of poetics in the pivotal fifth book.

Like her creator, Aurora has written successful ballads, but found them too confining. She has written pastorals that failed because they were not "humanised" (5.95). And certainly Barrett Browning must have been referring to her own medieval ballads when Aurora rejects the poet who "trundles back his soul five hundred years" (5.191). She rejects all the forms that the poetesses were allowed, thus privileging the masculine epic. The epic contains the age; it does not restrict the writer to a brief lyric "song." *Aurora Leigh*'s blank verse ties it to *Paradise Lost*; and like *The Prelude* it treats the growth of a poet's mind. And yet, as if naming her own autobiographical poem, Aurora declares that a poet should be "unscrupulously epic" and appropriate the form to her own uses:

> Trust the spirit,
> As sovran nature does, to make the form;
> For otherwise we only imprison spirit
> And not embody.
>
> [5.224–27]

She insists on the heroic in the ordinary, as did the Victorian novelists, which was at variance with much of Victorian poetic practice, which preferred classical or medieval heroes—or even the bishops, dukes, and intellectuals of Browning's work. And yet, though her book was wrung from her "life-blood" (5.356), Aurora is dissatisfied with her art. She feels its passion, yet: "There's more than passion goes to make a man / Or book, which is a man too" (5.398–99).

Aurora's use of "man" to describe herself as poet is both conventional and literal. Although she is a professional, something eludes her as a poet. She does not name this lack, but in essence describes it as she muses on herself as an artist:

> I am sad.
> I wonder if Pygmalion had these doubts

And, feeling the hard marble first relent,
Grow supple to the straining of his arms,
And tingle through its cold to his burning lip,
Supposed his senses mocked, supposed the toil
Of stretching past the known and seen to reach
The archetypal Beauty out of sight,
Had made his heart beat fast enough for two,
And with his own life dazed and blinded him!
Not so; Pygmalion loved,—and whoso loves
Believes the impossible.
                              But I am sad:
I cannot thoroughly love a work of mine,
Since none seems worthy of my thought and hope
More highly mated. He has shot them down,
My Phoebus Apollo, soul within my soul,
Who judges, by the attempted, what's attained,
And with the silver arrow from his height
Has struck down all my works before my face
While I said nothing. Is there aught to say?
I called the artist but a greatened man.
He may be childless also, like a man.

                                        [5.399–420]

Aurora identifies herself—as she must as creator—with Pygmalion, not Galatea. It is a significant choice of model; Pygmalion typifies the artist who creates woman according to his gaze, not her reality. Aurora, oblivious to this irony, claims that the difference between herself and Pygmalion as artists is due, not to gender, but to the fact that "Pygmalion loved," which allowed him to "believe the impossible." She, however, "cannot love a work of mine." Galatea proved a fertile muse for Pygmalion; whereas Aurora's muse, Phoebus Apollo, "soul within my soul, / . . . Has struck down all [her] works before [her] face." Her adoption of a male muse should indicate that she imagines herself a female poet. Yet her effort is fruitless, confirming the psychic contortions Aurora must undergo to imagine herself as a poet at all: "I called the artist but a greatened man. / He may be childless also, like a man." Pygmalion was a "greatened man"; she is "childless, like a man." Her identification as a poet has much to do

with gender; while the analogy between labor and the creation of
Art is a convention, Aurora imagines the poet here as specifically
male, deprived of the reproductive capacities that differentiate
him from the female. Her feeling "I am sad," if connected with
her childlessness, indicates her alienation from the procreative
potential that defines her sex. It suggests both Aurora's desire to
identify herself as a woman and the barrenness of not doing so.
Through her close contact with the procreative role of woman
enacted by Marian Erle in the second half of her story, Aurora
finally claims her female identity.

Although she cannot yet realize herself as a woman, Aurora
understands that love and passion are the price she has paid for
being an artist:

> How dreary 'tis for women to sit still,
> On winter nights by solitary fires,
> And hear the nations praising them far off,
> Too far! ay, praising our quick sense of love,
> Our very heart of passionate womanhood,
> Which could not beat so in the verse without
> Being present also in the unkissed lips
> And eyes undried because there's none to ask
> The reason they grew moist.
>
> [5.439–47]

Aurora writes here almost as a poetess, yet the epic context ele-
vates the "affections" described. Aurora recognizes the irony in
men's praising women for the "very heart of passionate womanhood" that imbues their "verse" while paradoxically condemning women artists not to feel it in their lives. That lovers respond
to the passion in her work while she sits alone leads her to admit
she's "hungry" (5.488–90). Her "mother-want" is transformed
into hunger for the "love of one" (5.481) rather than for the gen-
eralized love of all. Although she cannot name Romney, she both
muses on Pygmalion's love and envies her male contemporaries,
not for "native gifts or popular applause" (5.517) but for "a girl
. . . with brown eyes" (5.521–22)—a mother or a wife who sup-
ports them in their work. Aurora associates her doubts about her
work with her inability to give and take as the male poets, with
whom she aesthetically identifies, can from their mistresses or

wives. Prefiguring her union with Romney, Aurora here glimpses the fact that love is essential for art.

Yet publicly she can, on the very evening she begins writing her "better self," say to Lord Howe at his party:

> "you shall not speak
> To a printing woman who has lost her place
> (The sweet safe corner of the household fire
> Behind the heads of children), compliments,
> As if she were a woman. We who have clipt
> The curls before our eyes may see at least
> As plain as men do. Speak out, man to man."
>
> [5.806–11]

But in private afterwards she finds the separation of poet from woman intolerable. Whereas metaphorically she described herself as one who "clipt the curls before [her] eyes" like a man, she records:

> And I breathe large at home. I drop my cloak,
> Unclasp my girdle, loose the band that ties
> My hair . . . now could I but unloose my soul!
> We are sepulchred alive in this close world,
> And want more room.
>
> [5.1037–41]

Aurora can release the symbol of her womanhood, her hair, and reveal the female body within the clasping "girdle," but cannot fully inhabit her femaleness, her soul. Such denial feels like death, as surely as it did for the nun in "The Lay of the Brown Rosary"; Aurora feels "sepulchred alive," imprisoned. However, the hair she has loosened, even when she keeps her soul imprisoned, assumes the strength of Aurora's own repressed passions as she dwells on the prospective marriage of Romney and Lady Waldemar, "a woman still" (5.1124):

> My loose long hair began to burn and creep,
> Alive to the very ends, about my knees:
> I swept it backward as the wind sweeps flame,
> With the passion of my hands
>
> .   .   .   .

> ... made a knot as hard as life
> Of those loose, soft, impracticable curls.
>
> [5.1126-34]

The dramatic image of Aurora's "loose long hair . . . alive to the very ends," which Aurora must with "passion" repress into a "knot as hard as life," represents Aurora's passionate female life and its sublimation into masculinity. The force of the repression threatens to overwhelm her; imprisonment becomes unbearable.

Aurora finally acts on her need for "more room" to loose her soul from being "sepulchred alive." Her decision to leave England is as significant as Barrett Browning's own. Her raising money for her literal journey by selling both the "residue of [her] father's books" and also the manuscript (the writing of which liberated her from their influence), parallels Barrett Browning's transcendence of Milton's hold on her art and her rejection of her father's authority. Aurora is ready for her psychic journey, uniting poet and woman.

Whereas the first five books of *Aurora Leigh* were written at one time, the last four, written in Paris and Florence and spanning a three-year period, were written in several sittings. The second part is divided into Aurora's first sight of Marian in Paris (6.1-389); her discovery of Marian and their conversation (6.390-7.374); and their journey to Italy and Aurora's final reunion with Romney (7.375-9.964). Aurora comments on the journal style of this second half, "I have written day by day" (9.725).

In Paris, Aurora reveals she is initially in the sway of conventional patriarchal ideology. When she first glimpses Marian, she cannot acknowledge that Marian is holding a child: "The arms of that same Marian clasped a thing / . . . I cannot name it now for what it was" (6.344-46). She enacts both female silence about the reality of women's lives and also patriarchal horror at the "fallen woman," translating "stolen" sexual pleasure into the language of actual thievery:

> A child. Small business has a castaway
> Like Marian with that crown of prosperous wives
> At which the gentlest she grows arrogant
> And says "My child." Who finds an emerald ring
> On a beggar's middle finger and requires

> More testimony to convict a thief?
> A child's too costly for so mere a wretch;
> She filched it somewhere.
>
> [6.347–54]

Aurora dismisses Marian as "damned" (6.366), then catches herself: "Stop there: I go too fast; / I'm cruel like the rest" (6.366–67). Instead of stereotyping Marian, she imagines another explanation for the child—it is a neighbor's. Although Aurora is still incapable of accepting the child as Marian's, such questioning of her own responses determines her to find Marian, "And save her, if she will or will not—child / Or no child,—if a child, then one to save!" (6.388–89).

The transformation from imagining the child as a "thing" to determining to help both mother and child is Aurora's first altruistic move. Until this point, survival for her in a society that demanded woman's self-abnegation necessitated Aurora's absorption in her own affairs. But, as for many other Victorian characters, human maturity depends on what Maggie in *The Mill on the Floss* names the "abandonment of egoism"; indeed, even Pip in *Great Expectations* learns the importance of such abandonment if he is to render others intelligible to his own mind. Aurora's growth into a harmonious selfhood is achieved through love as well as art, and through a compassionate sympathy for Marian's situation on Marian's terms, not according to convention. Marian is the instrument of this transformation.[22]

When Marian told her story to Aurora in London, it was unthreatening; indeed it reinforced middle-class ideology about the working-class and evoked middle-class charity. But Marian's story in Paris, unlike her earlier London tale, directly assaults Aurora's values: she refuses to be defined by Aurora's middle-class ideology and language. Instead of a narrative "coloured . . . in after times" (3.829) and told more according to the "thing [she] understood so, than the thing [she] heard so" (4.155–56), Aurora records a story in which Marian insists on her version, refusing to "scrupulously hint / With half-words, delicate reserves, the thing / Which no one scrupled [she] should feel in full" (6.1222–23). The narrative technique is quite different from Aurora's earlier fiction objectifying Marian; in Paris Aurora records the dialogue whereby she first learns to articulate the subjectivity of female experience. Such dialogue is still suspiciously middle-class, underlining the fact that Marian's function is still to be absorbed into and exploited by Aurora's middle-class story, not dramatized as exemplifying the dilemmas of the poor.

When Aurora finds Marian in Paris, she is initially shocked at the ease with which Marian refers to her past and to Romney, and she asserts with patriarchal reticence: " 'Therefore come,' / I answered with authority.—'I think / We dare to speak such things and name such names / In the open squares of Paris!' " (6.475–78). The ambiguity here, as to whether "We dare to speak" represents a new freedom or a reprimand against Marian's assumption of such freedom, is resolved by Marian's silently accompanying Aurora in response. The affairs of women's lives are for the domestic interior, not for the "open squares," suggesting that Aurora endorses a prohibition against such naming in the "open squares" of poetry.

Silent at first, Marian "followed closely" where Aurora "went, / As if [she] led her by a narrow plank / Across devouring waters, step by step" (6.481–83), until she had to return to her child, necessitating that Aurora give up her authority and follow. She submitted to Marian's lead, and, whereas earlier Marian crossed the treacherous "devouring waters" into her domain, Aurora now experienced an equal threat to her own psychic structures:

> Then she led
> The way, and I, as by a narrow plank
> Across devouring waters, followed her,
> Stepping by her footsteps, breathing by her breath,
> And holding her with eyes that would not slip.
> [6.500–504]

Aurora's "breathing by [Marian's] breath" moves her from the circumscribed world of the "printing woman," who dared not speak of woman's experience except as "coloured" by the teller, into the subjectivity of Marian's world, that of the "common woman." A gulf initially separates the two women. Crossing that gulf has already proved treacherous for Marian, exploited by the middle-class world as an experiment, and it threatens Aurora now with loss of autonomy. She has hitherto resisted following

anyone's lead: outwardly she acquiesced in her aunt's upbringing,
while inwardly resisting; and, sensing the danger Romney posed
to her autonomy, she refused his proffered authority.

Aurora's emotions stir, watching the "extremity of love" (6.600)
between Marian and her son. Yet she still evokes patriarchal
morality about the "fallen woman" when, "trying to be cold"
(6.612), she suppresses her enjoyment of the mutual smiles between mother and child. Unless a mother be pure, she insists:

> "I would rather lay my hand,
> Were I she, on God's brazen altar-bars
> Red-hot with burning sacrificial lambs,
> Than touch the sacred curls of such a child."
>
> [6.620–23]

Marian, "plung[ing] her fingers in his clustering locks" and
speaking with "indrawn steady utterance," reproaches Aurora for
her piety, which cannot "find grace enough for pity and gentle
words" (6.624–30). Aurora insists in a "grave and sad" voice on
Marian's impiety in stealing the child; Marian is "no mother,
but a kidnapper," who will deprive her child of a "pure home,"
"pure heart," "pure good mother's name and memory" (6.631–
41). Whereas Aurora summons the pious platitudes of middle-
class religion to judge Marian, the latter responds with quite a
different social analysis. Comparing herself to "any glad proud
mother" with her "church-ring" who might evoke the law to
judge her, Marian declares:

> "I talk of law! I claim my mother-dues
> By law,—the law which now is paramount,—
> The common law, by which the poor and weak
> Are trodden underfoot by vicious men,
> And loathed for ever after by the good."
>
> [6.665–69]

When Aurora insists she "filched" her child, Marian rejects being blamed as victim:

> "What, what, . . . being beaten down
> By hoofs of maddened oxen into a ditch,
> Half-dead, whole mangled, when a girl at last

Breathes, sees . . . and finds there, bedded in her flesh
Because of the extremity of the shock,
Some coin of price! . . . and when a good man comes
(That's God! the best men are not quite as good)
And says 'I dropped the coin there: take it you,
And keep it,—it shall pay you for loss,'—
You all put up your finger—'See the thief!
'Observe what precious thing she has come to filch.
'How bad those girls are!' "

[6.676–87]

The very God whom Aurora imagines as judge Marian sees as
compensating her with the child for the brutality she has suffered. "Angry with the world," she turns Aurora's argument up-
side down to reveal its empty rhetoric:

"Ah, ah! he laughs! he likes me. Ah, Miss Leigh,
You're great and pure; but were you purer still,—
As if you had walked, we'll say, no otherwhere
Than up and down the New Jerusalem,

.   .   .   .

. . . the child would keep to *me*,
Would choose his poor lost Marian, like me best."

[6.710–18]

Aurora adamantly persists in her disapproval; yet her anger is
directed not at Marian, but at her own empathy with the young
victimized mother. Believing "a child was given to sanctify /
A woman" (6.728–29), she reproaches Marian for turning her
"faults" into "easy virtues." Marian, "with most despairing wonder," questions:

"What have you in your souls against me then,
All of you? am I wicked, do you think?
God knows me, trusts me with the child; but you,
You think me really wicked?"

[6.739–42]

When Aurora accuses her of being "complaisant," of committing
a "wrong" for "certain profits" from a seducer, Marian seems to
share her middle-class rhetoric and ideology when she claims she

had "chaste pulses" because she was not sexually willing, not "fouled in will / And paltered with in soul by devil's lust" (6.761–62), but was rather a victim of "man's violence" (6.1226). However, she rejects such a sexual economy:

> "What, 'seduced' 's your word!
> Do wolves seduce a wandering fawn in France?
> Do eagles, who have pinched a lamb with claws,
> Seduce it into carrion? So with me.
> I was not ever, as you say, seduced,
> But simply, murdered."
>
> [6.766–71]

Although she shares Aurora's horror at unlawful sexual complicity, she educates Aurora to the fact that often the "fallen woman" was not complicitous in her "fall" but a brutalized victim. She places the blame where it belongs, on men, rather than on its traditional recipients, women.

Marian speaks of female experience in a way quite new to Aurora. Her narrative disrupts Aurora's patriarchal discourse and transforms woman from scorned object to angry subject. Aurora is thereby empowered to identify herself as female:

> But I, convicted, broken utterly,
> With woman's passion clung about her waist
> And kissed her hair and eyes,—"I have been wrong,
> Sweet Marian."
>
> [6.778–81]

Her old attitudes "broken utterly," Aurora experiences her "woman's passion." She allows herself the physical expression of feelings suppressed since she first met her aunt and "clung about her neck," only to receive in return a kiss from "cold lips" before "with some strange spasm / Of pain and passion, she wrung loose my hands / Imperiously, and held me at arm's length" (1.314–26). She acts both as child again as she clings about Marian's waist and also as adult as she kisses her hair and eyes. Romney's criticisms and corrections had only served to harden Aurora's resolve to "walk at all risks," whereas Marian's serve to reunite Aurora with her repressed womanhood. However, her language and images are inappropriate for these new values: she switches from calling Marian harlot to identifying her as "Sweet holy Marian" (6.782). Earlier Marian refused to allow Aurora's patriarchal rhetoric to describe her experience as "fallen woman"; now she resists its cult of true womanhood. Aurora proclaims Marian "innocent" (6.785); Marian vehemently insists Aurora face the truth:

> that world of yours has dealt with me
> As when the hard sea bites and chews a stone
> And changes the first form of it. I've marked
> A shore of pebbles bitten to one shape
> From all the various life of madrapores;
> And so, that little stone, called Marian Erle,
> Picked up and dropped by you and another friend,
> Was ground and tortured by the incessant sea
> And bruised from what she was,—changed! death's a change,
> And she, I said, was murdered; Marian's dead.
>
> [6.804–13]

Aurora, complicitous in Romney's experiment, denied her affinity with the "common woman," and betrayed her.

Although Aurora still cannot unite her heart and speech, she does offer Marian practical help, a home for her and the child in Italy:

> "I am lonely in the world,
> And thou art lonely, and the child is half
> An orphan. Come,—and henceforth thou and I
> Being still together will not miss a friend,
> Nor he a father, since two mothers shall
> Make that up to him."
>
> [7.120–25]

Aurora provides for the mother and child; although no longer an artist "childless like a man," she does not imagine herself as "father" but assumes a mother's role. She thereby confirms her new role as a poet: to include the joyful and painful subjectivity of women's lives in her work. Although she can juxtapose Marian's language with her own platitudes, Aurora is still dependent on the fictions of the latter: "in my Tuscan home I'll find a niche / And set thee there, my saint, the child and thee" (7.126–

27). Aurora imagines Marian as a Madonna figure, but by including Marian's version of her experience in her autobiography, Aurora demonstrates the fallacy of such fictions, even while not fully able to reject them. Most important, she demonstrates that the reality of women's lives should be the subject matter of poetry.

Barrett Browning effects the transformation of woman as object into woman as subject via the stories of women who, like the runaway slave and Marian Erle, are outside the linguistic, social, and political systems typified by middle-class white men. Whereas Aurora, a middle-class woman, could assume a male identity as a poet, the slave and Marian are bound by their biological destiny. Through the stories of such marginal women Barrett Browning and her creation, Aurora Leigh, identify with the female voice essential to their true maturation. Although Barrett Browning is unusual among high Victorian poets in her concern for slavery and the working-class woman, there are ideological ramifications in such a gesture. In "using" under-class women— as the runaway slave and Marian Erle—to effect her own transformation into subjectivity, Barrett Browning exploits as well as dramatizes such women, who then disappear from the poems.

She was not, however, purely exploitative, as she reveals to Thackeray:

> I am not a "fast woman." I don't like coarse subjects, or the coarse treatment of any subject. But I am deeply convinced that the corruption of our society requires not shut doors and windows, but light and air: and that it is exactly because pure and prosperous women choose to *ignore* vice, that miserable women suffer wrong by it everywhere. Has paterfamilias, with his Oriental traditions and veiled female faces, very successfully dealt with a certain class of evil? What if materfamilias, with her quick sure instincts and honest innocent eyes, do [*sic*] more towards their expulsion by simply looking at them and calling them by their names? [*L*, 2:445]

It is analogous to, but with a quite different moral emphasis from, Wordsworth's focus on ordinary people.

Aurora records how she was powerfully moved by her "woman's passion" when Marian named the wrong she suffered; yet identifying herself as a woman is difficult and troubling for her:

> My head aches,
> I cannot see my road along this dark;
> Nor can I creep and grope, as fits the dark,
> For these foot-catching robes of womanhood.
>
> [7.147–50]

The "robes of womanhood" had been a potent image for Aurora since Romney first warned her that writing poetry "defiles / The clean white morning dresses" (2.95–96), and she herself acknowledged:

> A woman's always younger than a man
> At equal years, because she is disallowed
> Maturing by the outdoor sun and air,
> And kept in long-clothes past the age to walk.
>
> [2.329–32]

Only after hearing Marian's story, however, does Aurora understand she cannot escape her sex, try as she will to clip the "curls before [her] eyes" (5.810). This realization releases her suppressed feelings as she thinks on Romney, "the man I love—I mean / The friend I love" (7.173–74). She allows herself for the first time the feelings of a "common woman," yet in terror quickly subverts them:

> Poor mixed rags
> Forsooth we're made of, like those other dolls
> That lean with pretty faces into fairs.
> It seems as if I had a man in me,
> Despising such a woman.
>
> [7.210–14]

While Aurora has, through Marian, felt her woman's passion, it still discomforts her. Hearing that Kate Ward wears a cloak modeled on her own—representing, as her friend Vincent Carrington, the artist, says, "How women can love women of your sort" (7.613)—Aurora muses, "Kate loves a worn-out cloak for being like mine, / While I live self-despised for being myself" (7.706–

7). Yet she also acknowledges, "I've a heart / That's capable of worship, love, and loss; / . . . I'll be meek / And learn to reverence, even this poor myself" (7.734–37). She admits, "I'm a woman, it is true; / Alas, and woe to us, when we feel it most!" (7.740–41). Feeling "it most" means experiencing love and passion, yet Aurora imagines that her rejection of Romney has forfeited such a possibility.

Leaving England, her father's land, allowed Aurora, through Marian, to realize her subjectivity. Her fame as a poet and her return to Italy, her mother's country, enables her to inhabit that subjectivity. As if to confirm this she visits the house where she had lived with her father: "I rode once to the little mountain-house / As fast as if to find my father there" (7.1119–20). But the house is changed, and Aurora leaves: "That was trial enough of graves" (7.1142–43). She cannot assume her old role of wearing her father's masculine "doublet." While such separation makes her feel like a "restless ghost" (7.1161), she also finds in it a new freedom. Through extolling the virtues of being out of England, she expresses also a confidence in the "better self," a female one, she is creating:

> I'm happy. It's sublime,
> This perfect solitude of foreign lands!
> To be, as if you had not been till then,
> And were then, simply that you choose to be.
>
> [7.1193–96]

> possess, yourself,
> A new world all alive with creatures new,
> New sun, new moon, new flowers, new people—ah,
> And be possessed by none of them!
>
> [7.1200–1203]

But she has no model for how to possess this "new world" and succumbs, as de Beauvoir describes the state, to the "delusion" of "play[ing] at being a woman." Obsessed with what she imagines to be the loss of Romney—"Romney, Romney! Well, / This grows absurd!—too like a tune that runs / I' the head" (7.959–61)—she watches women at church, praying in their sorrow. Identifying with them, she "drop[s her] head upon the pavement too, / And pray[s]" that God will not hear her words but "only listen to the run and beat / Of this poor, passionate, helpless blood" (7.1266–71).

Being a "common woman" threatens to silence Aurora, enabling her only to feel, as Barrett Browning had once imagined Mary's feeling at the foot of the cross, "with a spasm, not a speech." And indeed, she sinks into passivity when "ended seemed [her] trade of verse":

> I did not write, nor read, nor even think,
> But sat absorbed amid the quickening glooms,
> Most like some passive broken lump of salt
> Dropped in by chance to a bowl of oenomel,
> To spoil the drink a little and lose itself,
> Dissolving slowly, slowly, until lost.
>
> [7.1306–11]

In terms reminiscent of her description of suffering her aunt to "dry out from [her] drowned anatomy / The last sea-salt left in [her]" (1.383–84), she now imagines herself passive, broken, bitter, and "lost." Her only models for being female are the women she has read about, her mother's picture, her aunt, her view of the monstrous Lady Waldemar and the saintly Marian, those of her readers like Kate Ward who look to her as their model, and the suffering women she sees in Italian churches.

If the end of Book 7 dissolves the "faulty artist," then the last two books create the "true poet."[23] Aurora wavered earlier between imagining herself as male or female. Now she falters between her cultural engendering and her subjectivity. In her creation of a "better self" who can "exhibit all the peculiar powers without the negations of her sex,"[24] she redefines woman by uniting the expression of her intellectual powers with the realization of "the very heart of passionate womanhood" (5.443).

The first sign that Aurora will rescue herself from the "delusion" of "play[ing] at being a woman" is her filling the "quickening glooms" with the fantasy of a mythic sea-king:

> Gradually
> The purple and transparent shadows slow
> Had filled up the whole valley to the brim,

> And flooded all the city, which you saw
> As some drowned city in some enchanted sea,
> Cut off from nature,—drawing you who gaze,
> With passionate desire, to leap and plunge
> And find a sea-king with a voice of waves,
> And treacherous soft eyes, and slippery locks
> You cannot kiss but you shall bring away
> Their salt upon your lips.
>
> [8.34–44]

Appropriately, Aurora finally activates her imagination both by hearing Marian laugh as she plays with her son (passionate womanhood) and also by reading (intellectual endeavor). Aurora has a "book upon [her] knees to counterfeit / The reading that [she] never read at all" (8.3–4). Marian's laugh startles her out of the "drowsy silence" so that she finally reads her book, "Boccacio's tale, / The Falcon's, of the lover who for love / Destroyed the best that loved him" (8.21–23).[25] Identifying with the protagonist, Frederigo, who killed his favorite falcon to feed his mistress, Aurora implies—by saying, "Some of us / Do it still" (8.23–24)—that she has destroyed the best part of herself, "my trade of verse," in her love for Romney. Aurora's response to Marian's laugh and Boccaccio's tale is to transform herself from a "passive broken lump of salt" into a poet: the "salt" on her lips expresses the subjectivity of her desire in imagining the male, the "sea-king," as object of her passion.

When Romney appears—almost as a physical manifestation of her imagined sea-king—Aurora (ignorant of his blindness) believes he is married to Lady Waldemar. She recognizes her love for Romney yet simultaneously accepts that she has lost him. In a lengthy discussion (8.309–1090) the cousins address the issues they first raised ten years previously on Aurora's twentieth birthday. Romney, impressed by Aurora's mature poetry, accepts now the status of object that men must necessarily have in woman's vision. Endowing her with the God-like power of the creator, he feels Aurora rightly "turned [him] from the garden" because of his arrogance:

> "*I* should push
> Aside, with male ferocious impudence,

The world's Aurora who had conned her part
On the other side the leaf! ignore her so,
Because she was a woman and a queen,
And had no beard to bristle through her song,
My teacher, who has taught me with a book."

[8.327–33]

The power of Aurora's poetry has convinced him that there is "the other side the leaf" from his. Previously, when Aurora crowned herself a poet, his gaze transfixed her to stone: now he understands how egocentric his vision was: "certainly / I stood myself there worthier of contempt, / Self-rated, in disastrous arrogance" (8.695–97). His arrogance toward Aurora was matched by his arrogance toward the world's poor, "one great famishing carnivorous mouth,— / A huge, deserted, callow, blind bird Thing" (8.396–97) whom only he could save. When the poor reject his methods, he understands the fallacy of his beliefs. He tells Aurora, "I yield, you have conquered" (8.470–71). In light of Aurora's later humbling of herself before Romney in a show of love and self-abnegation, Romney's self-derogation is crucial. As Romney will later say to her, so Aurora replies, "I am not so high indeed, / That I can bear to have you at my foot" (8.486–87).

Aurora's apparent self-debasement before Romney in her final declaration of love concerns critics, who refer to it as the poem's "conventional happy ending," "the self-abnegating servitude with which Aurora Leigh concludes," and the "perfection of self-sacrifice" that Aurora enacts to cope with the "guilt of self-centered ambition."[26] And indeed Aurora's declaration is disturbing as she begs Romney, "stoop so low to take my love / And use it roughly, without stint or spare" (9.674–75). It is, however, a logical stage in her maturation, and it parallels a similar one in Barrett Browning's life, recorded in the Sonnets from the Portuguese when the speaker queries, "How, dearest, wilt thou have me for most use?" (17). Indeed the very "competition" between Aurora and Romney as to who should sit at whose feet evokes the early correspondence between Barrett and Browning, each vying for position of humblest lover and weakest poet. It is also a persuasive stage within the terms set by the poem, Aurora Leigh. Aurora can confidently assert, "I'm an artist, sir, / And woman" (8.826–27), and outline her poetics by saying, "I'm plain at speech, direct in purpose" and "I use the woman's figures naturally" (8.1127, 1131). Yet her only model for a woman's experience of love is the self-abnegating one dictated by her culture. (Such an objectification Aurora saw at its extreme in Marian's experience, for all the subjectivity with which Marian insisted on in narrating it.) Romney's refusal to allow Aurora to objectify herself enables her to reject the "delusion" of this "play at being a woman." To be fully a woman does not necessitate rejecting the role of artist, but redefining it. On her twentieth birthday Aurora felt herself incomplete as both "Woman and artist" (2.2); her determination was to "complete" herself. By thirty she recognizes that she can only complete herself as artist by realizing herself as woman:

> Passioned to exalt
> The artist's instinct in me at the cost
> Of putting down the woman's, I forgot
> No perfect artist is developed here
> From any imperfect woman.
>
> [9.645–49]

What her long story, from her description of her mother's portrait to her declaration of love for Romney, has taught her is that in her very attempt to define herself as an artist, following the "high necessities of Art" (9.643), she violated her fundamental nature. To be fully a "common woman" is to own fully her passionate nature. As an artist she must fully own that nature to be a "true poet."

Aurora's final freedom is initiated when she hears that her ancestral home, inherited and lived in by Romney, burned to "a great charred circle, where / The patient earth was singed an acre round" (8.1032–33). Blinded subsequently by the shock, Romney is "turned out of nature," "a man, upon the outside of the earth" (9.564,71). Whereas Barrett in the Preface to *Poems of 1844* describes herself as an "exile," Aurora, with her father's and lover's house razed, records how the male is now exiled, on the "outside of the earth." He has become object. The final stage of Aurora's autobiography parallels her creator's. Romney's blindness means Aurora is no longer the object of his gaze, echoing Barrett's realization of her subjectivity in the *Sonnets* when her beloved's "divinest Art's / Own instrument didst drop down at [his] foot / To hearken what [she] said" (41).

In "The Poet's Vow," "A Vision of Poets," and "Lady Geraldine's Courtship" Barrett dramatized the convention of the female muse guiding the male poet. The enquiry into other possibilities for the figuration of poet and muse, begun at the end of "A Vision of Poets" and continued through *Casa Guidi Windows*, is consummated in *Aurora Leigh*.

Aurora's union with Romney, on a literal level a man with whom she can live as a sexual and intellectual equal, provides the book with its conventional happy ending. However, he functions symbolically as Aurora's muse, which transforms the conventional ending into a radical one. A male poet competes with the precursor father for the muse's favor; Aurora competed with the cultural definitions of woman, dramatized in the monstrous Lady Waldemar and the angelic Marian, for the favors of this male muse. Romney appears, therefore, to be the "composite precursor" exemplifying the dilemma Joanne Feit Diehl identifies as fundamental to the nineteenth-century woman poet: "For Rossetti and Browning as well as for Dickinson, the precursor becomes a composite male figure; finding themselves heirs to a long succession of fathers, these women share the vision of a father/lover that surpasses individuals. And so for them the composite father is the main adversary."[27] A male poet separates his precursor father from "the image of the fecund if idealized or distant muse" whom he may win from the father for himself. The nineteenth-century woman poet's dilemma is that her composite precursor and her muse are the same (male) figure. He always, therefore, retains the inhibiting power Milton's glory held over Barrett in "A Drama of Exile." Diehl identifies this problem for Barrett Browning in her reading of "A Musical Instrument" (*Last Poems*, 1862). Yet she acknowledges that Dickinson, Rossetti, and Barrett Browning do not "reveal identical pressures." Barrett Browning's work exemplifies an alternative to that engagement with the composite precursor which Diehl identifies as dominating Dickinson's work.

Unlike Dickinson, Barrett Browning approaches the dilemma by initially imagining a muse who is not such a precursor or father/lover. She identifies as muse one in the gender/power economy who bears a position analogous to the one the female muse holds in relation to the male poet. She imagines not a silent lover but an infant boy. Whereas the son was privileged over the mother in "Isobel's Child," after Barrett Browning's move from her father and England, she recasts that muse into one without such inhibiting power. Although the slave's son wants "the master-right" to become that inhibiting figure, his mother, burying him in the "dark earth," denies him that status, retaining the idealized relationship with him that male poets have with the muse, liberating her song. In *Casa Guidi Windows* the muse is initially an anonymous boy singing *"bella libertà."* However, Barrett Browning concludes the poem by evoking one to whom she has literally given birth—her son. Diehl claims that "for the male poet, the birth of a poem fulfills his maieutic impulse; he becomes both midwife and mother of his art"; Barrett Browning becomes midwife and mother to both her art and muse. The mother poet invites the muse infant, "Let me see thee more," and commands his total attention: "Now look straight before, / And fix thy brave blue English eyes on mine" (2.746–47). She thus summons the silent object of her desire to inspire her vision of the "new springs of life" (2.762).

In *Aurora Leigh* the figure of the muse changes. As demonstrated, Marian Erle is the agent of Aurora's transformation into subjectivity, thus evoking the earlier figure of George Sand's liberating the potential for her "woman's voice." However, Marian only gains that powerful function by virtue of her infant son. Her need to return to care for him necessitates Aurora's following Marian, "as by a narrow plank / Across devouring waters" (6.501–2). He is the silent object around whom the competing ideologies and discourses of Aurora and Marian whirl, until finally Aurora embraces her woman's passion. Aurora assumes the poet/mother role toward him; he "will not miss . . . a father, since two mothers shall / Make that up to him" (7.124–25).

Barrett Browning, therefore, imagines prior to the last book of *Aurora Leigh* a muse who is a silent other over whom she has power. The male poet separates the muse from the precursor, supplanting the father in her affections, reenacting thereby the oedipal struggle. Barrett Browning separates from the father/precursor by maintaining the privileged preoedipal affectional bond of mother and infant. Once that silent boy individuates into adult manhood, the danger is that he will assume the "master-right," become the composite precursor, and silence the woman poet with his inhibiting glory. It is this finally that Barrett Browning confronts in *Aurora Leigh*. Initially she rejects Romney who, disdaining her poetry, assumes the inhibiting role. She finds her woman's voice through the agency of Marian Erle and is confident of her maternal role in relation to the muse (a reversal of Wordsworth's throwing himself on nature's bosom). However, she rejects such gender/power arrangements as ultimately inadequate. The problematic nature of the ending—beyond its conventional narrative resolution—lies in the fact that when the blinded Romney becomes dependent on Aurora he will be as a young child, dependent on his mother. Yet in his blindness, evoking the new Jerusalem Aurora is to write, he is also the authoritative precursor—especially the blind Milton writing the old Eden. He is both infant son and father/lover, the muse both separate from and identified with the father. But when Leigh Hall burns he is exiled from that ancestral home. Although it is discomforting that he tells Aurora she is to write the new Jerusalem, his call for a poetics of how "the old world waits the time to be renewed" (9.942), for "new oeconomies, new laws, / Admitting freedom, new societies / Excluding falsehood" (9.947–49) echoes Thackeray's vision of "new laws, new manners, new politics, vast new expanses of liberties unknown as yet." Romney overrides the muse's conventional role and evokes a Biblical canonical text, but he also leaves to the woman poet's subjectivity the description of those "new societies," "vast new expanses of liberties unknown as yet." If Aurora does not write such a description, she does initiate a recentering of the sex/gender economy such that it can be written with woman as well as man as subject.

As I stated at the outset, Barrett Browning needs to be read on her own liberal humanist terms. As Marian Erle can only finally be conceived in middle-class rhetoric, so Aurora Leigh is limited by Barrett Browning's "traditional humanism [which is] part of patriarchal ideology."[28] Within that ideology, she resolves the dilemma of being woman and poet with a "Romantic rage" and a "discourse with a shattering revolutionary force."[29] Barrett

Browning rejects the composite precursor; finds a poetic authority in a maternal relation to the muse; embraces her woman's passion through her engagement with Marian Erle, on the latter's terms; and renegotiates her authority as poet in relation to Romney as father poet and lover within the gender and canonical terms of patriarchal discourse. Just as Shakespeare's muse in the sonnets, as Joseph Pequigney argues in *Such Is My Love*, was a young man, and Tennyson acknowledges Hallam as his muse in "In Memoriam" (103), so Barrett Browning confirms the multiple possibilities for the site of poetic authority and inspiration.

Once she is read on her own terms along with the three male high Victorian poets, then the more recent theoretical speculations about gender can be brought to bear on these four poets at this moment of literary history. Dorothy Dinnerstein, Nancy Chodorow, and the French theorists Julia Kristeva, Hélène Cixous, and Luce Irigaray privilege the preoedipal figuration between parent and infant over the triangular oedipal struggle. Barrett Browning's work suggests that this figuration may well also inform the construction of poet and muse, for both female and male poets.

CONCLUSION

When Barrett Browning wrote to Mrs. Martin about the reception of *Aurora Leigh*, she addressed the issue of "coarseness" that the reviewers had raised:

> [Y]ou will grant that I don't habitually dabble in the dirt; it's not the way of my mind or life. If, therefore, I move certain subjects in this work, it is because my conscience was first moved in me not to ignore them. What has given most offence in the book, more than the story of Marian—far more! —has been the reference to the condition of women in our cities, which a woman oughtn't to refer to, by any manner of means, says the conventional tradition. Now I have thought deeply otherwise. If a woman ignores these wrongs, then may women as a sex continue to suffer them; there is no help for any of us—let us be dumb and die. I have spoken therefore, and in speaking have used plain words . . . which, if blurred or softened, would imperil perhaps the force and righteousness of the moral influence. [*L*, 2:254]

To Anna Jameson, the art critic, she addressed herself to another issue raised by reviewers, namely the similarity between the endings of *Aurora Leigh* and *Jane Eyre*. She explained the difference; whereas Mr. Rochester was blinded by the fire,

> [I]f you read over again those pages of my poem, you will find that the only injury received by Romney in the fire was from a blow and from the emotion produced by the *circum-*

stances of the fire. Not only did he *not* lose his eyes in the fire, but he describes the ruin of his house as no blind man could. He was standing there, a spectator. Afterwards he had a fever, and the eyes, the visual nerve, perished, showing no external stain—perished as Milton's did. [*L*, 2:246]

In these two letters Barrett Browning engages the poetics that *Aurora Leigh* dramatized. Her task is to address the wrongs of women so that as a sex they do not "continue to suffer them." As a woman she must speak or be "dumb and die," like Margret, Rosalind, and the page. Her speech must be in "plain words" that do not disguise the truth. To realize this aesthetic Barrett Browning has to "tame" Milton. The direct analogy she makes between Romney and Milton suggests that Barrett Browning has finally made her peace with her precursor. *Aurora Leigh* thereby dramatizes those issues that Barrett Browning first addressed in the Preface of *Poems of 1844*. Eve will no longer suffer her "alloted grief" passively; women poets must speak out against it. Milton's glory can no longer inhibit Barrett Browning in her realization of this, because her vision has supplanted his. She enacts what she stated in *Casa Guidi Windows*: "We do not serve the dead . . . the past is past" (1.217). Aurora Leigh eats of the tree of knowledge and, while Romney rises as God's and Milton's specter to punish her, she refuses their prohibition and punishment: the "song" she sings with her assertive "I" is quite other than the "innocent distraction" to which Romney had earlier condemned her.

Aurora Leigh not only presents a new reading of *Paradise Lost* in Aurora's insistence on eating of the tree and on usurping the Adamic privilege of naming the world, but, in its treatment of the relationship between Aurora and Romney, it demonstrates how Barrett Browning empowered herself to do so: Milton/Romney (like Browning by the end of the *Sonnets*) becomes lover/muse, object of woman's passion and vision.

Barrett Browning's importance as a poet lies in this self-conscious demonstration of both the anxiety of influence and the anxiety of authorship as they affect a strong woman poet writing in a tradition which assumes that the poetic voice is male. *Aurora Leigh* provides a gloss for what Barrett Browning's previous work had shown. Initially the woman poet, like any young poet, must identify with her powerful precursors. This necessitates imagining herself as male, with woman as object of her vision. Eventually this "frustration" yields to a crisis in which she begins to identify herself as female, as she must in order truly to mature. Having no models for such a yoking of woman and poet, she responds by following the cultural models of woman that as a young poet she had rejected; she transforms herself into the object she has been delineating in her work. Saved from such total passivity by writing of self-abnegation even while fully imagining herself enacting it, she realizes her poetic maturity by embracing and recording her own subjectivity with man as object of her gaze.

Barrett Browning offers a paradigm for the study of women poets. The narrative of her work is an inevitable one for strong women poets as long as the male poetic voice is culturally privileged. For confirmation of this paradigm in the career of a contemporary American poet hear Adrienne Rich in "When We Dead Awaken":

> A lot is being said today about the influence that the myths and images of women have on all of us who are products of culture. I think it has been a peculiar confusion to the girl or woman who tries to write because she is peculiarly susceptible to language. She goes to poetry or fiction looking for *her* way of being in the world, since she too has been putting words and images together; she is looking eagerly for guides, maps, possibilities; and over and over in the "words' masculine persuasive force" of literature she comes up against something that negates everything she is about: she meets the image of Woman in books written by men. She finds a terror and a dream, she finds a beautiful pale face, she finds La Belle Dame Sans Merci, she finds Juliet or Tess or Salome, but precisely what she does not find is that absorbed, drudging, puzzled, sometimes inspired creature, herself, who sits at a desk trying to put words together. . . .
>
> I know that my style was formed first by male poets: by the men I was reading as an undergraduate—Frost, Dylan Thomas, Donne, Auden, MacNeice, Stevens, Yeats. . . .

I finished college, published my first book by a fluke, as it seemed. . . . by the time my [second] book came out I was already dissatisfied by those poems. . . .

About the time my third child was born, I felt that I had either to consider myself a failed woman and a failed poet, or try to find some synthesis by which to understand what was happening to me. . . .

In the late fifties I was able to write, for the first time, directly about experiencing myself as a woman. . . .

. . . The choice still seemed to be between "love"—womanly, maternal love, altruistic love—a love defined and ruled by the weight of the culture; and egotism—a force directed by men into creation, achievement, ambition, often at the expense of others. . . . We know now that the alternatives are false ones—that the word "love" is itself in need of revision.[1]

The parallels between Elizabeth Barrett Browning's career and Adrienne Rich's are illuminating, confirming, as Showalter says, how every generation of women writers finds itself without a history.[2] The parallels between Elizabeth Barrett Browning's career and Adrienne Rich's are tragic. Had the work of Barrett Browning, Christina Rossetti, Emily Dickinson, H. D., Edith Sitwell, alongside Frost, Dylan Thomas, Donne, Auden, MacNeice, Stevens, and Yeats, been a crucial part of the literary history to which the young Rich turned for "guides, maps, possibilities," maybe she would not have had to repeat the paradigm in her turn. Only by recognizing women poets' struggle to form the synthesis of woman and poet, to make woman and artist both complete, as a crucial and integral part of humanistic literary history, can we move beyond it.

NOTES

INTRODUCTION

1. Woolf, "Aurora Leigh," p. 183.

2. Rossetti, *Poetical Works*, pp. 460–61; Meynell, *Prose and Poetry*, p. 353.

3. Showalter, "Women's Time, Women's Space," p. 36.

4. Gardiner, "Mind Mother," p. 115.

5. Moi, *Sexual/Textual Politics*, p. 8.

6. Gardiner, "Mind Mother," p. 115.

7. Showalter, "Women's Time, Women's Space," p. 36

8. Barrett Browning, *Letters*, 2:254 (hereafter cited in the text as *L* followed by volume and page).

9. Gilbert, "From *Patria* to *Matria*," p. 200.

10. Feminist Studies of Barrett Browning's work are Julia Markus's introduction to *Casa Guidi Windows*; Alaya, "Brownings' Italy"; Cora Kaplan's introduction to Barrett Browning's *Aurora Leigh*; Gelpi, "Vocation of the Woman Poet"; Mermin, "Female Poet"; Blake, "Art versus Love," pp. 171–201; Rosenblum, "Face to Face"; Gilbert, "From *Patria* to *Matria*"; Auerbach, "Robert Browning's Last Word"; Rosenblum, "Visionary Aesthetic."
The following were published once this book was completed; they did not therefore contribute to my argument, but are valuable resources in the growing field of Barrett Browning studies: Mermin, "Barrett Browning's Stories"; David, " 'Art's a Service' "; Leighton, *Elizabeth Barrett Browning*; Friedman, "Gender and Genre Anxiety"; Blake, "Elizabeth Barrett Browning and Wordsworth."

11. See Eagleton, *Literary Theory*, pp. 11, 16; Froula, "When Eve Reads Milton," p. 322.

12. See Homans, *Women Writers and Poetic Identity*, chap. 1.

13. Although the term "poet" describes both men and women writers,

I use "poetesses" to refer to those women writers who, unlike Barrett Browning, Christina Rossetti, or Emily Dickinson, did not imagine themselves as centrally located within the mainstream of literary tradition. They saw themselves as confined to certain portrayals of women and constrained within a certain subject matter of the affections. Critics treated them differently from male poets. A discussion of their place and importance is documented in Hickok's *Representations of Women*. While I hesitate to use a term that can be interpreted as demeaning, it emphasizes the dual alienation Barrett felt as a serious woman poet—from both the male and female literary traditions available to her.

14. Barrett Browning, *Complete Works*, 2:143–44 (hereafter cited in the text as *W* followed by volume and page).

15. de Beauvoir, *The Second Sex*, p. 46. The idea of woman as "other" is graphically illustrated by Virginia Woolf in *The Years*, p. 361, where Peggy, a doctor, is talking to a male poet at a party:

Her attention wandered. She had heard it all before. I, I, I—he went on. It was like a vulture's beak pecking or a vacuum cleaner sucking, or a telephone bell ringing. I. I. I. But he couldn't help it. . . . He could not free himself. . . . He had to expose, had to exhibit. But why let him? she thought, as he went on talking. For what do I care about his "I, I, I"? Or his poetry? Let me shake him off then, she said to herself, feeling like a person whose blood has been sucked, leaving all the nerve-centres pale. She paused. He noted her lack of sympathy. He thought her stupid, she supposed.

"I'm tired," she apologized. "I've been up all night," she explained. "I'm a doctor—"

The fire went out of his face when she said "I." That's done it—now he'll go, she thought. He can't be "you"—he must be "I." She smiled. For up he got and off he went.

16. Mermin, Gelpi, Gilbert "From *Patria* to *Matria*," Auerbach, and Rosenblum have raised related questions in their discussion of specific poems. Suzanne Juhasz, author of *Naked and Fiery Forms* and *Undiscovered Continent* and editor of *Feminist Critics Read Emily Dickinson*; Diehl, *Dickinson and the Romantic Imagination*; and Homans, *Women Writers and Poetic Identity*, also query the woman poet's position in a literary tradition dominated by fathers and sons battling for a female muse.

17. For a discussion of the problems facing the woman poet see Gilbert and Gubar, "Woman Poet."

18. Notable exceptions were Pope, Keats, and Browning.

19. Annette Kolodny explores this issue in her reading of Charlotte Perkins Gilman's "The Yellow Wallpaper" and Susan Glaspell's "A Jury of Her Peers":

In both . . . the same point is being made: lacking familiarity with the women's imaginative universe, that universe within which their acts are signs, the men in these stories can neither read nor comprehend the meanings of the women closest to them—and this in spite of the apparent sharing of a common language. *It is, in short, a fictive rendering of the dilemma of the woman writer.* For, while we may all agree that, in our daily conversational exchanges, men and women speak more or less meaningfully and effectively with one another, thus fostering the illusion of a wholly shared language. . . . [symbolic] representations . . . depend on a fund of shared recognitions, and potential inference. For their intended impact *to take hold* in the reader's imagination, the author simply must . . . be able to call upon a shared context with her audience; where she cannot, or dare not, she may revert to silence, to the imitation of male forms, or, like the narrator in "The Yellow Wallpaper," to total withdrawal and isolation into madness. (Emphasis mine.)

Kolodny, "A Map for Rereading," p. 58.

20. Brontë, *Shirley*, p. 252.

21. See Moers, *Literary Women*, p. 84; Gilbert and Gubar, *Madwoman in the Attic*, chap. 6.

22. Thackeray, "De Juventute," in *Roundabout Papers* from *Works*, 20:62–63.

23. See Christ, *Finer Optic*, pp. 72, 93; Houghton and Stange, *Victorian Poetry and Poetics*, p. 163.

24. See, for example, Gilbert, "Soldier's Heart," pp. 422–50.

25. Kaplan, "Varieties of Feminist Criticism," p. 48.

26. I use the name Barrett (rather than her maiden name, Barrett Barrett) to refer to the poet before her marriage, and Barrett Browning to refer to her after it. If this proves confusing, it replicates the confusion that exists over the naming of women in Western culture.

27. Barrett Browning and Browning, *Letters of Robert Browning and Elizabeth Barrett Barrett*, 1:168–69, 196, 408 (hereafter cited as *RB&EBB* in the text followed by volume and page).

28. Julia Markus uses these terms, referring to the speaker of "Casa Guidi Windows," in her introduction to Barrett Browning, *Casa Guidi Windows*, p. xxx.

CHAPTER I

1. Wilson, "Christopher in His Cave," p. 279.

2. Barrett Browning, *Autobiography* (hereafter cited in the text as *A* followed by page).

3. Barrett Browning, *Diary*, p. xix (hereafter cited in the text as *D* followed by page).

4. Ellis, *Women of England*, pp. 149–50.

5. Watts, *Literary Souvenir*. Barrett's comments on the poems are in an unpublished pocket notebook in Wellesley College Library (from

Sotheby Lot 110—Barrett's pocket diary for 1823 and notebook for 1824–25).

6. *Examiner*, pp. 387–88; *Athenaeum*, pp. 466–68 (the reviewer was probably Henry Fothergill Chorley); Wilson, "Christopher in His Cave," pp. 279–84; *Quarterly Review*, pp. 382–89; *North American Review*, pp. 201–18 (George S. Hillard was probably the reviewer); Warburton, *English Review*, pp. 259–73. Reviews also ran in the *Sunbeam*, p. 243; *Metropolitan Magazine* (London), pp. 97–101; *Monthly Review*, pp. 125–30; *Monthly Chronicle* (London), p. 195; *Atlas*, p. 395; *Literary Gazette*, pp. 759–60; *Arcturus, A Journal of Books and Opinions* (U.S.), pp. 171–76.

7. For a discussion of how this was also true for women novelists see Showalter, *Literature of Their Own*, chap. 3.

8. Donaldson, "Motherhood's Advent in Power," pp. 52–53.

9. Woolf, "Professions for Women," pp. 237–38.

10. Hayter, *Mrs. Browning*, pp. 82–83.

11. Taplin, *Life of Elizabeth Barrett Browning*, p. 62.

12. This theme of the womanly woman dying is taken up twenty years later in *Aurora Leigh*, when Aurora's aunt who "liked a woman to be womanly" (1:443) educated Aurora to understand woman's "Potential faculty in everything/ Of abdicating power in it" (1:441), so that Aurora feels her aunt has "dried out from [Aurora's] drowned anatomy / The last sea-salt left in [her]" (1:383–84) such that visitors worry that "she will die" (1:498).

13. Margaret Homans delineates this scenario in her discussion of the difficulties confronting Dorothy Wordsworth, Emily Brontë, and Emily Dickinson as writers. Homans, *Women Writers and Poetic Identity*.

14. See Hayter, *Mrs. Browning*, p. 31:

The 1838 volume first started the charge, so often brought against her, of imitating Tennyson—in "The Romaunt of Margret" said the *Atlas*; in "Isobel's Child" said the *Quarterly*. "It always makes me a little savage when people talk of Tennysonianisms!" she told Browning. "I have faults enough as the Muses know,—but let them be *my* faults! When I wrote the 'Romaunt of Margret,' I had not read a line of Tennyson." . . . "Nearly everything in the 'Seraphim' was written before I ever read *one* of his then published volumes," she told Horne in 1844.

CHAPTER 2

1. Miller, *Robert Browning*, pp. 93–101.

2. Barrett Browning and Browning, *George Barrett*, Appendix 2, pp. 343–44.

3. Elaine Showalter's discussion, in *Literature of Their Own*, p. 268, about the onset of Woolf's madness in early adolescence illuminates

Barrett's "considerable debility," her mysterious sinking into a career of illness.

4. Quoted in Ehrenreich and English, " 'For Her Own Good,' " p. 90.

5.   I only thought
            Of lying quiet there where I was thrown
            Like sea-weed on the rocks, and suffering her
            To prick me to a pattern with her pin,
            Fibre from fibre, delicate leaf from leaf,
            And dry out from my drowned anatomy
            The last sea-salt left in me.
                                    [*Aurora Leigh*, 1:378–84]

6. Certainly Barrett's great admirer, Emily Dickinson, perceived her illness as a reaction rather than inherent sickness: "That Mrs. Browning fainted, we need not read *Aurora Leigh* to know, when she lived with her English aunt." Dickinson, *Letters*, 2:376.

7. Florence Nightingale, "Cassandra," in *Practical Deductions*, vol. 2, *Suggestions for Thoughts to Searchers after Religious Truth*, prepared for private printing in 1859. "Cassandra" was not published in Nightingale's lifetime. Its first widespread availability was as an appendix to Ray Strachey, *The Cause: A Short History of the Women's Movement in Great Britain* (London: G. Bell and Sons, 1928). It is now available as Florence Nightingale, *Cassandra* (New York: Feminist Press, 1979) from which page references are given here.

8. One reason Barrett hypothesized for her father's opposition to her wintering in Italy was that the previous time she had gone away, to Torquay, for her health, her favorite brother, Edward, had drowned in a boating accident. Barrett was consumed with grief and guilt; against her father's will, she had begged that Edward be allowed to stay with her in Torquay for company. While aware of her father's harshness in forbidding her to go away, she also appreciated some of his reservations: "He was generous & forbearing in that hour of bitter trial, & never reproached me as he might have done & as my own soul has not spared— never once said to me then or since, that if it had not been for *me*, the crown of his house wd not have fallen. . . . Nothing, except that I had paid my own price . . & that the price I paid was greater than his loss . . his!!" (*RB&EBB* 1:169, August 22, 1845).

9. For a similar identification of protector with jailer see Gilman, "The Yellow Wallpaper," pp. 317–34, in which the protagonist's doctor husband confines her, for her health, in an attic room, which eventually drives her crazy.

10. Woolf, "Aurora Leigh," p. 183.

11. See for example Donoghue, "Heart in Hiding," pp. 51–53, a review of Paddy Kitchen, *Gerard Manley Hopkins: A Biography*, in which he discusses the issue of the priesthood as a limiting factor in Hopkins' poetry: "Some poets, like Wallace Stevens, thrive on limitation; a little experience goes a long way with them, they could do nothing with the

freedom except lose themselves in it. Besides, experience is not circumstance, but what we make of circumstance."

12. See for example the history of this idea in relation to Jane Austen criticism in Dyson, *English Novel*, pp. 146–53.

13. Adams, *Westminster Review*, pp. 381–92. R. H. Horne in *New Spirit of the Age* writes of Barrett as "confined entirely to her own apartment, and almost hermetically sealed." (For Barrett's collaboration on some of the other articles in this book see *Life of Elizabeth Barrett Browning*, Taplin, pp. 116–17.)

14. Meynell, Introduction to *Prometheus Bound*, pp. x–xi.

15. Forman's paraphrase of Barrett's notes is in *A*, 1:xxxv.

16. This imperative is still active as reports of research show in Chesler, *Women and Madness*.

17. Gilbert and Gubar, *Madwoman in the Attic*.

18. Thomson, *George Sand and the Victorians*.

19. Ibid., p. 47.

20. See for example *Jane Eyre* or *Aurora Leigh* (1). See also Moers, *Literary Women*, p. 175.

21. It can be argued that Barrett is imagining a sexually democratic heaven, one where the earthly distinction between male and female becomes irrelevant, but one for which an earthly female is as fit as an earthly male. However, that the poem can only imagine such a possibility after death emphasizes the fact that Sand's and Barrett's focus is the questioning of religious and literary prescriptions for women on earth.

22. Edgar Allan Poe, *Broadway Journal*, p. 20.

CHAPTER 3

1. Warburton, *English Review*, p. 272; *Tait's Edinburgh Magazine*, p. 722; *Literary Examiner*, p. 628; Sarah Flower Adams, *Westminster Review*, p. 386.

2. *Athenaeum*, p. 763.

3. Barrett wrote of Keats: "I finished Keats's Lamia, Isabella, Eve of St. Agnes & Hyperion, before breakfast. The first three disapointed [*sic*] me. The extracts I had seen of them, were undeniably the finest things in them. But there is some surprising poetry—poetry of wonderful grandeur, in the Hyperion" (*D*, 93, August 18, 1831). To Browning she wrote: "but nobody who knew very deeply what poetry *is, could*, you know, draw any case against him. A poet of the senses, he may be & is, . . . but then it is of the senses idealized; & no dream in a 'store-room' wd ever be like the 'Eve of St. Agnes,' unless dreamed by some 'animosus infans,' like Keats himself" (*RB&EBB*, 1:187).

4. For a comparison of Barrett Browning's attitude toward sex and marriage with those of her male poet contemporaries see Johnson, in

Sex and Marriage, who discusses how Arnold, Tennyson, and Browning wrote about sexuality and marriage often with a frankness and complexity—if also a tact—that belie the twentieth-century view of them as "prudish."

5. Quoted in Hayter, *Mrs. Browning,* without source, p. 188.

6. Miles, *Eras and Modes,* p. 117. See also Kaplan, *Miracles of Rare Device,* p. 12: "The greatest achievements of Romantic poetry are in the short poem or in sections of the larger ones. . . . The dominant Romantic forms become the ode, the ballad, and the variable lyric."

7. At least one reviewer, however, seems to have missed this aspect of the ballads, preferring to see in them what he felt should be there: "Never were generosity, and self-sacrifice, and loyalty so perpetually chosen for themes as now—rarely have they been more nobly illustrated." *New Quarterly Review* 5 (1845): 93.

8. Taplin, *Life of Elizabeth Barrett Browning,* p. 64.

9. See, for example, Viola and Orsino in *Twelfth Night,* Rosalind and Orlando in *As You Like It,* and Portia and Bassanio in *The Merchant of Venice.*

10. Taplin, *Life of Elizabeth Barrett Browning,* p. 77.

11. Barrett to her sister, Arabel, postmarked July 15, 1843, in the Berg Collection, New York Public Library, New York.

12. The date of composition can be assumed from the reference to 1843 in the poem's "Conclusion."

13. Carlyle to Ruskin, February 9, 1871, quoted in Springer, *What Manner of Woman,* pp. 129–30.

CHAPTER 4

1. Barrett Browning, *Letters to Mrs. David Ogilvy,* p. 30.

2. Hayter, *Mrs. Browning,* p. 105.

3. Gray, "Texts," from abstract.

4. Mermin, "Female Poet," pp. 363–65.

5. Christina Rossetti addresses the issue of the woman speaker of sonnets in her preface to her own sonnet sequence, "Monna Innominata." Alice Meynell wittily refers to woman as the sonneteers' object in *Prose and Poetry,* pp. 49–51.

6. Johnson, *Sex and Marriage,* p. 213.

7. Mermin, "Female Poet," p. 354.

8. Tennyson, "In Memoriam," Epilogue.

9. She was later reconciled with her brother, George Barrett.

10. Taplin, *Life of Elizabeth Barrett Browning,* p. 194; Hayter, *Mrs. Browning,* p. 20; Donaldson, "Poetic and Feminist Philosophies," pp. 149–50.

11. For a full discussion of the history of Barrett Browning's slave-owning family see Marks, *Family of the Barrett.*

12. Brownmiller, *Against Our Will*, pp. 153–70.
13. Marks, *Family of the Barrett*, p. 190.
14. Brownmiller, *Against Our Will*, p. 165.

CHAPTER 5

1. Rosenblum, "Visionary Aesthetic," pp. 61–68.
2. For a detailed discussion of the way in which Italy figured as a trope for Victorian women writers see Gilbert, "From *Patria* to *Matria*," pp. 195–98.
3. *Prospective Review*, p. 320.
4. *Athenaeum*, p. 598.
5. *Eclectic Review*, p. 317.
6. *Spectator*, p. 617.
7. Alaya, "Brownings' Italy," pp. 9–10.
8. Ibid., p. 10.
9. Of course neither she nor Browning could engage in Italian politics, but Barrett Browning knew she was debarred from political activity even in her own country.
10. Eliot, *George Eliot Letters*, 4:15.
11. For a detailed description of the celebration see Barrett Browning's letter to her sister, Henrietta, in Barrett Browning, *Casa Guidi Windows*, Appendix, pp. 65–70.
12. In her focus on the costumes of power Barrett Browning prefigures, but with a different emphasis, Virginia Woolf's essay, *Three Guineas*. Whereas Woolf explores how men use uniforms to encourage and maintain competition, which ultimately leads to sexual and class oppression at home and war abroad, Barrett Browning focuses on how men believe that power is synonymous with costume, rather than with their own integrity and commitment.
13. For a discussion of Victorian hero worship see Houghton, *Victorian Frame of Mind*, pp. 305–40.
14. Carlyle, *On Heroes*, p. 261.
15. Ibid., pp. 265–66.
16. Alaya, "Brownings' Italy," pp. 1–41, has shown how unfounded is criticism that Barrett Browning was unthinking and overly emotional in her hero worship such that she trusted both Pope Pius IX and Duke Leopold. First, her views represented those commonly held by the Anglo-Florentine community, and substantially by Browning. Second, she was, in fact, judicious in her comments on these men as possible Italian leaders, as *Casa Guidi Windows* reveals.
17. Elshtain, *Women and War*, pp. 3–13, 140–49.
18. *Eclectic Review*, pp. 312–13; *Athenaeum*, p. 597.
19. Ruskin, "Of Queens' Gardens," p. 107.

CHAPTER 6

1. See Introduction, n. 16.

2. Barrett Browning, *Aurora Leigh*, p. 16.

3. Rich, *On Lies, Secrets, and Silence*, p. 175.

4. Moers, *Literary Women*, pp. 173–211.

5. It is suggestive in light of Barrett Browning's revision of the Miltonic tradition that instead of twelve books, Barrett Browning gives birth to Aurora in nine.

6. Quoted in Taplin, *Life of Elizabeth Barrett Browning*, p. 311.

7. Swinburne, "Aurora Leigh," 6:3.

8. *Athenaeum*, p. 1425.

9. *Dublin University Magazine*, p. 465.

10. *Westminster Review*, p. 221.

11. Castan, "Structural Problems," p. 77.

12. Eliot, "Belles Lettres," p. 168.

13. It is important to remember that Mrs. Ellis was also a spokeswoman for such patriarchal beliefs; however, her act of writing her many books undermines her commitment to the ideology of woman that those books uphold. While her work suggests no original thinking, it does dramatize the fact that, for the hours she spent writing her books and seeing them through the publishers, she was not being a very "relative creature."

14. *Blackwood's*, p. 40; Patmore, *North British Review*, p. 454.

15. See Introduction, pp. 3–4, for a discussion of de Beauvoir's terms. For an examination, through a discussion of the poem's metaphors, of Aurora's transformation from identifying herself as "learned, poetic, and masculine" to reconciling herself with the power of her womanhood, see Gelpi, "Vocation of the Woman Poet," pp. 35–48. Gilbert examines the transformation of Aurora's "fragmentation of self" into a "reconstitution" of that self in terms of England and Italy, the *patria* and *matria*, in "From *Patria* to *Matria*," pp. 194–211.

16. Castan, "Structural Problems," p. 75.

17. I am not convinced by Castan's argument that in Books 8 and 9, necessarily related at one time after Aurora's reconciliation with Romney, Barrett Browning "sacrificed realism" in order to suggest a narrator who does not know what the final outcome of her story will be until the final moment. It is also possible that the narrator chooses not to present a stance of "mature retrospectivity," but rather to set her readers up to experience the outcome of her story as she did.

18. *National Review*, 4, p. 262.

19. While her mother's and father's deaths thrust Aurora into the repressive care of her aunt, they also freed her in a way for which Florence Nightingale envied novel heroines, when her own mother refused to allow her to learn nursing: "What are novels? What is the secret of the charm of every romance that ever was written? . . . The heroine has

generally no family ties (almost *invariably* no mother), or, if she has, these do not interfere with her entire independence." Nightingale, *Cassandra*, p. 28.

20. The fact that 120 years later Adrienne Rich writes about the same dilemma of being a woman and a poet reveals how crucial was Barrett Browning's location of this as a central issue for women poets: "To be a female human being trying to fulfill traditional female functions in a traditional way *is* in direct conflict with the subversive function of the imagination. The word traditional is important here. There must be ways, and we will be finding out more and more about them, in which the energy of creation and the energy of relation can be united." (Rich, *On Lies, Secrets, and Silence*, p. 43)

21. Gelpi, "Vocation of the Woman Poet," p. 42.

22. Gilbert and Rosenblum also read Marian as the agent of Aurora's transformation: Gilbert sees Aurora's encounter with Marian in Paris as a "process of reunification that will regenerate both these wounded daughters" (From *Patria* to *Matria*," p. 204); Rosenblum recognizes that the "symbolic instrument of [Aurora's] resuscitation is Marian Erle. . . . On a narrative level, the birth of Marian's child delivers her from her numbing exclusion from society; on the symbolic level, the woman who has been set beyond the boundaries of signification altogether—"fallen" to her death—becomes a powerful figure for the female as originator of meaning" ("Visionary Aesthetic," p. 65). Neither critic, however, demonstrates how Marian functions in this way.

23. *National Review*, p. 267.

24. Eliot, "Belles Lettres," p. 27.

25. Boccaccio, "Frederigo's Falcon," The Fifth Day, Novel 9, *The Decameron* 2:55–60.

26. Cora Kaplan in introduction to Barrett Browning, *Aurora Leigh*, p. 11; Gilbert and Gubar, *Madwoman in the Attic*, p. 580; Showalter, *Literature of Their Own*, p. 23.

27. Diehl, *Dickinson and the Romantic Imagination*, p. 15.

28. Moi, *Sexual/Textual Politics*, p. 8.

29. Gilbert and Gubar, *Madwoman in the Attic*, p. 580; Kaplan, introduction to Barrett Browning, *Aurora Leigh*, p. 11.

CONCLUSION

1. Rich, *On Lies, Secrets, and Silence*, pp. 39–47.

2. Showalter, *Literature of Their Own*, pp. 11–12.

BIBLIOGRAPHY

WORKS BY ELIZABETH BARRETT BROWNING

Aurora Leigh and Other Poems. Introduced by Cora Kaplan. London: Women's Press, 1978.

Casa Guidi Windows. Edited by Julia Markus. New York: Browning Institute, 1977.

The Complete Works of Elizabeth Barrett Browning. Edited by Charlotte Porter and Helen A. Clarke. 6 vols. New York: Thomas Y. Crowell & Co., 1900. Reprint. New York: AMS Press, 1973.

Diary by E.B.B.: The Unpublished Diary of Elizabeth Barrett Barrett, 1831–1832. Edited by Philip Kelley and Ronald Hudson. Athens: Ohio University Press, 1969.

Elizabeth Barrett Browning: Hitherto Unpublished Poems and Stories with an Inedited Autobiography. Edited by H. Buxton Forman. Boston: Bibliophile Society, 1914.

Elizabeth Barrett Browning's Letters to Mrs. David Ogilvy, 1849–1861. Edited by Peter N. Heydon and Philip Kelley. New York: New York Times Book Co., Quadrangle, and Browning Institute, 1973.

Elizabeth Barrett to Mr. Boyd. Unpublished Letters of Elizabeth Barrett Browning to Hugh Stuart Boyd. Edited by Barbara P. McCarthy. London: John Murray, 1955.

The Letters of Elizabeth Barrett Browning. Edited by Frederic C. Kenyon. 2 vols. New York: Macmillan Co., 1897.

The Letters of Elizabeth Barrett Browning to Mary Russell Mitford, 1836–1854. Edited by Meredith B. Raymond and Mary Rose Sullivan. 3 vols. Armstrong Browning Library of Baylor University, Browning Institute, Wedgestone Press, and Wellesley College, 1983.

WORKS BY ELIZABETH BARRETT BROWNING AND ROBERT BROWNING

Letters of the Brownings to George Barrett. Edited by Paul Landis with Ronald E. Freeman. Urbana: University of Illinois Press, 1958.

The Letters of Robert Browning and Elizabeth Barrett Barrett, 1845–1846. Edited by Elvan Kintner. 2 vols. Cambridge: Harvard University Press, Belknap Press, 1969.

SECONDARY SOURCES

Alaya, Flavia. "The Ring, the Rescue, & the Risorgimento: Reunifying the Brownings' Italy." *Browning Institute Studies* 6 (1978): 1–41.

Auerbach, Nina. "Robert Browning's Last Word." *Victorian Poetry* 22, no. 2 (Summer 1984): 161–74.

Blake, Kathleen. "Elizabeth Barrett Browning and Wordsworth: The Romantic Poet as Woman." *Victorian Poetry* 24, no. 4 (Winter 1986): 387–98.

———. "Elizabeth Barrett Browning (and George Eliot): Art versus Love." In *Love and the Woman Question in Victorian Literature: The Art of Self-Postponement*, pp. 171–201. Brighton, England: Harvester Press; Toyota, N.J.: Barnes & Noble Books, 1983.

Boccaccio, Giovanni. *The Decameron*, translated by J. M. Rigg. 2 vols. Florence: G. Fattorusso, 1950.

Brontë, Charlotte. *Shirley.* New York: E. P. Dutton & Co., Everyman's Library, 1975.

Brownmiller, Susan. *Against Our Will: Men, Women, and Rape.* New York: Simon & Schuster, 1975.

Carlyle, Thomas. *On Heroes, Hero-Worship, and the Heroic in History.* Philadelphia: Henry Altemus, 1894.

Castan, C. "Structural Problems and the Poetry of *Aurora Leigh.*" *Browning Society Notes* 7, no. 3 (December 1977): 73–81.

Chesler, Phyllis. *Women and Madness.* New York: Avon Books, 1972.

Chodorow, Nancy. *The Reproduction of Mothering.* Berkeley and Los Angeles: University of California Press, 1978.

Christ, Carol. *The Finer Optic.* New Haven and London: Yale University Press, 1975.

Cixous, Hélène. "The Laugh of the Medusa." In *New French Feminisms*, edited and introduced by Elaine Marks and Isabelle de Courtivron, pp. 245–64. Amherst: University of Massachusetts Press, 1980.

———, and Clement, Catherine. *The Newly Born Woman.* Minneapolis: University of Minnesota Press, 1986.

Cooper, Helen. "Working into Light: Elizabeth Barrett Browning." In *Shakespeare's Sisters: Feminist Essays on Women Poets*, edited and introduced by Sandra M. Gilbert and Susan Gubar, pp. 65–81. Bloomington: Indiana University Press, 1979.

David, Deirdre. " 'Art's a Service': Social Wound, Sexual Politics, and *Aurora Leigh*." *Browning Institute Studies* 13 (1985): 113–36.

de Beauvoir, Simone. *The Second Sex*. Translated by H. M. Parshley from the first French edition, 1949. New York: Bantam, 1961.

Dickinson, Emily. *The Letters of Emily Dickinson*. Edited by Thomas H. Johnson and Theodora Ward. 2 vols. Cambridge: Harvard University Press, Belknap Press, 1958.

Diehl, Joanne Feit. *Dickinson and the Romantic Imagination*. Princeton: Princeton University Press, 1981.

Dinnerstein, Dorothy. *The Mermaid and the Minotaur*. New York: Harper & Row, 1976.

Donaldson, Sandra M. "Elizabeth Barrett Browning's Poetic and Feminist Philosophies in 'Aurora Leigh' and Other Poems." Ph.D. dissertation, University of Connecticut, 1977.

_____. "Motherhood's Advent in Power: Elizabeth Barrett Browning's Poems about Motherhood." *Victorian Poetry* 18, no. 1 (Spring 1980): 51–60.

Donoghue, Denis. "The Heart in Hiding." Review of *Gerard Manley Hopkins: A Biography*, by Paddy Kitchen. *New York Review of Books*, September 27, 1979, pp. 51–53.

Dyson, A. E., ed. *The English Novel: Select Bibliographical Guides*. Oxford: Oxford University Press, 1974.

Eagleton, Terry. *Literary Theory*. Oxford: Basil Blackwell, 1983.

Ehrenreich, Barbara, and English, Deirdre. " 'For Her Own Good'—The Tyranny of the Experts." *Ms.*, December 1978, pp. 90–98.

Eliot, George. "Belles Lettres." *Westminster Review* 67 (January 1857): 168.

_____. *The George Eliot Letters*. Edited by Gordon S. Haight. 9 vols. New Haven: Yale University Press, 1954–78.

Ellis, Sarah Stickney. *The Women of England*. London: Fisher, Son & Co., 1838.

Elshtain, Jean Bethke. *Women and War*. New York: Basic Books, 1987.

Friedman, Susan Stanford. "Gender and Genre Anxiety: Elizabeth Barrett Browning and H. D. as Epic Poets." *Tulsa Studies in Women's Literature* 5, no. 2 (Fall 1986): 203–28.

Froula, Christine. "When Eve Reads Milton: Undoing the Canonical Economy." *Critical Inquiry* 10, no. 2 (1983): 321–47.

Gardiner, Judith Kegan. "Mind Mother: Psychoanalysis and Feminism." In *Making a Difference: Feminist Literary Criticism*, edited by Gayle Greene and Coppélia Kahn, pp. 113–45. London and New York: Methuen, 1985.

Gelpi, Barbara Charlesworth. "*Aurora Leigh*: The Vocation of the Woman Poet." *Victorian Poetry* 19, no. 1 (1981): 35–48.

Gilbert, Sandra M. "From *Patria* to *Matria*: Elizabeth Barrett Browning's *Risorgimento*." *PMLA* 99, no. 2 (March 1984): 194–211.

———. "Soldier's Heart: Literary Men, Literary Women, and the Great War." *Signs* 8, no. 3 (Spring 1983): 422–50.

Gilbert, Sandra M., and Gubar, Susan. "Introduction: Gender, Creativity, and the Woman Poet." In *Shakespeare's Sisters: Feminist Essays on Women Poets*, edited by Sandra M. Gilbert and Susan Gubar, pp. xv–xxvi. Bloomington: Indiana University Press, 1979.

———. *The Madwoman in the Attic: The Woman Writer and the Nineteenth-Century Literary Imagination*. New Haven: Yale University Press, 1978.

Gilman, Charlotte Perkins. "The Yellow Wallpaper." In *The Oven Birds*, edited by Gail Parker, pp. 317–34. New York: Anchor Books, 1972.

Glaspell, Susan Keating. "A Jury of Her Peers." In *American Voices, American Women*, edited by Lee R. Edwards and Arlyn Diamond, pp. 359–81. New York: Avon Books, 1973.

Gray, Lorraine. "The Texts of Elizabeth Barrett Browning's *Sonnets from the Portuguese*: A Structural Reading." Ph.D. dissertation, University of Detroit, 1978.

Hayter, Alethea. *Mrs. Browning: A Poet's Work and Its Setting*. London: Faber & Faber, 1962.

Hemans, Felicia. *The Poetical Works*. London: Peacock, Mansfield & Co.

Hickok, Kathleen. *Representations of Women: Nineteenth-Century British Women's Poetry*. Westport, Conn.: Greenwood Press, 1984.

Homans, Margaret. *Women Writers and Poetic Identity*. Princeton: Princeton University Press, 1980.

Horne, R. H. *A New Spirit of the Age*. London: Smith, Elder and Co., 1844.

Houghton, Walter E. *The Victorian Frame of Mind, 1830–1870*. New Haven and London: Yale University Press, 1957.

———, and Stange, G. Robert. *Victorian Poetry and Poetics*. Boston: Houghton Mifflin Co., 1968.

Irigaray, Luce. *Speculum of the Other Woman*. Ithaca, N.Y.: Cornell University Press, 1985.

———. *This Sex Which Is Not One*. Ithaca, N.Y.: Cornell University Press, 1985.

Johnson, Wendell Stacy. *Sex and Marriage in Victorian Poetry*. Ithaca, N.Y.: Cornell University Press, 1975.

Juhasz, Suzanne. *Naked and Fiery Forms*. New York: Octagon Books, 1978.

———. *The Undiscovered Continent: Emily Dickinson and the Space of the Mind*. Bloomington: Indiana University Press, 1983.

———, ed. *Feminist Critics Read Emily Dickinson*. Bloomington: Indiana University Press, 1983.

Kaplan, Fred. *Miracles of Rare Device*. Detroit: Wayne State University Press, 1972.

Kaplan, Sydney Janet. "Varieties of Feminist Criticism." In *Making a Difference: Feminist Literary Criticism*, edited by Gayle Greene and Coppélia Kahn, pp. 37–58. London and New York: Methuen, 1985.

Kolodny, Annette. "A Map for Rereading: Or, Gender and the Interpretation of Literary Texts." In *The New Feminist Criticism: Essays on Women, Literature, and Theory*, edited by Elaine Showalter, pp. 46–62. New York: Pantheon Books, 1985.

Kristeva, Julia. *Desire in Language*. New York: Columbia University Press, 1980.

Landon, Letitia. *The Poetical Works of L. E. L. Landon*. Boston: Phillips, Sampson and Co., 1853.

Leighton, Angela. *Elizabeth Barrett Browning*. Brighton, England: Harvester Press; Bloomington: Indiana University Press, 1986.

Marks, Jeanette. *The Family of the Barrett: A Colonial Romance*. New York: Macmillan Co., 1938. Reprint. Westport, Conn.: Greenwood Press, 1973.

Markus, Julia. Introduction to *Casa Guidi Windows* by Elizabeth Barrett Browning, edited by Julia Markus, pp. xv–xl. New York: Browning Institute, 1977.

Mermin, Dorothy. "The Female Poet and the Embarrassed Reader: Elizabeth Barrett Browning's *Sonnets from the Portuguese*." *ELH* 48 (1981): 351–67.

———. "Barrett Browning's Stories." *Browning Institute Studies* 13 (1985): 99–112.

Meynell, Alice. *Prose and Poetry*. London: Jonathan Cape, 1947.

———. Introduction to *Prometheus Bound and Other Poems* by Elizabeth Barrett Browning, pp. v–xv. London: Ward, Locke & Barden, 1896.

Miles, Josephine. *Eras and Modes in English Poetry*. Berkeley and Los Angeles: University of California Press, 1964.

Miller, Betty. *Robert Browning*. New York: Charles Scribner & Sons, 1953.

Moers, Ellen. *Literary Women: The Great Writers*. New York: Doubleday & Co., 1976.

Moi, Toril. *Sexual/Textual Politics: Feminist Literary Theory*. London and New York: Methuen, 1985.

Nightingale, Florence. *Cassandra*. New York: Feminist Press, 1978.

Pequigney, Joseph. *Such Is My Love*. Chicago and London: University of Chicago Press, 1985.

Rich, Adrienne. *On Lies, Secrets, and Silence: Selected Prose, 1966–1978*. New York: W. W. Norton & Co., 1979.

Rosenblum, Dolores. "*Casa Guidi Windows* and *Aurora Leigh*: The Genesis of Elizabeth Barrett Browning's Visionary Aesthetic." *Tulsa Studies in Women's Literature* 4, no. 1 (Spring 1985): 61–68.

———. "Face to Face: Elizabeth Barrett Browning's *Aurora Leigh* and Nineteenth-Century Poetry." *Victorian Studies* 26, no. 3 (1983): 321–28.

Rossetti, Christina. *The Poetical Works of Christina Georgina Rossetti.* With Memoir and Notes by William Michael Rossetti. London: Macmillan & Co., 1904.

Ruskin, John. "Of Queens Gardens." In *Sesame and Lilies.* Orpington and London: George Allen, 1894.

Showalter, Elaine. *A Literature of Their Own.* Princeton: Princeton University Press, 1977.

―――. "Women's Time, Women's Space: Writing the History of Feminist Criticism." *Tulsa Studies in Women's Literature* 3, nos. 1/2 (Spring/Fall 1984): 29–43.

Springer, Marlene, ed. *What Manner of Woman.* New York: New York University Press, 1977.

Swinburne, Algernon Charles. "Aurora Leigh." In *The Complete Works of Algernon Charles Swinburne,* edited by Sir Edmund Gosse and Thomas James Wise. 6 vols. London: William Heineman; New York: Gabriel Wells, 1926.

Taplin, Gardner B. *The Life of Elizabeth Barrett Browning.* New Haven: Yale University Press, 1957.

Thackeray, William Makepeace. *The Works of William Makepeace Thackeray.* With biographical introductions by Lady Ritchie. 26 vols. New York and London: Harper & Brothers, 1911.

Thomson, Patricia. *George Sand and the Victorians.* New York: Columbia University Press, 1977.

Watts, Alaric A., ed. *The Literary Souvenir; or, Cabinet of Poetry and Romance.* London, 1825.

Woolf, Virginia. "Aurora Leigh." In *The Second Common Reader.* 1932. Reprint. New York: Harcourt, Brace & World, Harvest Books, 1960.

―――. "Professions for Women." In *The Death of the Moth and Other Essays.* 1942. Reprint. New York: Harcourt Brace Jovanovich, Harvest Books, 1974.

―――. *Three Guineas.* New York: Harcourt, Brace & World, 1938.

―――. *The Years.* New York: Harcourt, Brace & World, 1937.

REVIEWS

Reviews of *Aurora Leigh*
 Athenaeum, November 22, 1856, 1425–27.
 Blackwood's Edinburgh Magazine 81 (1857): 23–41.
 Dublin University Magazine 49 (1857): 460–70.
 Eliot, George. "Belles Lettres." *Westminster Review* 67 (January 1857): 168.
 National Review 4 (1857): 239–67.
 Patmore, Coventry. *North British Review* 26 (1857): 443–62.
 Westminster Review 68 (1857): 220–28.
Reviews of *Casa Guidi Windows*

Athenaeum, June 7, 1851, 597–98.
Eclectic Review 94 (1851): 306–17.
Prospective Review 7 (1851): 313–25.
Spectator, June 28, 1851, 616–17.
Reviews of *Poems of 1844*
 Adams, Sarah Flower. *Westminster Review* 42 (1844): 381–92.
 Athenaeum, August 24, 1844, 763–66.
 Literary Examiner, October 5, 1844, 627–29.
 New Quarterly Review 5 (1845): 77–104.
 Poe, Edgar Allan. *Broadway Journal* 1 (1845): 20.
 Tait's Edinburgh Magazine 3 (1844): 720–25.
 Warburton, [?]. *English Review*. December 1845, 259–73.
Reviews of *The Seraphim, and Other Poems*
 Arcturus, a Journal of Books and Opinions (U.S.) 1 (February 1841):
  171–76.
 Athenaeum, July 7, 1838, 466–68.
 Atlas, June 23, 1838, 395.
 Examiner, June 24, 1838, 387–88.
 Literary Gazette, December 1, 1838, 759–60.
 North American Review 55 (1842): 201–18.
 Metropolitan Magazine (London), August 22, 1838, 97–101.
 Monthly Chronicle (London) 2 (1838): 195.
 Monthly Review, n.s. 3 (1838): 125–30.
 Quarterly Review 66 (1840): 382–89.
 Sunbeam, September 1, 1838, 243.
 Warburton, [?]. *English Review*, December, 1845, 259–73.
 Wilson, John [Christopher North, pseud.]. "Christopher in His Cave."
  Blackwood's Edinburgh Magazine 44 (1838): 279–84.

INDEX

Adams, Sarah Flower, 54–55
Aeschylus, 9; *Prometheus Bound*,
  E. B. Browning translation of,
  15; influence of, in *The Sera-
  phim*, 22, 25
Alaya, Flavia: on *Casa Guidi Windows*, style of, 127–28
Albert, Charles, 143
Arnold, Matthew, 8, 17, 162;
  works, 19th-century and, 8–9;
  Preface to "Poems, 1853," 130
Athenaeum: review of *The Seraphim*, 22, 24; "The Book of the
  Poets" in, 37; review of ballads
  in *Poems of 1844*, 68; on *Casa
  Guidi Windows*, 126, 129, 138;
  review of *Aurora Leigh*, 148–49,
  152
Auden, W. H., 191–92
Author, and text: relationship of,
  in traditional humanism, 2–3;
  relationship of, in French feminist theory, 3; male definition
  of, and E. B. Browning, 9–10

Ballads: poetesses and, 31–32; me-
  dieval setting, popularity of, 97;
  E. B. Browning's rejection of,
  97–98
Barrett, Alfred, 52
Barrett, Arabel: E. B. Browning to,

on "The Lay of the Brown Ro-
  sary," 79
Barrett, Edward (brother): E. B.
  Browning and, 36, 46–48
Barrett, Edward (father): and E. B.
  Browning, subjugation of, 51–
  52, 67; and children, marriage,
  and sexuality of, 52, 100; E. B.
  Browning on, to R. Browning,
  52–53; slavery and, 114
Barrett, Henrietta, 16–17, 50; E. B.
  Browning and, 35; and father,
  52, 100; marriage, 100
Barrett, Richard, 111
Barrett family: slavery and, 117
Beauvoir, Simone de, 14, 153, 180;
  The Second Sex, on woman as
  "other," 4–5
*Blackwood's Edinburgh Maga-
  zine*: review of *The Seraphim*,
  12, 22–23; review of *Aurora
  Leigh*, 152
Bloom, Harold, 2; on men, and po-
  etry, 5; on poets, and poetic
  past, 145
Boston National Anti-Slavery Ba-
  zaar, 11
Boyd, Hugh, 13–14, 22; E. B.
  Browning and, 16–17, 49; E. B.
  Browning to, on "The Runaway
  Slave at Pilgrim's Point," 111